Memories Are Made of This

Deana Martin is an actress, entertainer, and author living with her husband in Beverly Hills, California. She is the director of the Deana Martin Foundation, and producer and driving force behind the annual Dean Martin Festival.

Foreword by Jerry Lewis

Memories Are Made of This

DEAN MARTIN

THROUGH HIS DAUGHTER'S EYES

DEANA MARTIN

WITH WENDY HOLDEN

PAN BOOKS

First published 2004 by Harmony Books
A division of Random House Inc., New York

First published in Great Britain 2004 by Sidgwick & Jackson

This edition published 2005 by Pan Books
an imprint of Pan Macmillan Ltd
Pan Macmillan, 20 New Wharf Road, London N1 9RR
Basingstoke and Oxford
Associated companies throughout the world
www.panmacmillan.com

ISBN 0 330 49064 8

1 3 5 7 9 8 6 4 2

A CIP catalogue record for this book is available from
the British Library.

Printed and bound in Great Britain by
Mackays of Chatham plc, Chatham, Kent

For John, Mickey, Hunter, and Jagger

The men in my life

PHOTOGRAPHS

ACKNOWLEDGMENTS

THIS BOOK WILL, FOR THE FIRST TIME, SET THE RECORD straight about my family. It will explore the reasons for their successes and failures and give people a greater insight into what motivated them to make their life choices. As a parent, I now know how difficult it is to juggle children, work, ambition, and emotional demands. We are each the sum of our experiences, and none of us is perfect. Sometimes we rise to a challenge and sometimes the challenge takes a lifetime.

My parents gave me their love—unconditionally, irrevocably, and eternally. Now, as an adult, making my way in the world, I still feel their love, and it links me to them. For that I will always be grateful.

There are many people who made this project possible, and whom I now thank. First and foremost, Dad's fans. Thank you for your love. He never forgot you and he never stopped being grateful. My lifelong friend Lorna Luft, for giving me the courage to undertake such a cathartic and monumental task. Jerry Lewis, whose professional guidance and friendship I cherish. For his honesty. For being my father's partner and for letting me into his heart. Tony Oppedisano, for a lifetime of stories. Patti Lewis, for sharing her memories and photographs. My mother, Jeanne, for giving me a home, watching me grow, loving and protecting me. My dear brother Craig, for being one of the sweetest people on earth. My sister Gail, who helped raise me—thank you for your sense of humor and your strength. My brother Ricci for filling my world with laughter. My sister Gina, who will always be younger, for her positive outlook on life. My brother Dean Paul and my beautiful sister Claudia, thank you for being my guardian angels. Aunt Anne, for her remarkable memory and insights into our lives.

My son Mickey; we grew up together. Thank you for helping us find our way in the world. Now that you are married with children of your own, you finally understand what it means to be a parent, the joy and the pain and the wonder of it all. Mostly, I hope that when you read this book, you will finally understand what my father meant to me. Paola, for giving us Hunter and Jagger, our two beautiful grandsons.

And to my darling husband, John, my true love, for giving me the strength, direction, and focus to make this book possible. In the words of one of my father's best-known songs—"Your love made it well worth the waiting, for someone like you."

I would like to thank Alan Nevins, my talented agent at The Firm. Wendy Holden for helping me organize my thoughts. Shaye Areheart, my publisher, and Kim Meisner, my editor, for believing in my vision. Jeffrey Lane, Tara Gilbride and Penny Simon, my publicists, for spreading the word. Shane Rosamonda and Rene Reyes, for helping me sort and catalog my material. And Ingrid Connell for her work in the U.K.

Rose Angelica and the Dean Martin Festival Committee for their hard work and dedication. The people of Steubenville, who always had a special place in Dad's heart, and I now understand why. Neil Daniels and The Dean Martin Fan Center. Sonny King, Hal Needham, Alan King, Shirley MacLaine, Dennis Farina, Henry Silva, Larry Manetti, and Bruce Charet for sharing their adventures.

It is with appreciation and a special fondness that I remember the following people: Pola and Robert Ellis Miller, Bob and Barbara Leone, Elena Melgar, the Ladies of Bodies by Deana, Diane Crocetti, Archie Crocetti, Richard and Rose Crocetti, Tom Vecchione, Gina Vecchione, Ane Vecchione, Randy Vecchione, Mary Crocetti Vecchione, Grace Braeske, Mindy Costanza, Julia McDonald, Lou Panebianco, Dohrman Panebianco, Harry Greenberg, Mario and Mitzi Camerlengo, Violet Nelson, Virginia Fato, Helen Bonitatibus, Joe Perrone, Ida DiSarro, Anna Yannon, Victor Gillette, Julia Charmor, Tina and Art Baker, Jim and Debbie

Monoco, Kim Jascula, Roy and Sue Galuzzi, Kim Johnson, Rich Angelica, Joe DiAlbert, Mario DiCarlo, Steubenville Post 33 American Legion, Ron and Skip Lucas, Al DeMayo, Mike Berarducci and DiNovo's, the City of Steubenville, Mayor Domenick Mucci, Officer Roger Badger and Officer Joel Walker, Joe and Donna Staffilino, Naples Spaghetti House, Sue Delatore, Steubenville High School, Rico and Linda Schettini, Steubenville Bakery, Lou Tripodi, the Steubenville Rotary Club, Reno Saccoccia, Capitol Records, and a very special thanks to Father Tim Shannon of St. Anthony's Church. The Deana Martin Foundation Board of Directors: Richard Delatore, Dr. Laura Meeks, Bob Martin, Adam Scurti, Richard Sunyoger. The people who helped make Dean Martin Day possible: Governor Bob Taft, Senator Greg DiDonato, Representative Eilene Krupinski. The Dean Martin Committee: Carol Weber, Bob and Mel Martin, Judy Porco, Les and Von Stuckemeyer, Cliff and Jackie Rick, Mario Camerlengo, Felicia Borkowski, Nellie Hardy, Dan Calabrese, Assunta Olivieri, Maria Pittera, Lucia Scaffidi, Jan Watson, Joe and Edna Michetti, Yolanda Manella, Philomenia DiCarlontonio, Juanita Meszaros, John and Julie Charmor, Delphia and Sheila Ksiazek, Ann Febo, Domenick Lamone, Freda Bates, and Sharon Ranallo.

Sid Avery, Allan Grant, Bob Martin, and Guy Webster, the masters, for their beautiful images. Diana Avery, Ron Avery, and all our friends at the Motion Picture and Television Photo Archive, and Karin Grant, thank you.

There are far too many to thank personally. I have mentioned some of you in the text, and hope that those who have been inadvertently overlooked will forgive me.

—Deana Martin

FOREWORD

by Jerry Lewis

I SUSPECT THAT WHEN WRITING A FOREWORD TO SOME-
one's work, the tough part is thinking of all the nice things to
say ... but I didn't have that problem writing this. Probably
because the work is impeccable and so is the author. But I've felt this
way about her since around 1955, when I realized how impeccable
she was even then. And now she writes about another element, also
a part of my life—a great part—a part that made me qualified to
write anything.

Writing this is one exquisite rush for me, and more than likely will be the same for you when reading her love letter. Now, understand, Deana is good, but what makes her book terrific is that she is terrific—terrific in her ability to get on paper what is in her heart. And for her to write about her hero makes this read an exceptional one . . . and one you'll be glad you read. I felt my spirit soar from the get-go, and it kept me riveted—not so much because I love the subject matter as much as she does, if that's possible, but because I was there. I saw it all, I felt it all, and now I relive it all through the talent and commitment of a marvelous young lady who I adore more than ever before.

My recollections of Deana as a child are pretty sketchy, only in that I wasn't much older than she was at the time, and rather than adore that child as most adults do, I was too busy adoring myself. I should be somewhat ashamed to make that admission, but seeing that I was only eighteen or so, it doesn't sting as hard. And Deana was just arriving: this dark-haired, incredible beauty who broke every button on Dean's shirt . . . he carried 8¥10s in his wallet! Okay, I'm kidding, but he did have a slew of photos of Deana, the other kids, and himself. And, at the time, who could afford photography? So all the pictures he had were of him and Deana in strips of four poses running vertically, you know, the ones you get for a quarter in a photo machine at the arcade. Dean was in there more than he was at the bar (I'm kidding). But he was crazy nuts over her. He felt the same way about the other kids, sure, but the sparkle in his eyes when he picked her up was like a beam from the lighthouse on the Jersey shore.

I have to say I loved reading what Deana wrote—maybe because she bit the bullet, she was courageous, up-front, tenacious, and so totally forthright. I read it with tremendous pride and love, and I know other readers will feel the same emotions I felt. I love this author for a myriad of reasons, but especially for how she honored my partner.

—Jerry Lewis

Sweet, sweet the memories you gave to me
You can't beat the memories you gave to me
Memories are made of this . . .

Memories Are
Made of This

Prologue

I LOVED BEING CALLED DEANA MARTIN, EVEN WHEN I was very small. Dad was such a positive influence on people's lives, that to be so closely associated with him was always a blessing. People can't help but smile when they think of my father, which has to be the greatest legacy of all.

When people hear my name for the first time, they often ask the same question:

"Any relation?"

"Yes," I reply proudly, "he's my father."

They smile and, with tremendous affection and obvious enthusiasm, cry, "Oh, I love your father! I've loved him all my life."

Then come the inevitable comparisons. "But of course you're his daughter! My goodness, I can see it in your eyes, your smile. You're the spitting image of him. How wonderful to meet you."

Total strangers reach out to touch me, to make some direct physical connection with the Dean Martin they know. They want me to sign anything they have on hand, to stand next to them and smile for their cameras, and to tell them what it is really like being his daughter. They range in age from their teens to their nineties. They are of all races and nationalities. My father's appeal transcends class, color, and creed.

Some take their hero-worship seriously, impersonating Dad at the numerous Dean Martin conventions around the world, dressing up in a black tuxedo with a red pocket square in the breast pocket. They comb their hair like Dad and try to re-create his laid-back air of cool sophistication and his charismatic singing style. Others devote whole sections of their homes to the extraordinary memorabilia they've collected over the years—photographs, magazine clippings, concert tickets, record albums—an endless array of items that hold individual memories. They seem to know more about my family than I do, telling me everything from the date I graduated from high school to the full names of each of my siblings and their families. Some simply own a Dean Martin compilation album, have seen a few of his movies, some with Jerry Lewis, and remember his long-running number one rated television show. Such minimal contact was enough to make them lifelong fans.

Whatever their background, Dad's songs provided the soundtrack to their lives, and his image filled their living rooms and cinema screens for over sixty years. He was the regular guy who'd made it, and yet, he was the suave, sophisticated king of cool. The son of an Italian immigrant from humble beginnings who not only worked his way to the top, but became someone many aspired to be. Because of the easy familiarity they always felt toward my dad, his fans often pose deeply personal questions they'd never normally dream of asking a complete stranger:

"Did he really drink?" "What was the true reason behind the split with Jerry Lewis?" "What was Frank Sinatra like?" "How many brothers and sisters do you have?"

Like Dad, I've learned to smile and deflect their deepest probing with a joke, a noncommittal answer, or a laugh.

Sometimes, just sometimes, they ask me the most important question of all:

"Was he a good father?"

To their surprise, I shake my head and smile. "No," I reply candidly. "He wasn't a good father, but he was a good man."

Where Dad came from, that meant a great deal more.

One

INSIDE EACH OF US IS A SMALL, DARK PLACE WE CAN escape to when we're in pain. It is a silent sanctuary where comforting thoughts and memories wash over us, providing a soothing balm for the fear we're feeling inside. I first discovered mine when I was quite small. Cared for by an aunt while my mother disappeared for three days, I was sent to live with my father, a man I barely knew despite the name I bore.

I can vividly recall standing in the foyer of his opulent Beverly Hills mansion, along with three big boxes of clothes belonging to me and my two older sisters. A woman I knew as my stepmother picked up each item between her thumb and forefinger. "No, not this," she'd say, or, "This looks clean, we'll keep it," or—with a sympathetic look—"This can go to Goodwill." One of the boxes was mine, and I stood staring at my only possessions being picked over and graded.

That first interminable summer in my father's house, I remained completely mute, breaking my silence only occasionally to whisper my fears to my sisters, from whom I became inseparable. My arms were pocked with hives, my skin raw from nervous scratching. While my father worked hard to maintain his position in Hollywood, revered by his millions of fans, his little Deana sat clutching the banister every night. Dressed in one of my stepmother's baby-doll nighties, I dripped silent tears on the top step of his grand staircase, grieving for a loss too enormous for a nine-year-old child to comprehend.

ON AUGUST 19, 1948, the day I was born in the Leroy Sanatorium, New York City, my father was busy doing what he did best. I emerged into the world at the very same moment a desperate woman threw herself from the window of the Russian embassy across the street. The media throng that gathered outside to cover the mystery suicide had no idea that Dean Martin's fourth child was bawling for attention just feet away.

Dad was on the other side of the country at the time. He was with his comedy partner, Jerry Lewis, playing at Slapsy Maxie's Café, a popular new nightclub on Wilshire Boulevard in Los Angeles. Theirs was the hottest ticket in town, and regularly filling front-row seats were friends like Humphrey Bogart, Tony Curtis, and Janet Leigh. Sitting alongside them would be stars like Fred Astaire, Clark Gable, Joan Crawford, Jane Wyman, James Cagney, and Gary Cooper, as well as just about every studio head and entertainment executive in town. Dad opened each show with a song. The minute he walked out onto that stage, the atmosphere was electric. His image, his style, his magnetism, class, and talent just lit up the club. Hollywood's brightest settled back into their seats, eagerly anticipating what lay ahead.

Dad and Jerry were superstars, earning around ten thousand dollars a week just after the end of the Second World War. They were about to sign a ten-movie, five-year deal with Paramount Studios worth $1,250,000. They also had a separate recording contract with Capitol Records and a radio deal with NBC. With three young children and my recent arrival, Dad was finally succeeding in paying off the debts that had dogged him for years, and funding the fairy-tale lifestyle he hoped to create for us all.

My mother, Betty, called Dad at the Hollywood Roosevelt Hotel the night I was born to tell him he had a new daughter to add to his family. He was so deeply asleep when he took the call that he thought it was someone fooling around and hung up. Hours later, Dad rang back to see if his hazy memory of the previous night was correct. It was true. Mother had given him a daughter. Between them, they settled on the name Deana Angela. Dad had always wanted at least some of his children to be named after him. Having successfully chosen the names Craig, Gail, and Claudia, Mother was only too happy to comply with Dad's request. At the hospital, the registrar misspelled my name, writing it as Dina on my birth certificate, much to Mother's annoyance. It was a mistake that was to be repeated throughout my life. When the gossip columnist Walter Winchell wrote in his Sunday column that my name was Dinah, my mother was exasperated. She sang the line from the song, "Dinah? Is there anyone finah in the state of Carolina?" and muttered, "Can't Winchell get anything right?"

It was two months before my father finally met me. His West Coast debut of *The Martin & Lewis Show* and his first movie role with Jerry in the film *My Friend Irma* kept him more than three thousand miles from 315 West 106th Street and Riverside, New York. That was where I shared an apartment with my mother, brother, and sisters and our housekeeper, Sue. Staying with us were my maternal grandmother, Gertrude, and my young aunts Anne and

Barbara, who'd come from Philadelphia to help with my arrival. In the apartment above us was the singer Lena Horne, whose children played with us from an early age.

I finally came face to face with my father in Philadelphia, where Patti Lewis, Jerry's wife, accompanied the Martin family to a long-awaited reunion. Having taken me in his arms, he beamed adoringly into my big hazel eyes. Dad then announced that we were all moving to California. We returned to New York almost immediately to start packing, while my mother's family traveled home, their task complete. It was an emotional parting. To add to the tears, Mother's close friend, the actor Jackie Cooper, came to bid her good-bye.

"I wish you weren't going to Hollywood, Betty," he told her, giving her a warm embrace. "I just know it's gonna break your heart." Mother wondered what he knew.

♦♦♦

FOR A BRIEF PERIOD after my arrival, my parents enjoyed real happiness. Dad loved being a family man, and reveled in being a star. He could hardly believe how much his fortunes had changed. "Who'd have thunk it?" he would say. "For a boy from Steubenville, Ohio?"

He was always proud of where he came from, and mentioned it whenever he could. My grandfather Gaetano Crocetti had traveled to Steubenville shortly after arriving at Ellis Island in New York in 1913. A nineteen-year-old farm laborer, he came from Montesilvano, Italy, near Pescara on the Adriatic coast, following his two elder brothers to eastern Ohio. Steubenville was thirty-five miles west of Pittsburgh and had a large Italian immigrant population. Once settled, my grandfather became a barber. He embraced his new life but never lost his impenetrable Italian accent or his love for the old country.

My grandmother Angela Barra was born in Fernwood, Ohio, to parents who emigrated from Italy. She was raised by German nuns who taught her all the things that a young lady needed to know: The art of cooking, caring for a home, and, most important, they taught her how to sew. This was a skill that she developed into a lucrative profession, as she became known as the finest seamstress in the region. Because of her, all of the boys in the neighborhood had beautifully handcrafted clothes, either new or altered from older suits. When we were children she made many of our finest outfits, all matching, and it was she who gave my father his impeccable sense of style. She also gave my grandfather his American nickname "Guy." On Sunday, October 25, 1914, at the age of sixteen, Angela married Guy at St. Anthony of Padua Church in Steubenville, Ohio. Their first child, Guglielmo, known to me as Uncle Bill, was born on June 24, 1916. Dad, who was baptized Dino Crocetti at the same church, was their second child. He was born June 7, 1917.

My grandmother was an excellent homemaker and a wonderful cook. Her sons were raised on traditional Italian cuisine such as spaghetti and meatballs, veal or sausage with peppers, and Dad's favorite—pasta fagioli. My grandfather was a respected barber, and his sons were *never lacking for anything*. All he ever wanted was their health and happiness. He also hoped that one day they might work alongside him in his barbershop.

Dad grew up in a close-knit neighborhood that served as an extended family. With his cousins John, Archie, and Robert, he played bocce ball and baseball in the lots behind their houses and swam in the Ohio River. There was church every Sunday, where Dad and Uncle Bill were altar boys; Boy Scouts, where he was the drummer; and the Sons of Italy social events. Until he was five years old, Dad spoke predominantly Italian, but that changed when he started going to school.

Learning English as a second language gave Dad a slow and easy style of speaking that remained with him for the rest of his life. Like all children, he began picking up phrases and expressions from his school friends and soon sounded just like them. Unlike his studious brother, Dad spent much of his spare time watching westerns at the local movie house, the Olympic. Sometimes he would hang out at the poolrooms and nightclubs that were opening to cater to the increasing numbers of steelworkers in the town, which became known as "Little Chicago." It was great entertainment, and all done openly within a few yards of his father's shop.

For a time some of Dad's friends joked that the only chair he was heading for was not the swiveling type in his father's barbershop. Dad even added a funny line about that into the song "Mr. Wonderful" years later, that went, "Back home in Steubenville, they're doubting all this, I swear. / They're still betting six-to-five I get the chair."

Dad once told an interviewer, "I had a great time growing up in Steubenville. I had everything I could possibly want—women, music, nightclubs, and liquor—and to think I had all of that when I was only thirteen."

My father learned from an early age that charm, good looks, and a smile could help him find everything from employment to hot bread at the Steubenville Bakery. He was, at different times, a milkman, a gas station attendant, and a store assistant.

He loved to sing, which he did at any opportunity, never passing up an invitation to entertain. He had a beautiful voice and enjoyed sharing it. The idea of making a living from singing first came to him when some friends pushed him onto the stage of a club called Walker's Café. He was sixteen. "Go on," they urged, "you can do it."

Cracking jokes between songs, with lines like "You should see my girlfriend, she has such beautiful teeth . . . both of them!"—Dad won over the crowd and soon started to pick up a few extra dollars singing at other venues around town. His role models were the Mills Brothers, who were fellow Ohioans, and Bing Crosby, whose records he played on a wind-up gramophone until he wore them out. Dad looked good and sang great, was well mannered, and had impeccable taste in clothes and girls. The combination made for a heady mix.

But the salary for a nightclub singer was meager at best. Forever humming tunes in his snap-brimmed hat, he began running errands for those making the most of Prohibition. He did everything from dealing at illegal card games to delivering bootleg whiskey throughout the area—the alcohol he claimed was so potent he could have run his car on it. He was a card dealer at the Rex Cigar Store, where he slipped so many silver dollars down his trouser legs and into shoes that he jangled when he walked. It was money his bosses didn't begrudge him, and which he quickly spent.

My aunt Violet used to say to him, "Dino, you never have any money."

He'd smile and reply, "I don't need money, Vi, I'm good looking."

Dad kept working, taking on different jobs, and accepting donations from friends who subsidized his pay so that he would keep singing. His only alternative was a career in the steel mills of Ohio and West Virginia—something he tried briefly. "I couldn't breathe in that place," Dad told me many years later, shaking his head. "I have nothing but respect for those guys. They're tough, but it wasn't for me."

He took up prizefighting briefly, under the pseudonym Kid Crochet, for ten dollars a match, breaking and permanently disfiguring the little finger on his right hand. He traveled the state, working as a croupier or a roulette stickman in numerous clubs across Ohio. By the time he was in his late teens, he was a worldly-wise young man earning twice as much as his father. He knew what he wanted—the world beyond the river. The dream was crystallized by a road trip to California with a friend in 1936. There he soaked up the atmosphere of Hollywood and wondered wistfully if one day he would be part of its magic.

His greatest desire was to pursue his singing career, and in 1939 he was finally offered a full-time job as the lead singer in the Ernie McKay Band in Columbus, Ohio. He was twenty-two. It was Ernie who gave him his first stage name, Dino Martini, in the hope of cashing in on the popularity of a heartthrob Italian singer named Nino Martini. Not long afterward, Dad was lured to Cleveland by Sammy Watkins and his orchestra. Sammy insisted on another name change, and this time it would stick. In a rented tuxedo and under an entirely new identity—Dean Martin—Dad sang the liltingly romantic songs that were to become his own. The stars were aligning.

IT WAS 1941 and my mother, Elizabeth (Betty) MacDonald, was eighteen years old and a student in Swarthmore, Pennsylvania, when she first met Dad. Pretty, a world-class lacrosse athlete with a good singing voice and a tremendous sense of fun, she was one of five sisters much admired by the local young men. She was in Cleveland with her father, Bill MacDonald, who was being relocated there as a senior salesman for Schenley Whisky.

It was in the Vogue Room of the Hollenden Hotel where Dad was rehearsing that my mother first set eyes on him. Twenty-three years old, with dark wavy hair, and billed as "The Boy with the Tall, Dark, Handsome Voice," Dad was the best-looking man she'd ever seen. The mutual attraction was instant, and Dad fell for the Irish twinkle in Mother's eyes.

As an added insurance policy, Mother—who, having four sisters, knew how to attract attention—arrived at his show later that night wearing a big red sombrero. "Just to make sure he noticed me," she'd say, glowing from the memory.

Dad proposed just a few weeks later, after taking her home to meet his parents. They were relieved she was Catholic and quickly warmed to the innocent young girl their son Dino had fallen for. Grandma Angela crafted Mother a stunning wedding dress. They were married in St. Ann's Church in Cleveland Heights in October 1941, while my aunts Anne and Barbara, aged six and four respectively, scattered flowers and sang "I'll Be with You in Apple Blossom Time." The newlyweds spent their wedding night at the hotel where they'd met. They were young and in love and excited about their future. They didn't have long to wait, because the next morning Mother joined Dad on a six-week bus tour with the Sammy Watkins Band, bumping along from town to town.

When Dad left for another tour on the increased salary of fifty dollars a week, Mother stayed behind. She was already pregnant with my brother Craig and wanted to prepare their new apartment for the baby. Pearl Harbor was bombed while Dad was away, and his draft notice arrived soon after. The thought of losing him to the war terrified Mother, but the double hernia he didn't even know he had kept him out of the war.

BY JUNE 1944, Dad was recording for radio and had his own show, *Songs by Dean Martin*, broadcast on WMCA from New York. Whenever he called Mother long distance, there'd be an excited flurry of activity in the house.

"I did a new recording," he would tell her, his voice echoing hollowly down the line. "I'll be on WLAC tonight at six-thirty."

Her eyes bright, baby Craig in her arms, Mother would gather everyone around the wireless and listen breathlessly as Dad's seamless, subtle voice sang "Oh, Marie," reaching out to her from across the miles.

"He's so much better than Bing Crosby," Mother would sigh.

Two years later Dad signed his first recording contract, with Diamond Records. This coincided with a lucrative engagement at the Riobamba in Manhattan, his first big break. The previous singer had been Frank Sinatra, whose cancellation had opened a door. With a new salary of $150 a week, Dad moved Mother and Craig to New York City and hoped the good times were about to roll.

MOTHER WOULD join Dad whenever she could at the Riobamba, sitting at the front table, beaming up at the love of her life as he stood singing to her as if she were the only woman in his world. One day he'd be a star, of that she was certain. One day he'd stay at home with her to enjoy the fruits of his success.

In 1944 Dad went on tour again, to Canada and the East Coast, and Mother moved back to Pennsylvania with her parents, where she gave birth to my sister Claudia. Returning to Manhattan, she discovered Dad had been evicted for nonpayment of rent and was sleeping on the floor of his agent's hotel bedroom. He was living there with another singer, Sonny King, and a young comic named Alan King. Practical jokes were common among the three entertainers. Whoever was last in at night ended up sleeping in the bathtub. "You didn't want to be the one in the tub," Alan recounted, "because when Dean would use the bathroom at night, he'd see one of us sleeping in the tub and just before he left, he'd turn on the taps." Dad's roommates were also careful not to leave any spare change around. "Your father would pick it up and put it in his pocket and be happy to loan it back to you when you needed money later."

Despite their situation, Dad always looked great. "We all looked up to your dad," Alan said. "Even though we were all struggling, he never looked like he was."

At New York's popular Nedick's Restaurant, famous for their hot dogs and orange soda, they had a breakfast special. A refillable cup of coffee, two doughnuts, and an orange soda for a nickel. "Your dad," Sonny King told me, "would go in first and have his coffee, one of the doughnuts, and half the orange soda. Then I would walk in and say, 'Hey, Dean, you have to go, you have a very important contract to sign.' Then your dad would jump up and say, 'Okay, Sonny, why don't you eat my other doughnut? Don't let it go to waste.' Then he would run out and I would sit down.

"This went on until the owner finally said, 'You don't have to do this every day, guys. I'll tell you what, you can both come in and have doughnuts, coffee, and an orange drink for one nickel and when you're finally successful . . . you pay me back.'

"And we did pay him back," Sonny told me. "Years later we hunted that guy down and we each gave him $25,000. You should have seen the look on his face. He couldn't believe it. But that's the way Dean and I were raised, and that's the kind of guys we are."

Leaving my brother and sister with my grandparents, Mother visited Dad for several days at a time, giving him her support and helping with the chores. That overcrowded double room—number 616 in the Bryant Hotel—was where my sister Gail was conceived.

The times were tough, but Sonny told me, "It was fun. We would pool our money and your mother would walk across the street to the grocer and make dinner for us all on less than a dollar."

When Alan wanted to propose to his girlfriend Jeanette, he needed a ring. Someone told him, "You don't need to pay fancy prices. I know where we can get one." Alan told me years later, "I took Betty to see a guy who had a stash of hot jewelry laid out in the back of his car. It wasn't quite what she expected, but being a good sport, squashed in there, side by side, she picked me out a beautiful diamond ring. Outgrowing that ring years later, Jeanette had another cut to match it and has worn them as earrings ever since."

It's hard for me to imagine how lonely it must have been for Mother, separated from Dad for such long periods of time and raising her children virtually alone. By her early twenties, her hair had turned white. Whenever she and Dad were reunited, life was beautiful at first. Many times, in some small way, he'd try to show her how much she meant to him. They had a unique bond, connecting in all sorts of ways, whether it was playing cards, going to the movies, or playing badminton. She had fallen in love with Dino Crocetti, an aspiring and penniless singer. He always appreciated that she loved him even though he had nothing, and showed it often with a look, a touch, or an embrace. Those who knew them back then said there was never any doubt that they were in love.

However, the stress of his long absences was unbearable for her, and they'd argue about everything. Sometimes their difficulties seemed insurmountable, with rumors that Dad was having affairs on the road. My father was not without fault, but I don't think he ever intended to break Mother's heart. He loved her too deeply for that. Mother, who was by now living with Dad's parents in Steubenville, had a fiery Irish temperament. Once she slapped him across the cheek, threw a drink in his face, and threatened to leave him. Afterward, without a word, he walked out, leaving her wondering if he was ever coming back. He did, a few days later, laden with flowers and gifts.

Telegrams flew between their two mothers. "Good news, Dean and Betty have reconciled," Grandma Angela wrote to Grandmother Gertrude, who adored Dad but whose Catholicism railed against his character flaws. Gertrude had at least four of those telegrams.

After several years of dividing her time between New York, Philadelphia, and Steubenville, Mother learned the hard way what it was like being married to someone in "the business." While Dad was away, she was nursing her children through the usual childhood diseases and trying to pay the bills. She practiced her Italian and learned the art of Italian cuisine from Grandma Angela, who also taught her how to sew. I loved the stories my grandmother would tell me, about when she and my mother would sit at night making the same sort of beautiful clothes for us that she had made for my dad.

When my parents' relationship was at its best, Mother became the only person in Dad's universe. She repeatedly followed her mother's advice to "let things blow over." She nurtured Dad and took care of his every need, pressing his clothes on the floor of his hotel room for his next show, while their latest child slept in a dresser drawer. When Dad failed two screen tests because the studios said he couldn't speak properly, Mother worked tirelessly, teaching him proper pronunciation and diction.

"My English was lousy in those days, baby," he admitted to me years later. "I could barely hold a conversation. At times it was embarrassing."

It was Mother who smoothed his rough edges, making him pronounce his *g*'s at the ends of words like "singing." He'd say "dem" and "doze" and she'd tell him, "No, Dean, it's 'them' and 'those.'" Friends remember her gentle direction to him while he ate, repeating, "You don't go down to the soup. The soup comes up to you"; something I also recall her teaching me as a child.

Dad was a willing student and took her coaching in good grace, grateful for her polishing. Mother was articulate and literate and frequently wrote poetry and even her own songs. She helped Dad select which tunes to include in his act and worked out his arrange-

Two

MY PARENTS' FAVORITE FILM WAS *BRINGING UP BABY*,
with Cary Grant and Katharine Hepburn. They'd watch it repeatedly, each identifying strongly with the characters. I guess they saw
it from their two separate perspectives—Dad for the humor and
Mother for the romance. The only difference was that *Bringing Up
Baby* had a happy ending.

Dad was determined to make it as big as Cary Grant, and my
mother continued to encourage him. While he enjoyed modest success as a young singer, billed as "New York's latest radio singing

sensation," there was plenty of competition from the likes of Bing
Crosby, Frank Sinatra, and Perry Como, and major engagements
were hard to find. It was then that fate led him down a path he
couldn't possibly have predicted—a partnership in one of the unlike-
liest yet the funniest double act in show-business history.

He and the young comic Jerry Lewis had worked the same bill in
a number of New York clubs. Jerry's wacky stage show, described
as "pantomimicry," in which he lip-synched a number of famous
operatic arias while changing clothes and making funny faces,
appealed to Dad's innate sense of humor. "You're a funny kid," Dad
told Jerry backstage.

Inherently mischievous, Dad—waiting to go on at the Havana-
Madrid Nightclub in Manhattan one night—bounced the needle on
Jerry's record so that his lips were no longer in synch with the
music. At first Jerry was furious, but when the audience started
laughing, he encouraged Dad to carry on. When it was Dad's turn to
sing, Jerry dressed up in a waiter's white jacket and started dropping plates and spilling drinks. Rising to the bait, Dad soon had the
audience howling as he heckled Jerry mercilessly from the stage. At
one point, Dad went backstage, picked up a suitcase, and walked out
through the crowd, yelling to Jerry, "Lock up when you're through."
The crowd begged for more.

When New Jersey nightclub owner Skinny d'Amato needed a
singer to replace someone who'd fallen ill at his 500 Club in Atlantic
City, a nineteen-year-old Jerry (who was also on the bill) suggested
Dad. To this awkward young genius, riddled with neuroses, Dad was
the epitome of elegance and style. What Dad omitted to tell Jerry
was that he'd recently been declared bankrupt and was desperate
for a financial break. What Jerry failed to mention was that Skinny
didn't just want a singer, he wanted a comedy act. It was only when
Dad got there that Jerry told him the truth. Re-creating what they'd
been doing at the Havana-Madrid, their show was a smash hit. They
were soon doing six shows a night, and the more people laughed, the
more they realized that they had inadvertently created something
Jerry called "Magic in a Bottle."

The pair worked so well together they decided to promote their "sex and slapstick" act on the beach. Jerry would put on a swimsuit and pretend to almost drown while Dad gave him mouth-to-mouth resuscitation. Returning Dad's "kiss" with mock passion, Jerry would jump up and tell shocked onlookers, "If you think that's funny, folks, come and see our act at the 500 Club tonight!" The ensuing lines around the block testified to just how original their humor was. It was the summer of 1946, and Martin & Lewis were topping the bill.

Although they were the same height—six feet—Jerry was always known as "the kid" or "the little one." He stooped constantly, giving the impression of being smaller and the easily intimidated fool to his fraternally indulgent, sophisticated friend. Dad, who cut Jerry's hair into his trademark crew cut, always stood tall and erect. Unknown to Dad, Jerry had special lifts fitted to Dad's shoes to make him appear even taller. The pair became affectionately known as "the organ grinder and the monkey."

It was very much Dad's show. His was the nightclub act that Jerry constantly interrupted to wreak havoc. Each time Dad began to sing, Jerry would burst onto the stage or do something crazy in the audience. Dad retained his cool throughout, playing the patient older brother. With tremendous affection, Jerry played the tempestuous nine-year-old, pushing the limits of outrageousness. The way he handled it made the audience laugh with Dad and feel comfortable with some of the crazier antics, like cutting off men's ties with scissors. If Jerry had been working alone, it would never have worked. As Dad's friend Steve Allen told me, "They were brilliant. They knew exactly how far to push the boundaries and what was funny. If you take a pair of scissors and cut off someone else's tie, that's funny. If you cut off your own, it isn't."

Asked once why they'd changed their surnames to Martin and Lewis (Jerry's real name was Joseph Levitch), Dad replied, "We didn't think Crocetti and Levitch sounded so good."

Dad told Jerry that his name would have to come first on the billing, because it should be alphabetical.

"What?" said Jerry, knowing that *L* came right before *M*.

"No," said Dad, with typical humor, "*D* comes before *J*." And so it stuck.

Their first official engagement together as "Martin & Lewis" was in January 1947 at Loew's State theater in New York. Their fee was $1,500 a week. It was the start of a multimillion-dollar, ten-year partnership that would see them make sixteen motion pictures together and become the hottest radio and television comedy act in history. Good times were finally on the way.

♦♦♦

DAD'S AGENT, Abby Greshler, booked them for several months at the Loew's before they were snapped up by other theaters such as the Chez Paree in Chicago and the Copacabana in New York, run by Jack Entratter. Jack was so desperate to hire them that he offered them five thousand dollars a week in a postwar era when the average national income was fifteen hundred dollars a year. Dad finally moved out of the Bryant Hotel and rented a ten-room apartment on Riverside Drive. The Martins were a proper family at last.

Mother was sitting right at the front of the stage when Dad and Jerry opened at the Copacabana in April 1948. She was five months pregnant with me and positively glowing. Jerry clowned around with his false buck teeth as he and Dad took their standing ovation. A photograph taken of my parents backstage after the show has Dad standing behind her smiling, his hands protectively around her bulging stomach. They looked blissfully happy.

One day shortly afterward, however, Mother went to see Dad perform at the Copa, and discovered in his dressing room confirmation of a telegram he'd just sent. It was addressed to the actress June Allyson and read, "I'm still tingling."

Dad and Jerry were onstage and had just started their act, but that didn't faze her one bit. The evidence in her hand, Mother went out into the nightclub to confront Dad, who hid behind Jerry and tried to make it look like part of the act. Knowing that Mother would eventually reach him and, fearful of her Irish temper, he jumped off the stage, fled straight through the bewildered audience and out the front door. Even she had to laugh.

Forgiven for his indiscretion with Miss Allyson, Dad appeased Mother. When Martin & Lewis played Slapsy Maxie's in L.A. for the first time, Mother and Patti Lewis flew out for the show and watched proudly from the dance floor. "Your mother was very animated that night," Patti told me. "She sensed that this was the start of something great, and that her long-suffering patience with Dad was about to pay off. She put on a beautiful gown, paid special attention to her hair, and made sure that everyone would notice the adoring and heavily pregnant Mrs. Dean Martin at ringside." The club was full of famous faces, movie stars like Doris Day, Lana Turner, and Danny Kaye. Mother had a serious crush on John Wayne by then, and asked Patti if she thought he might turn up. With her playful sense of humor, she told Patti with that famous twinkle, "If John Wayne walks into this room, I'd better have a mattress on my back!"

The show went brilliantly. Dick Stabile and his orchestra provided the music, and Dad and Jerry were so impressed that they hired Dick as their bandleader. Dick Martin was a bartender that night and always maintained that it was seeing Martin & Lewis perform that inspired him to become a comedian.

Sitting alongside my grandfather Guy and grandma Angela, Mother enjoyed the music and the wine before reluctantly leaving for her hotel room. She had to relieve the babysitter and prepare for her journey back to New York the following day. Patti Lewis stayed alone for the second performance. Just as it was about to begin, Jeanne Biegger, a twenty-year-old whom Dad had first met at the Beachcomber Club in Florida, slipped quietly into Mother's seat and sat gazing up at Dad adoringly. Patti was so angry at Dad for blatantly flaunting his latest girlfriend on such a night that she didn't speak to him for the rest of the evening.

The first inkling Mother had that Dad had a new woman in his life was when boxes of Florida oranges arrived at our home, addressed to him from "an admirer." Patti refused to tell Mother anything, but Vi Greshler—Abby's wife—could always be relied upon to fill in the name of Dad's latest flame. When Dad had an affair with Rita Hayworth just before he started seeing June Allyson, Vi informed Mother immediately. Now that Rita and June were both history, Vi didn't hesitate to let Mother know who sent the fruit—Jeanne Biegger, a model from Miami, and a former handmaiden to the University of Miami Orange Bowl Queen.

"She pronounces her name Jeannie," Vi pointed out helpfully, just before Mother threw her out.

Having invited Jeanne to follow him to Los Angeles, Dad moved her into the home of Dick Stabile, where he could visit her at his leisure. Poor Patti, who had to endure sitting next to Jeanne several times since that first encounter, could never bring herself to tell her best friend. "He absolutely considered himself a free man," she told me years later, with a sigh. "Even though he was married and had kids, Dean was always free. That's just the way he was. Jerry was the same. Betty and I had to put up or shut up."

From the day Mother found out about Jeanne from Vi, the boxes of oranges were unceremoniously trashed. She hoped that Jeanne would eventually suffer a similar fate.

◆◆◆

THERE ARE some early photographs of Dad playing with us in the garden of our new home in Hollywood, and in them he looks truly contented. Dapper as always, he wore pressed pants, argyle socks, and a perfectly tailored shirt. He'd scoop up one of us in his arms, an unruly strand of hair falling over his tanned face, and kiss us for the camera. His love for us was unquestionable; he enjoyed having a large family and being the proud father. He was thirty-two years old and on the brink of superstardom; he could feel it. He had a beautiful family and a devoted wife who'd given up everything to be with him. At last the long years of separation and loneliness were about to pay off.

I don't think Mother saw what was coming. Whatever the rumors about his life on the road, and there were many, he had always come home to her. And home was wherever he wanted that to be. Having left New York and moved to a six-hundred-dollar-a-month mock Tudor house at 850 Stone Canyon Road in Bel-Air, we settled into our new environment and began to live Dad's California dream. My grandparents Angela and Guy—who'd retired to Long Beach from Steubenville a few years earlier—moved in with us for a time to smooth the way.

To the outside world, we seemed like the perfect Hollywood family—the successful young East Coast singer and comic arriving in Bel-Air with his devoted wife and four little children, grandparents too. The glossy magazine spreads featured "Mr. and Mrs. Dean Martin at Home." It was idyllic but for one fact. My father's life was about to take him in a different direction.

I CAN'T recall the day my father told my mother he was leaving us. It was February 1949, and I was less than a year old. My brother and sisters, who would have been seven, five, and three respectively, have blocked the event from their collective memory. The first my mother's family knew that anything was wrong was when they were back home in Pennsylvania, listening to Louella Parsons's popular Sunday-night radio broadcast from Hollywood. "Just who does Dean Martin think he is," she said, "walking out on a wife and four children, one of whom is just a few months old?"

Knowing that her family would have heard the broadcast, Mother rang home a few minutes later, to confirm the news. "Oh, Betty," my grandmother said. "I'm so very sorry." Mother had been keeping the details from them, hoping that the affair would blow over. But instead, Dad moved into a small rental house on Sunset Boulevard with his new love.

YEARS LATER, during the only conversation I ever had with him about why he'd abandoned Mother and us, he said simply, "I fell in love with Jeanne, and I was fed up having to come home and cook dinner for you kids." I was too young to remember, but my brother and sisters tell me Dad would often come in from a hard day at work and, discovering they hadn't eaten, would fix them all fried-egg sandwiches, one of his favorites. The implication was that my mother was no longer capable. It is certainly true that men of his generation just didn't fix the dinner. He would have regarded having to do this as a failure on Mother's part. As for me, I would have thought it might be a fun thing to do sometimes—prepare some food for your kids—especially when you hadn't seen them all day. His suggestion that it was a burden or a reason for leaving us kills me. I guess Dad was just trying to keep everything together.

Upon hearing the news of the breakup, my grandmother and aunts Anne and Barbara flew to L.A. and stayed for a year. They shared the Spanish-style house Mother bought for us at 551 South Beverly Glen Drive. They returned home a year later after my grandfather Bill followed them out and unwisely tried to intervene in Mother's muddled financial affairs. Having angrily sent her family back to the East Coast, my mother was now utterly alone.

Refusing to give Dad a divorce, she was granted a legal separation and custody of us kids, but stayed in L.A. as she continued to hope that he might come back. The gossip columnists fueled the flames, suggesting that Dad's decision to walk out on his family could be detrimental to his career. But his first film with Jerry, *My Friend Irma*, did so well at the box office that they immediately started filming a sequel, *My Friend Irma Goes West*. One day Mother spotted Dad walking openly down Sunset Strip with Jeanne on his arm, each in matching Sy Devore outfits. Days later she learned that friends had already received fancy, gold-embossed invitations to Dad and Jeanne's wedding, even though he and Mother were still married.

But the news that shocked her the most was when Dad told her that Jeanne was pregnant. Fearing for Jeanne's unborn child, and believing that abortion was a mortal sin, Mother felt that there was no other choice. Dad must do the right thing.

Utterly defeated, she acceded to his request for a divorce and moved to Las Vegas for a six-week residency. She lived at the newly opened Flamingo Hotel and Casino to qualify for the more lenient Nevada divorce laws. She took seven-year-old Craig with her while the rest of us stayed home with Grandma Gertrude and our aunts.

Mother went to Vegas against all advice. Her parents, sisters, parents-in-law, and friends tried to persuade her not to make it so easy for Dad, but Mother said, "There's a baby on the way, for goodness' sake, and anyway, this is just one affair too many." She had friends in Vegas, including the comedian Jan Murray. He married one of the daughters of Bugsy Siegel, the gangster credited with creating the gambling city.

By the time her required residency was up, she'd had six weeks of dancing, drinking, and having fun. She was determined to carry on with the lifestyle that helped numb the pain of both her separation and the news that Jeanne wasn't pregnant after all, which came as a bolt from the blue. Aunt Anne always said that was the unkindest cut of all. "If she'd known Jeanne wasn't pregnant, she wouldn't have allowed the divorce," she told me later. "By the time she found out, it was too late. That divorce was rushed through the courts in double-quick time. Dean was in love and just wanted to marry Jeanne as quickly as possible. There was never any time for Betty to think or change her mind."

The divorce papers were signed in the summer of 1949 and took effect on August 24. It was five days after my first birthday, which I spent without either of my parents to help me blow out the striped candle on my cake.

My mother was completely alone when she attended Clark County Court in Las Vegas to hear Judge Frank McNamee announce the end of her eight-year marriage on the grounds that Dad had caused her "extreme mental anguish and grievous suffering." The judge decreed their bonds of matrimony "wholly dissolved, set aside and held for naught." Finding a bar afterward, Mother drowned her sorrows.

A few days later, Mother arrived home and surrounded herself with friends and family. She pretended that her heart wasn't breaking when Dad married Jeanne in a simple civil ceremony at the Beverly Hills mansion of Herman Hover, the owner of the nightclub Ciro's. Jerry Lewis was Dad's best man, and a reluctant Patti Lewis was matron of honor. Jerry told me years later that moments before the ceremony Dad broke down in tears.

"What's the matter, partner?" Jerry asked, putting an arm around his shoulder.

"I really never wanted to hurt Betty," he told him. "I love her and my kids. Trouble is, I've fallen in love with Jeanne, too."

"Holy smokes!" cried Jerry. But with Dad's lovely new bride waiting outside and the divorce irrevocable, the ceremony went ahead.

They spent their honeymoon at the Del Mar races and then at the Flamingo in Las Vegas, which Mother had only just vacated. Jeanne sat in the front row of the Martin & Lewis shows twice nightly before watching Dad win at blackjack.

The new Mrs. Martin returned to L.A., eager to start a family, just as soon as Dad stopped to catch his breath. He and Jerry were filming their third movie, *At War with the Army*, based on the successful Broadway show about a frustrated sergeant-cum-singer and his goofy sidekick. They were appearing regularly on the NBC radio network. Martin & Lewis were also headlining in several nightclubs across the country. They were hosting the popular Sunday night television show *The Colgate Comedy Hour*, and Dad was making record after record for Capitol. He recorded twenty-six songs in 1950 alone. Times should have been good.

But suddenly they were embroiled in bitter litigation. Abby Greshler, their agent, hadn't paid the Internal Revenue Service any tax on their behalf, and they owed thousands of dollars in back taxes. Everyone from Lou Costello to Dad's original bandleader, Sammy Watkins, was demanding a piece of the pie. Before he knew it, Dad was officially broke.

"The people I knew back then either wanted nothing at all to do with me or they wanted half of everything I was making," Dad told me years later. "I was earning plenty, on paper, but I never knew where it all went."

Unable to meet his hefty alimony payments, he stopped sending Mother child support, so she took him to court. The judge had little sympathy and stung Dad for a further eight thousand dollars in legal costs. It hurt Mother dreadfully that Dad and his new bride were attending parties and mixing with Hollywood society, while applying to pay her less, but she never once had a bad word to say about him and never let us see her distress. From Dad's point of view, I honestly don't think there was ever any intention of hurting us. He'd already paid Mother a large amount of money in a lump sum and knew we had a roof over our heads and enough food on our plates. In hindsight, it seems he was merely planning to postpone keeping up his crippling monthly payments until his financial affairs were in a better state. Whatever his reasoning, it's definitely not okay with me that he stopped paying alimony and child support. If he had taken the time to think about what the decision meant for us, I am sure he would have felt terrible about it. But Dad was never great at taking responsibility. He wanted anything unpleasant in his life to simply disappear. As he so often did, he hid his head in the sand and hoped bad things would go away.

Mother also did not complain when she learned that Dad had been invited back to Steubenville—a place she'd lived humbly for a number of years while he was on the road. There was to be a grand parade and a town celebration of Dean Martin Day. My brother Craig went with them.

Mother's friends were not always so charitable. Ella Logan, the musical comedy singer and original star of Broadway's *Finian's Rainbow*, threw a huge party and invited Dad and Jeanne. Going to Saks Fifth Avenue to buy herself a new dress, Ella bumped into Jeanne, who was there to collect her own dress for the party.

"Oh, let me see," Ella cried, and Jeanne—delighted and surprised at the sudden interest—put on the gown and paraded for the woman who'd sung with Ella Fitzgerald and Frank Sinatra.

Later that night, poor Jeanne arrived at the party in her beautiful new gown only to discover that all the waitresses were wearing the same dress, kindly bought for them by their generous hostess.

Three

DESPITE DAD'S ASSESSMENT OF THE SITUATION AND THE consensus, I suspect, among others, I don't ever recall Mother being incapable in those early stages of their separation. On the contrary, she went to extraordinary lengths to conceal her drinking and her heartache from us, laughing, playing, and planning fun things to do, to an almost manic degree. Later she undoubtedly lost control, but not in ways that were terribly obvious to a young child.

"He'll come back," she'd tell friends and family gaily. "This divorce means nothing. My Dean always comes back." She honestly

believed that once the novelty of Jeanne had worn off, Dad would
come running home. All she had to do was wait and keep us kids
amused in the meantime.

I don't remember missing my father as a little girl. I guess I was
so young when he left that I had no memories to miss. As far as I
was aware, it had always been just Mother and Craig, Gail, Claudia,
and me. The only variation to our little group was provided by the
occasional visits of grandparents and aunts. I know that we must
have visited my father every now and then, because I have the photos—some taken by Jeanne—but I have little or no recollection of
those encounters.

I have spent much of my adult life wondering why Dad took such
a limited part in his children's early years. There were, I believe,
many reasons, chiefly that he worked so hard at making movies and
recording albums that he simply didn't have the time. I know it
wasn't Jeanne's influence that kept him so distant. On the contrary,
it was she who seemed to instigate most of the contact. Mother was
always happy for us to spend time with him, so the problem was
really his reluctance or inability to spend time with us. Maybe he
couldn't cope with the Catholic guilt of leaving us. Maybe he just
wanted to put all that behind him and start a new life. Maybe he was
just too darned tired to play with four little kids. I know it wasn't
because he didn't love us—that has never been in question—but I
can't pretend it doesn't hurt like hell.

Having effectively been a single parent all along, Mother did her
best to rise to the challenge of caring for us all admirably, cooking
dinner when the mood took her, or when she was between maids.
Intensely proud of her Irish heritage, she'd make us mashed potatoes dyed green and scooped into ice cream cones on St. Patrick's
Day, when she'd dress us in green from head to toe. Barney's
Beanery, an Irish pub in Hollywood, became our regular hangout.

An extremely tactile woman, Mother was constantly hugging
and kissing us, telling us how much she loved us. Strict on manners
and table etiquette, she'd whack our elbows if we placed them on the
table and tell us, "Children are to be seen and not heard. Respect

your elders. Never interrupt and always say 'excuse me.'" She joined in the fun too, though, and whenever we'd ask her the time, which we did often just to get her response, she'd say, "Time for all you little doggies to be dead. Don't you feel sick?" Laughing, we'd ask her again and again. What a family!

With her considerable alimony being paid monthly, her dressing room was filled with gowns and fabulous shoes, all looking as though they'd come from the set of her favorite television show, *I Love Lucy*. There were brightly colored polka-dot dresses with full skirts and high cuffs, striking black and white blouses and shoes, shoes, and more shoes. My sisters and I would pull on Mother's satin dresses and plaster our faces with her makeup and pretend to be her, while she was sleeping or downstairs preparing for one of her parties.

As the maids came and went and Mother began to take less of a hands-on role, we started to lead increasingly less-structured lives. Washed but unironed clothes piled up on the floor of our bedrooms and we ate whatever leftovers were in the refrigerator. The only meal I can ever recall Mother teaching me to make was meat loaf. I remember cracking an egg and pouring ketchup onto ground beef before dunking a piece of bread in milk, and adding it to the mix. Mother seasoned it and told me, conspiratorially, "Now for my secret ingredient: Lipton's onion soup. My mother used it and now I'm telling you." One would have thought it was a hundred-year-old recipe handed down through the generations. Bless her. She let me mix it all up with my tiny hands and cram it into a little pan. Making meat loaf with her is one of my happiest early memories.

♦♦♦

THE NIGHTS were always the best. After a few cocktails, Mother was in her element, throwing Hawaiian luau parties, for which she'd import beautiful floral leis from Honolulu and set up flaming tiki torches around the back lawn. There'd be food everywhere, proper grown-up food, not just stale doughnuts or greasy bacon or the remnants of some pasta she'd made days earlier. The house would be full of musicians and writers and politicians. Everyone would be smoking cigarettes and drinking fancy cocktails adorned with miniature umbrellas and exotic fruit. We children would be included in the fun, and introduced to Mother's guests—who included Sheila MacRae, Rocky Marciano, Lenny Bruce, and Adlai Stevenson. (In 1952, Stevenson lost the presidential election to Eisenhower.)

The young actor Tony Curtis was a great friend and a regular at the parties. He also used to come over to our house every afternoon to borrow Mother's tape recorder. Sitting in the den in his white turtleneck sweater, he'd practice his elocution in an attempt to lose his Bronx accent, while Mother listened and advised, just as she had with Dad. Tony was going through his "tights" phase, when he seemed to be dressed permanently in medieval costume for such movies as *The Black Shield of Falworth* or *The Purple Mask*. Mother helped Tony constantly, getting him to say "father" rather than "fodder." By the time he filmed *Trapeze* (more tights), he had become a star and we began to see less and less of him.

My mother was not good at managing her finances, and began to run up huge debts. My father had paid her plenty of money—$60,000 cash and $3,600 a month alimony, including $1,000 child support ($250 a month for each of us). Never having dealt with such large sums before, she mismanaged it, losing much to fraudulent investors. One of the first-ever Ford Edsels was parked in our driveway, we ate at expensive restaurants, and had plush furnishings and beautiful clothes. She gave us music and ballet lessons at the Buddy Ebsen School of Dance. Our grandfather Guy, who'd by now moved with Grandma Angela to a house in Inglewood paid for by my father, drove us to our dance classes every weekend.

"Call me 'Pop,' not 'Grandpa,' " he'd insist, his Italian accent as thick as homemade gnocchi. " 'Grandpa' just makes me feel old." He was "Pop" from that day on, and we soon came to adore the eccen-

tric Italian with the funny way of speaking and the pockets full of
change for gelato or ice cream.

When Mother wasn't holding court in L.A., she transferred her
parties to more exotic locales. She rented a fabulous house in
Laguna for one vacation, inviting all her friends. Another time she
drove us to the fabled Rosarito Beach Hotel in Mexico, where we
rode horses on the beach, ordered huge meals from room service,
and went deep-sea fishing. It was tremendous fun. We kids were
largely left to our own devices while all-day pool parties turned into
all-nighters and the number of guests grew and grew. They only disappeared when it was time for Mother to pick up the tab.

Mother finally accepted the fact that Dad wasn't coming back.
She started dating a handsome man called Rainbo for his penchant
for bright Hawaiian shirts. His real name was Frank Jackson, and
his brother was married to Mother's sister Mary. Rainbo had been
everything from a World War II Marine to a policeman. I have nothing but fond memories of him; he was the first real father figure in
my life. He moved in with us for a while, helping out around the
house, remodeling the basement, taking us kids to the park, cooking
us meals, and trying to hold Mother together. He never raised his
voice, even when Mother had some of her more volatile moments,
and he would always try to protect us.

Raising her voice to us, she would say, "Get to your room or
you'll get the back of my hand." She could put the fear of God in us
all without having to do a thing. Sometimes it felt as if it was just
Rainbo and us against the world. When he eventually left, unable
to handle Mother's drinking, it left a huge hole in our lives and our
hearts.

As she had when Dad left, Mother threw herself into socializing
to help numb the pain. She continued to throw parties, dress us up
at every opportunity, and fill the house with friends. Around midnight the real fun would begin. We'd usually be tucked into bed by
then, worn out by the evening's celebrations and desperately trying
to get some rest before school the next morning. Mother would come

to our second-floor bedroom with its four little beds in a row and shake each of us awake.

"Hey, sleepyheads, get up," she'd say excitedly. "The grunion are running! We're going grunion-hunting!" And that's exactly what we'd do. We'd pull on some pedal-pushers and T-shirts, join a convoy of gleaming limousines down to Santa Monica, and run to the edge of the waves. Thousands of grunion would be glistening silver in the moonlight, flapping helplessly as they laid their eggs in the wet sand, and we'd try to catch as many as we could with our bare hands.

Those are my happiest memories of my mother, seeing her standing on the shore, still in her evening gown, wet to her waist, covered in sand, her head thrown back and laughing as we and her guests tried to catch those slippery little fish. We'd flop into bed at dawn, exhilarated and exhausted, with enough happy memories to feed on for the rest of our lives.

Mother read a story in the newspaper in 1954 that touched her heart. An American hero, Marine Corporal Ira Hamilton Hayes, had been arrested on drunk and disorderly charges. Ira Hayes was one of the highest decorated soldiers from World War II, receiving the distinguished Medal of Honor, our nation's highest military citation. He was one of the men immortalized in the Pulitzer Prize–winning photograph taken at Mount Suribachi on Iwo Jima, as they raised the American flag signaling the end of Japanese control. Mother was outraged and thought it was a disgrace that the country that he had served so bravely would not raise a hand to help him. So she contacted Ira and gave him a job.

He was grateful and promised that he would not drink and said, "You can count on me . . . I'll never let you down."

He was her right-hand man. He handled everything from the house to the driving. Ira told me stories of his childhood, growing up as a young Pima Indian on the Gila River Reservation in Arizona. He told me how proud he was to become a Marine and how he received his nickname of Chief Falling Cloud from his pals in the USMC Parachute School. He was an extraordinarily kind man,

someone who would sit and chat with me for hours. Then one day
Mother received a phone call from the Santa Monica Police department. Ira had been arrested for public intoxication. She immediately went to the station and bailed him out. She told him he still
had a job and said, "We can beat this, together." All was well again,
until the court date. "All he needs is a second chance," Mother told
Aunt Anne on the way to the courthouse. He never showed up.
Mother kept searching for him. We finally heard that he returned
to his home in Arizona. Sadly, Ira never recovered from the loss of
his comrades during the war. Months after leaving us, he died of
exposure to the cold on January 24, 1955. Mother always blamed
herself, saying, "He didn't want to let me down . . . I feel I let him
down."

⧫⧫⧫

MOTHER THREW parties regularly, so on "ordinary" nights we'd
be on our own, Craig, Claudia, Gail, and I. We had such fun, playing
games of make-believe and kidding around. One day Craig covered
himself with ketchup and lay out on the grass behind the Beverly
Glen house, pretending he'd been stabbed when Mother saw him.
For a moment Mother was horrified, but then she looked closer and
started to laugh. We'd all been in on his secret, but never let on.

Aunt Anne, who'd returned to California to marry, was now a
regular visitor at our home. She was appalled. "Aren't you going to
punish them for teasing you so?" she asked Mother.

"No!" she cried, still laughing. "I can't just punish Craig. They
were all to blame, and I'd much rather they stuck together against
me than tattled on each other."

Poor Craig. I think it must have been toughest on him, losing his
father and then Rainbo. He was seven when Dad left home. Anne
remembers one particular day when Dad had promised to come over
and pick up Craig to spend the day with him. He was filming at
Paramount Studios with Jerry, and promised he'd take him onto the

set. Craig got ready, put on his coat, and sat on the top step outside the front door, waiting. Hours passed, and still he waited.

"Don't you want to come inside and wait, honey?" Mother or Anne would ask in turn.

"No," Craig said, shaking his head firmly. "He's coming. My dad will be here any minute."

Hours passed while Mother tried desperately to get in touch with Dad on the telephone to remind him of his commitment. Craig sat outside, waiting. He sat there all day. He sat there until the sun was setting and nobody came. He never waited for his father again.

Later Craig went to live with Grandma Angela and Pop. Mother couldn't cope with four children, and Craig would be better off with them. It's true that with our grandparents—especially madcap Pop—Craig could relax and be a teenager, without having to look out for the rest of us. An intensely private and gentle person, Craig had been attending the Urban Military Academy in Brentwood. From an early age he had set his sights on becoming a member of the armed forces, just as soon as he was old enough. We missed him desperately.

That left us girls alone with Mother and she did her best to keep us entertained. After school she played card games like Hearts or Pokeno with us. Sometimes she'd pack us into the station wagon with pillows and blankets and take us to a drive-in movie. We'd sit mesmerized, eating homemade Italian sandwiches and watching wonderful films like *Peter Pan* or *20,000 Leagues Under the Sea*. When the refrigerator was empty, she would take us to places like the Ming Room at Bruce Wong's on La Cienega Boulevard. She loved the paper-wrapped chicken, washed down with a cocktail for her and fizzy pink Shirley Temples for us. We enjoyed going to Barney's Beanery for a hamburger and a Coke, where Mother would stand us on the worn wooden bar and we would sing and dance for the customers. Many times we would go to La Cienega Lanes, a bowling alley where Mother first taught us how to bowl. She would wave to us from the lounge while we played . . . and she flirted with the male customers. Life seemed to me to be one exciting event after another, but I was a very young child.

◆◆◆

MOTHER NEVER spoke badly about Dad or his new wife. She would even invite the young Jeanne to spend the occasional evening with us when Dad was out of town, which was often.

"I am the only other woman in L.A. who knows how lonely it is being Mrs. Dean Martin," she would tell her successor. Then Mother would smile and fix Jeanne a drink as she sat curled up like a teenager in the den, eating popcorn in front of the television.

Jeanne arranged for us to visit with Dad when he was in town. There are home movies and photos of all of us in the pool, with Dad throwing us around, but I recall very little about those days. On Halloween, Mother would take us over to Dad's for a party. She loved Halloween and would always dress us up for trick-or-treating. One year I was a little clown, and she shyly pushed me toward the camera as Jeanne, very pregnant, filmed home movies. When I look at those films today, Mother looks uncomfortable as the camera pans over to her. It seems as if she is consciously hiding behind a corner while coaxing me out into the room so I can be filmed along with the other children. How difficult that time must have been for her.

After a while, Jeanne began inviting us over for another reason. She wanted us to meet our new brother. His name was Dean Paul Martin Junior, but he was to be known to us for many years simply as "Dino."

The only indication we had of how Mother took the news that Jeanne had given Dad a son was that she became an insomniac. Night after night, she couldn't sleep unless she took a pill, usually washed down with a cocktail. She lay in bed so late into the morning that we had to get ourselves up, dressed, and off to school. Breakfast was whatever was in the refrigerator, usually powdered sugar doughnuts from Dantes's Carmel Market. Then came that time in my life, as with most young girls, when I wanted to join the

Brownies. I went to Mother and asked for the money for my uniform and initiation dues. Knocking nervously on her door, I called, "Mom, Mom, it's Deana. I need two dollars. I want to be a Brownie."

Eventually, she called out, "Come back at lunchtime, baby."

Dismayed, I answered, "But Mom, it is lunchtime."

I never got to wear the Brownie uniform.

ON THE rare occasions when Dad came to visit us at Mother's house, like at Christmas, she'd dress us up in the beautiful clothes Grandma Angela had made for us, tie ribbons in our hair, and make sure we were well behaved and polite.

"Sit up straight!" she'd say. "Elbows off the table. Mind your p's and q's." If we bit our fingernails we had to sit on our hands.

My earliest memory of Dad is one of those first Christmases. He and Jeanne had rented a big house on Woodruff Drive, less than a block away. He walked to our home, laden with presents. We were too shy to run and embrace him, so we kept our distance and thanked him coyly for each gift he gave us. He was always impeccably dressed and smelling of his special cologne, Fabergé Woodhue, which he wore until the day he died.

He had the most enormous hands, all wrinkled and fleshy, and he'd scoop us up in them and hold us to him. Whenever he played jacks and pick-up sticks with us, we were amazed because he could easily pick up the entire collection with just one hand. I remember him placing my hand in the palm of his one day and laughing at me.

"Why, Deana, baby," he said, his eyes sparkling, "your hand's so tiny."

Dad was always so sweet to us; he'd never raise his voice or tell us what to do. He loved us and enjoyed being with us, but—as with everything in his life—only in small doses.

Once his all-too-brief visit had ended and we were tucked up in bed, reliving every magical moment in our minds, Mother would unscrew the knob from her bedroom door and cry herself to sleep.

Her rhythmic sobs, night after night, echoing along the landing, were the closest thing we had to a lullaby.

THE IRS came after both my parents when they found some serious discrepancies in their joint tax returns, which Abby Greshler had submitted years before. Dad left everything up to Abby and his business managers and was once again shocked to learn there was a problem. Typically, though, he didn't fire Abby immediately. Always willing to give someone a second chance, he gave him the opportunity to sort things out. There was a lot of sorting out to do; the IRS estimated that he and Jerry owed them in excess of $600,000.

Mother knew nothing about it until the IRS demanded that she pay back almost $100,000 of her alimony, cash she no longer had. Unable to raise the funds, she asked Dad for help, but he couldn't afford to pay his own bill. He was busy making his next film with Jerry, *The Stooge*, which was one of Jerry's favorite Martin & Lewis movies.

After months of negotiations with the IRS, they finally seized our house—the only home I'd known for seven years. Their action left Mother—and us—officially homeless. We were too young to understand how devastated Mother must have been.

"We're going on a big adventure," she told us, her eyes bright. "I've found somewhere great for us to live, so pack your things and let's get in the car." She always made everything seem like fun. It was her way of protecting us.

With the help of some good friends, she managed to retrieve her furniture, belongings, and personal records. She put them into storage, but then failed to meet the payments, so they too were seized by default. Ella Logan rented us her large Spanish-style house on Bristol Circle, Brentwood. Mother continued to live as flamboyantly as ever, throwing parties that went on all night. Once again she never let us know that her world was crumbling around her, and she made everything that was happening seem like something wonderful.

We were watching television when Elvis Presley made his first appearance on the *Ed Sullivan Show*. This show was originally called *The Toast of the Town* and Dad and Jerry had been the guest stars on the very first show. We'd also watch Dad and Jerry fooling around together hosting *The Colgate Comedy Hour*, which also featured Jack Benny, George Raft, Bob Newhart, Phyllis Diller, Mel Brooks, and Jimmy Durante. How we'd laugh at their silly antics. I remember one hilarious sketch where Dad played a ventriloquist to Jerry's dummy. We laughed so much our ribs hurt.

Although I loved watching the program on our black-and-white television with my brother and sisters, I don't think at the time I realized Dean Martin, the man with the beautiful voice and the winning smile, was anyone remotely related to me. Mother, however, sat enthralled, a glass pressed to her cheek as she watched his image flickering before her on the screen.

Dad and Jerry had just been voted the "Number-One Stars of Tomorrow" in a newspaper poll, and Dad was hailed as a triumph playing a freshman football star in his fourth movie with Jerry, *That's My Boy*. At thirty, Mother was very beautiful and seemed to have an abundance of cash, so there was no shortage of admirers to flatter her and help her spend it. Some persuaded her into investments that almost always mysteriously failed. She might have known these men for fifteen years or fifteen minutes, you could never tell. Most were perfectly fine, but some weren't.

One summer evening, Gail ran into the kitchen and pleaded with Emma, our cook, to call us all early for dinner.

"Why, honey?" Emma asked with a smile.

"Please," Gail whispered, her face pale. "Just come into the living room."

When Emma followed her in, wiping her hands on her apron, she was horrified to find one of mother's guests sitting opposite us, his pants around his ankles, exposing himself. I was about six years old.

Mother was summoned, and immediately she called the police. My older sisters remember being interviewed by a police officer and telling him, very bashfully, that the nasty man had showed us his "thing." That sordid little episode was the first in a series of incidents that alerted the outside world that all was not right with the way we were being raised. Unbeknownst to us, these events were to change our lives forever.

memo to DEAN MARTIN

Bett

Dean and first wife, Betty, before they split. Then, she never took a drink. Now she pitches all-night binges for some of the most unsavory characters in Hollywood.

Four

NOT LONG AFTERWARD, *CONFIDENTIAL* MAGAZINE PUB-
lished a malicious article that only added to my mother's woes.
Titled "Memo to Dean Martin," it described Mother as "one of the
hardest drinkers in all Los Angeles," and went on to say that "her
companions on week-long bouts of guzzling are, for the most part,
some of the most unsavory characters in Hollywood." The Bristol
Circle house was said to be "the drinkingest house in Hollywood." It
claimed the police had been called there on several occasions, includ-

ing once to arrest a man for violation of parole on a statutory rape charge. Presumably this was our flasher. The article went on,

> The kids? Well they could tell you plenty about what goes on there. They could tell you about living on a pot of spaghetti for as long as a week at a time while Betty tosses champagne binges for her hoodlum friends on the three and a half thousand dollars a month you give her. Betty's own menu would frighten a confirmed alcoholic. Day after day, she'll start off with vodka and orange juice or tequila and lime juice for breakfast, switch to pink champagne and follow that up with quarter-hourly slugs of Scotch until far into the dawn.
>
> But you've been too busy to know all this, Dean. You dropped by the house a couple of times last spring but didn't stay long enough—either time—to learn what was really going on.... It's a tough problem ... but don't lose sight of something important. There's something special about 12812 Sunset Boulevard. Your children live there too!

The article was sensationalized and unnecessarily cruel. Mother was beside herself. She went to see Aunt Anne, clutching a copy of the magazine in her hand. Anne had never seen her so upset.

"Somebody sold me out," she wailed, trembling. "Somebody was paid money to tell them terrible, untrue things." No matter how she tried, Anne couldn't calm her down. Mother couldn't afford to sue for libel, even though the reporter who wrote the article had never attempted to contact her or her friends to tell her side of the story. *Confidential* magazine was eventually shut down because of the type of unconfirmed articles it ran.

With reporters and paparazzi on our heels, and unable to meet the rent, we had to quickly move from the Bristol Circle house. Mother woke us at two o'clock in the morning, and told us to get up.

"Hey, kids, we're going on a great excursion," she cried. "I bought us a horse ranch in Las Vegas, and we're going to move there right now. Get up and put your clothes on."

"Why are you waking us up, Mother?" we asked, our eyes full of sleep. "What time is it?"

"Time for all you little doggies to be dead, don't you feel sick?" she replied. Only this time we didn't laugh.

Climbing into Mother's new Cadillac, we arrived in Vegas just as the sun was rising over the desert, silhouetting the cactus. Only it wasn't a horse ranch after all, just sand with a chain-link fence and bunk beds—and the horses were too wild to ride. The house was beige, the land was beige, and the sky was beige. I remember asking Mother, "Can't we live somewhere with color?"

We enrolled at the Sunrise Acres School, which was also beige, but we didn't stay long enough for the teachers to remember our names. Instead, we returned to L.A. with two German ranch hands (one of whom didn't speak English), and turned up on the doorstep of Aunt Anne's one-bedroom apartment in Culver City.

"Hi, Anne, dear, can you put us up for a while?" Mother asked. Anne watched as all six of us trooped in and we stayed for two weeks, including Christmas. The German ranch hand Kurt regaled us with strange tales of his time in the Hitler Youth before the war.

Unable to stay there any longer, we moved again. This time to a rustic split-level house on Horseshoe Canyon, in the mountains north of Beverly Hills. We'd entertain ourselves by throwing Mother's Dinah Washington and Billie Holiday LPs like frisbees off into the canyon below from the wooden deck. At this house, Mother threw some of her wildest parties yet.

Regardless of the exaggerations of the *Confidential* article, Dad must have believed every word, because he cut Mother off without a penny. His brother Bill eventually persuaded him not to stop the child support, but her alimony was stopped. She'd lost her house, she was about to lose her car, and most of the friends who had only stuck around for the parties and the free booze evaporated. Many were torn between their allegiance to Dad and Mother, and ultimately they chose Dad.

Mother, by contrast, was now an insomniac with a drinking problem who'd been publicly vilified. She had never been more isolated.

Her parties continued, regardless. We didn't mind because they were always such fun and it was a lifestyle to which we had grown accustomed. I thought everyone lived like this—waking up to a house full of empty Lancers or Mateus rosé bottles, with cigarette butts floating in them.

Mother didn't like housework, and after a while the maids disappeared. She hated doing the laundry and would rather buy us new clothes in bulk than wash the old ones. However, school clothes needed to be clean, so my sister Gail made sure we were neat and tidy for classes. She'd sift through the great mound of clothes on the bedroom floor and find us something decent to wear. She'd wash and iron three shirts, as well as Mother's full-skirted dresses. Gail took care of us all. She'd make us snacks of peanut butter on celery when we were hungry, wash the dishes, and walk me to school. Without Gail, we'd never have held it together. And sometimes, late at night, during Mother's more raucous parties, Gail would lock us in the closet to keep us safe.

Mother was tremendous fun. She was smiling, loving, generous to a fault, and incredibly warm-hearted. She adored us kids and loved to be surrounded by people and laughter. God knows how she managed it, but our lives were crammed full of ballet, tap-dancing, and riding lessons, beach trips, parties, and grunion-hunting. If we weren't at school, we were riding bikes or playing ball or going to the bars with her. She made sure there was never a dull moment, for her or for us.

Endlessly reading the gossip columns, fearful of what she might find, Mother snipped any cutting she could find about Dad, as she had when they were together. She'd marvel at the crowds that mobbed the hotel when he and Jerry took their show to New York and revel in his critical acclaim on the silver screen. Never once did she seem bitter about how well he was doing. On the contrary, it seemed like vindication for all the time she'd put in teaching him manners and pronunciation to help make him a star.

Occasionally, Dad's latest tunes would come on the jukebox in whichever bar we were in, and Mother would sit listening, enthralled as he sang "Come Back to Sorrento" or "Until."

"That's my husband, the father of these children," she'd tell anyone who'd listen, dragging the graying hair from her eyes and smoothing down her skirt.

"Sure, lady," would come the reply.

◈

I CAN'T remember having many friends as a young girl—a result, I think, of moving around so much. Nor can I recall many childhood birthdays or social gatherings other than Mother's parties. I only know that between the ages of seven and nine, it seemed as if I went through third grade three times because every time I arrived at a new school, I was in a new third grade class.

On yet another first day at a new school, Wonderland Avenue, the teacher stood with me at the front of the class and said, "This is Deana, and Deana has some special news, don't you, Deana?"

I looked up at the teacher with a smile, surprised and delighted if that was so. "I do?" I said, wondering what it was.

"Yes," the teacher replied. "Can I tell everyone, Deana? Is that okay?"

"Okay," I said, shrugging my shoulders, as eager as the rest to hear it.

"Deana is Dean Martin's daughter!" the teacher announced excitedly. I looked up at her and back at my applauding classmates and wondered why they were clapping.

At another school, the Bel-Air Town & Country, if I was good and attended class all term, I'd be allowed to sit in the principal's office and drink hot chocolate by the open fire. I loved that school, with its old-fashioned rituals and navy blue uniforms, but I was there a very short time. I was sad to leave and told my sisters so.

"But I like it here," I said to Gail.

"I know, Deana," she said, stroking my hair. "We like it too."

"I was the May queen," said Claudia, "and I've never been that before."

"You looked beautiful," I told her, smiling. "With the flowers in your hair, the maypole, and the ribbons."

"But you know, sometimes we have to do things we don't like," said Gail. "You know Mother. Off we go. So let's just make it easier for her. Okay?"

One of Gail's closest friends was Liza Minnelli, who she knew through Mother's friendship with Judy Garland. From what we heard, Liza's home life was pretty much the same as ours. Liza called Mother "Mop," I don't know why. My mother adored Liza and her mother, who was always great fun. Mother also adored Liza's father, Vincente, who'd come by to collect his daughter and usually stayed for a drink. Liza's half sister, Lorna Luft, was younger and became a friend. We'd go over to their house on Mapleton, where her mother would usually be doing something fun. Gail, Liza, and I put on a little play for Judy in the yard. Liza and Gail sang and danced, and I played a tree. Judy loved every minute. Clapping her hands delightedly, she told me, "You were the best tree I ever saw." I was so proud.

Another thing I remember about Judy was that she had the most amazing ability to apply her bright red lipstick perfectly without looking in the mirror. Judy had such a fabulous talent; she was a huge star. I'd seen *The Wizard of Oz* a dozen times, and here was Dorothy, all grown up. She was very much like my mother in many ways—gaining weight, losing weight, drinking and having parties, smart, sassy, and funny to be around.

Mother had introduced us to her boyfriends in the past, like Rainbo and the actor Nicky Blair, but I'd never really thought of her as having relations with these men.

One night, however, I awoke with a raging thirst. As I shuffled past Mother's room, I noticed that her door was ajar. "Mother?" I called, pushing open the door. "I'm thirsty."

Lying in bed with my mother was Ed Townsend, a popular singer at the time. The words of his hit song "For Your Love" were written by Mother for Dad after he'd left: "More hopeless I grow with each heartbeat."

I was so shocked to see Ed in bed with Mother, I just stood there staring.

"Okay, baby," my mother replied, pulling the sheets around them, "you know where the kitchen is. Get yourself a glass of water and go right back to bed."

◆◆◆

MY FATHER was as busy as ever, recording albums, making movies and money as if there were no tomorrow. I'm sure that was why he rarely dropped by. As a child in what was effectively a single-parent family, I had never known what it was like to have a father around all the time, so what I didn't know, I didn't miss. It was only when I grew up that I realized how little Dad had featured in my early years. Protecting myself from the hurt, I began to make excuses for him—something I have continued to do throughout my life. The truth was that he didn't take the time to see his children very often and, with all the yearning of the shy little girl that I was, I now sincerely wish he had.

He could read sheet music, but he liked to learn new songs by just listening to them a couple of times and then recording. Eager not to waste unnecessary hours in the studio, and possessing the fantastic ability to get it right the first time, he took only two days to record an average album. His public loved it, buying his songs almost as fast as he made them.

He had also made a series of films in quick succession. *Sailor Beware* had him playing the serious friend to Jerry's misunderstood idiot. *Jumping Jacks* was shot at Fort Benning, Georgia; its story had Dad leaving a successful show-business partnership to join the army, pursued by his sidekick. It was hailed as one of their best films ever.

Their ratings pushed the unlikely team into superstar status, along with screen idols like Gregory Peck, Bette Davis, and Cary Grant, with whom their films vied for box-office receipts. Their ongoing popularity on the silver screen and on *The Colgate Comedy Hour* crossed all age, nationality, and gender barriers. Entire families would stay home, waiting for them to be beamed into their living rooms, or go see their movies repeatedly, trying to catch the gags they'd missed.

Dad and Jerry hosted their first charitable telethons to raise money for muscular dystrophy and for a new cardiac hospital. They had a cameo role in a popular Bob Hope and Bing Crosby movie, *Road to Bali.* They renegotiated their contract with Paramount, increasing their salary to a million dollars a year. They completed *Scared Stiff,* a comedy horror film starring Carmen Miranda. In it, Dad sang the memorable "You Belong to Me," which turned into yet another recording hit. There was no medium he could not conquer.

Mother saw every movie Dad ever made and usually took us along. We thought Jerry was hysterical and loved to watch his crazy antics, while Dad acted the straight man. I can remember standing in line outside one theater in Westwood to see their latest film and staring openmouthed at Dad's name on the billboard.

"That's your father's name up there," Mother told me.

"And you remember the spelling we did yesterday, Deana?" Gail added.

"Yes," I said, unable to take my eyes off the giant letters.

"Well, see Dad's name, spelled D-E-A-N?"

"Yes."

"Well, that's exactly the same as yours. You just add an *a.*"

For the first time in my life, I realized the connection between us.

◆◆◆

DAD AND Jeanne separated briefly in early 1953, something that happened every now and again, as it had with Mother. As a young child, living somewhere else, I had no idea they had separated, least of all why. It was only a long time later that I discovered things had not always been as rosy between them as they liked people to believe. Not that they would ever talk about it. The family mind-set was "Don't dwell, don't go crazy about issues, get over them." From my earliest days I can remember being encouraged to pick myself up and then move past problems, and never let them get me down. "This is tough, but it's tougher for other people. At least we're good looking," was one of Jeanne's favorite sayings. To her credit, Jeanne rarely spoke openly of the problems she and Dad had; the closest she came was when she'd complain that Dad never had any time for her. For Mother and us in those busiest days of his career, that certainly rang true. Jeanne claimed Dad was never home and had treated her as little more than a housekeeper and nanny in the four years they'd been married.

"He never talks. There's just no communication going on at all, I'm completely shut out," she'd say. "He's the quietest man in the world." The honeymoon was well and truly over.

It was almost over with Martin & Lewis as well, even though they were nominated for an Emmy and had been voted America's biggest box-office draw. Dad was going through a difficult time with his demanding, egotistical partner. In the movie *The Caddy*, they played a comedy duo looking back on how they met. The film produced one of Dad's biggest recording hits, "That's Amore," which immediately sold more than two million copies and warranted an Academy Award nomination for best song. But his grueling film and recording schedule was taking its toll. He and Jerry traveled to England for a series of shows. For a time it seemed as if things were turning sour between them.

Mother childishly believed that Dad might come back to us once he and Jeanne split, but it wasn't to be. Waiting at home for him to call, she read in the celebrity pages of the newspapers that he'd returned to his young bride when he found out she was pregnant with their second child. He promised to spend more time with her, and in an effort to patch things up he told her to look for a new house in Beverly Hills. Just as Jeanne discovered the perfect home, 601 Mountain Drive, my brother Ricci was born.

On learning the news, Mother smashed just about every glass we owned in the house. Gail and Claudia and I had to clean up the shards for days.

Dad continued to make movies with Jerry. Their twelfth film together, in 1954, was *3 Ring Circus* with Zsa Zsa Gabor, and it was then that the tensions between them really started to show. Dad didn't like his character and was given just one solo song, which he had to perform to a cage full of animals. Jerry, who likened himself to Charlie Chaplin with his skills in acting, filmmaking, and directing, began pushing his partner out.

Jerry was jealous of Jeanne and the hold she had over Dad, and they became rivals for Dad's affection. Jerry admitted to me years later that he had, indeed, been unkind to Jeanne.

"Dean was my partner and I wanted him all to myself," he said.

It was an impossible situation for Dad, and he withdrew into himself, barely speaking to Jerry and rarely socializing with him off the set. Patti and Jeanne weren't the best of friends, either, and Jerry surrounded himself with rising stars like Tony Curtis and Janet Leigh. Dad and Jerry's new agent, Herman Citron, urged them to make up for their continuing club dates and their next three movies, *You're Never Too Young*, *Artists and Models*, and *Pardners*. It wasn't easy for Dad, and if you watch those films now, you can tell.

Dad and Jeanne separated briefly again, and she moved to Palm Springs temporarily. At the same time, the IRS came down hard on Dad over unpaid taxes. The government even froze his bank accounts for a while. His financial situation was bleak, his marriage was in trouble, and he was tiring of his partner. There were high points, such as the continuing success of "That's Amore" and, a little later, "Memories Are Made of This," which sold more than a million copies. He returned to Jeanne when he discovered she was pregnant again with their third child.

Dad's patience with Jerry was running out. Neither of them was speaking to the other, and he was looking for a way out. Their final film was a road movie aptly titled *Hollywood or Bust*, about two friends who drive across America. The director, as exasperated with Jerry as Dad was, ordered Jerry off the set, and when he returned, Dad lost his legendary cool. He was tired of Jerry's ego and his need to control just about every aspect of their productions.

Then the day came when Dad just couldn't take it anymore. He was angry and hurt. Jerry insisted he dress up as a policeman in their next movie, *The Delicate Delinquent*.

"But I hate uniforms. Why can't I play a detective?" Dad had asked him.

"Because the script calls for a cop."

"You wrote the damn script, change it. I don't want to play a cop," Dad replied.

"Then we'll have to get someone else," Jerry said, staring Dad in the face.

"Start looking, boy," Dad replied, before turning and walking away.

ALTHOUGH DAD had enjoyed considerable success with his records, it was a brave and—many thought—foolish decision to walk out on such a moneymaking partnership. The pair were still involved in dozens of lawsuits, everything from unsettled tax cases to private suits from individual agents and writers who wanted a piece of the pie. At one point it was estimated that they were being sued for a total of almost $12 million.

The nation held its collective breath when the news of the split broke in the spring of 1956. Lou Costello and Jackie Gleason placed ads in the trade papers begging Dad and Jerry to change their minds for the sake of their fans. Nobody could quite believe that this unique team was parting after ten years. Before Dad or Jerry even had a chance to reply, Abbott and Costello had split as well.

Kids would come up to me at school and ask, "Is it true? Are Martin and Lewis really breaking up?"

"I don't know anything," I'd reply truthfully, and flee from their suspicious stares.

I was as disappointed as anybody. As a child, one of my favorite movies was *At War With the Army*, which Jeanne had invited us up to Mountain Drive to see. Dad and she had a 16-mm projector with a screen that came down from the ceiling in the living room. I can vividly remember sitting on Dad's lap in that big room, my arm hooked around his neck, laughing as he and Jerry and the rest of the cast constantly shuffled in and out of doors. They were so good together, and made so many people laugh, that like everyone else in the country I couldn't imagine it was over.

After fulfilling a few joint obligations, including some packed final club dates, Martin & Lewis parted for good. When Jerry wrote an article criticizing both Dad and Jeanne, claiming that all Dad wanted to do was play golf and do the minimum, the gloves came off.

In Dad's own inimitable style, he announced, "I've severed all connections. As far as I'm concerned, Jerry Lewis doesn't exist anymore in my life." It was nearly twenty years before they made up.

⚜

LIFE FOR my mother was becoming increasingly difficult. More than a year had passed since the *Confidential* article, and Dad was still withholding funds. She must have been worried sick about our future and her own, and yet she rarely confided in anyone, even her sister Anne. Her only solace was the privacy of her own room, with a glass in her hand. We certainly knew little about her problems, except that maybe the laundry was piling higher and the house growing a little shabbier. This was when she really started to lose control, I now realize. She spent more and more time in her room with the doorknob removed, and my sisters had to walk me to school.

Unable to meet the bills at the house on Horseshoe Canyon, Mother announced we were moving in with a friend. She told us, "Pack a little suitcase and your schoolbooks, girls. We'll come back for the rest later." We knew we had never returned to any place before, so we grabbed our most precious belongings and our favorite games and climbed into the car.

"Does this mean we have to go to another school, Mother?" I asked from the backseat as we pulled away from the house. The idea of yet another first day at a new school, the enrollment, and the inevitable announcement that I was Dean Martin's daughter, filled me with dread.

The parents of the other children never quite believed who we were. "If these are Dean Martin's children, why are they not at a private school in Beverly Hills?" they'd ask. The question would be handed down to their children. It was easier for Gail and Claudia to get away with it. But little Deana—Dean with an *a*—wasn't so lucky.

Our new home belonged to Mother's friend, a nightclub singer named Jackie Garcia. She lived with her husband, Kenny, and their son, Kevin, in a tiny bungalow on Harper Avenue in Hollywood. Claudia, Gail, and I slept in the same bed as Mother, in a small guest room.

We didn't like the change. It seemed our homes were shrinking. But we tried to make the best of a bad situation. Gail, Claudia, and Mother got out the cards, and we played games that reminded us of happier times. No matter how limited our means or space, playing hearts and Pokeno was always a way of escaping.

A few weeks after we moved in, Jackie won the *Queen for a Day* television contest, chosen from a group of contestants who competed for the saddest story of misfortune. She was a dear, sweet woman and we were very happy for her when she won. She was picked up in a limousine and taken to buy a new television, clothes, and food. If the newspapers had only known that Dean Martin's kids were living with her at the time, they'd have gone crazy.

Dad certainly didn't know. He was in Rome with a pregnant Jeanne making his first picture without Jerry, *Ten Thousand Bedrooms*. His co-star was Anna Maria Alberghetti (whom he always referred to as "Anna Maria Spaghetti"). He played a millionaire who buys a hotel in Rome to find romance. The script called for him to hold Miss Alberghetti's face in his hands, but when he did, her tiny, almond-shaped features completely disappeared.

It was while living with Jackie Garcia and attending Rosewood Elementary School that I was involved in a serious traffic accident. A truck hit the school bus broadside in a driving rain one afternoon and pushed us off the road. I hit my head and was cut, but not too badly. The press came and took my photograph as I was being taken away in an ambulance. Mother was there, screaming and crying, "My baby, what happened to my baby!" I was allowed to return home later and, apart from being a little shaken, I was fine.

The newspapers ran the story of the accident the next day: DEAN MARTIN'S DAUGHTER IN BUS ACCIDENT!, with a photo of me looking like a little orphan. Mother kept the clipping, but she hated the photograph of herself so much that she neatly removed her own image with scissors.

There was another story in the papers around that time, which Mother didn't clip. Jeanne gave birth to her third child, my baby sister Gina. Mother was devastated.

"Oh, gee," she told Aunt Anne, "I wish ours had been the only girls."

Gina's arrival finally made it clear to her that Dad was never coming back to us, and she didn't know how to face life without him.

Five

FOR A TIME, DAD WONDERED WHAT HE WOULD DO NEXT.
The critics expected him to sink without a trace after he split from
Jerry. As he turned forty, he realized that aside from branching out
on his own in films, his only hope of making money was to rekindle
his act as a nightclub entertainer.

He sought the advice of Ed Simmons, a talented comedy writer
he'd previously worked with on *The Colgate Comedy Hour*. With
Ed's help, Dad perfected his stage persona of the lovable lush singer,
cigarette and glass in hand and wisecrack at the ready. He'd played

a drunk successfully once before, in *The Stooge* with Jerry, and he revived some of the best lines he'd learned back then. He also modeled his character on the recently retired comedian Joe E. Lewis, whom he'd always found amusing. One of his favorite lines was, "You're not too drunk if you can lie on the floor without holding on."

Las Vegas seemed the most likely spot for his new character's debut. He felt at home among the bars and blackjack tables, and he went there to seek his fortune. On March 6, 1957, he performed his first forty-five-minute act at the Copa Room of the Sands Hotel and Casino. The owner was Jack Entratter, the former manager of the Copacabana in New York, who'd first helped Dad and Jerry make their name.

Dad's friend and fellow singer Frank Sinatra was king of the nearby Desert Inn, and there was a taste in town for the kind of smooth Italian crooner who appealed to both men and women. Despite Jack Entratter's familiar face, Dad was anxious about his debut. This was his first live public appearance without Jerry in years. The last time they'd appeared in Vegas was in 1950. Fortunately, Dad had the moral support of his companion Mack Gray, his accompanist Ken Lane, and his dresser Jay Gerard. Ken had been a voice coach at Paramount until Dad hired him as his bandleader. Jay was a former extra who'd been Dad's stand-in in *My Friend Irma*, and who became his wardrobe assistant shortly afterward. Mack, whose real name was Maxie Greenburg, had been an actor in the 1930s and 1940s. He was a former boxing manager who knew how to handle himself and others. Dad poached him in 1952 from one of his heroes, the actor George Raft, for whom Mack had worked as an assistant for over twenty years. Mack was to become Dad's most loyal friend and musical coordinator, and was by his side on that historic night.

Strolling woozily to the edge of the stage, singing a few tunes and fooling around with the audience, Dad unveiled his new character. A glass of apple juice masquerading as scotch in his hand, he perfected a role that was going to become, to many, indistinguishable from the real Dean Martin.

He spoke of his family and made us the affectionate butt of some of his best jokes. "I forgot to tell you about Jeanne's terrible accident," he told the audience. "She drank my orange juice at breakfast." Another line was, "I have seven beautiful kids." The audience would applaud and he'd hold up his hand. "Don't clap, it only took seven minutes." The crowd, which included his friends Lucille Ball, Desi Arnaz, Debbie Reynolds, and Jack Benny, went berserk. The management of The Sands booked him for a five-year run, at $25,000 per week. It was the start of a twice-yearly, six-week booking that Dad happily performed for more than thirty years.

WHEN HE returned to L.A. from a nationwide tour of the most prominent East Coast clubs, he paid a surprise visit to Mother to ask her advice. She had, after all, been his main source of support and encouragement for years when he was first starting out, and he valued her opinion. It must have taken a lot for them to set aside all their differences and sit down together. She responded with generosity of spirit.

Dad needed all the help he could get. *Ten Thousand Bedrooms* had flopped. Critics described it as lacking in pace and style, and the audience had showed its disdain for Dad's decision to leave Jerry and go it alone. One reviewer commented, "It isn't just Jerry that's missing." Another said, "Apart from Lewis, Mr. Martin is a fellow with a little humor and a modicum of charm." To make matters worse, Jerry was doing well, both in his own films and, amazingly, for the first time as a recording artist with an album that went gold.

"Things aren't working out," Dad told Mother, miserably. "It's been tough since I split with Jerry. I now have two wives and seven children to support and, apart from some success in Vegas, I've had to go back to working the clubs in places like Pittsburgh. I've been given a break—a part in a war film called *The Young Lions* with a couple of big shots, Montgomery Clift and Marlon Brando. It's terrible money, but I'd virtually pay them to do it. Only trouble is I'm scared. I don't know if I'm going to be able to pull it off."

Mother sat him down. "Listen to me, Dino Crocetti," she told him, taking him firmly by the shoulders. "You can do this. You're going to be a big star. I've always known that. They're probably terrified of working with someone like you, who can stand on a stage live and completely win over a crowd. Don't you dare have a crisis of confidence now."

Dad said later that the two greatest turning points of his career were meeting Jerry Lewis and leaving Jerry Lewis. "I became a real actor because of those two things," he added.

In *The Young Lions* he portrayed a Broadway singing star, Michael Whiteacre, who avoids being drafted into the army. Whiteacre ends up in the heat of the action in Europe, caught between a disgruntled Nazi officer, played by Marlon Brando, and a shy, Jewish-American GI played by Montgomery Clift. Frank Sinatra had scooped an Oscar the previous year for his impressive acting skills in *From Here to Eternity*. Dad's agent, Herman Citron, hoped Dad might do the same.

In the end it was Montgomery Clift who helped him through. The brilliant young actor with the tortured soul, his face recently shattered by a car accident, taught Dad method acting and helped him learn his lines. Dad never forgot his kindness and became Monty's friend and drinking partner while on location in Paris. He helped him through some of the worst excesses of his drug abuse and enjoyed socializing with him. The two men formed a special bond that transcended any public criticism over Monty's homosexuality. As with Jerry, Dad was never afraid to show the critics that two men could have a healthy and close relationship regardless of their sexuality.

Brando was trickier. A perfectionist, he asked for take after take until he was satisfied with his performance. When he finally shot Brando in the closing scene, Dad quipped, "That was great. All I ever killed so far was time." For me, Dad's role in *The Young Lions* was one of his finest performances as an actor. It was certainly the one of which he was proudest. He was paid less for that movie than he received for a week at The Sands, but he didn't care. This film, above all others, brought him something money couldn't buy—the respect of his peers. If he'd stayed with such serious roles, instead of accepting some of the more frivolous ones he was too afraid to turn down, I think he could have developed into an Oscar-winning actor.

After three months' filming in Paris under the direction of Edward Dmytryk, Dad was thrown a glittering welcome-home party at the Villa Capri by Jeanne and their friends. He was glad to be home. He did not enjoy Europe, claiming Barney's Beanery served better food than any he'd had there. The lyricist Sammy Cahn hosted the evening and made an audio recording of it, he said, "to be used at Dean's trial." I still have a copy, which I listen to every now and again, and it makes me smile. It is a timeless cameo from a world long gone, an age of elegance, style, and humor. Dad, the ultimate icon of cool, had become Hollywood royalty, and yet the superstars breathing the same rarefied air around him were just his pallies.

The Hollywood gossip columnists were clamoring at the door to find out what was going on inside the Villa Capri. Everyone who was anyone was there from Dad's co-stars in the film, such as the stunning actress May Britt, to the established legends. With Sammy Cahn on the piano and Frank Sinatra heckling in the background, Dad sang a special version of "Alone" that Sammy had written for him. It went, "Alone, all alone in a plane I was Paris-bound, alone with no Jeanne and no Mack around . . . Alone in a berth wide enough for three, alone with only a pillow where Jeanne should be . . . Dmytryk tried my spirits, time and time to lift, Dmytryk ain't no neat trick and neither is Clift. Alone in the bistro, alone in the bar. Alone with Marlon who just talks and talks the part. It's no fun getting off, my friends, by transatlantic phone. Believe me, chums, it's the last time I'll go alone."

Jo Stafford stood up and sang a song about Dad: "He didn't know the art of method acting, which started new careers. The mumbled lines, that's halted and retracting, Dean's been talking like that for years."

Sammy then sang a version of "The Poor People of Paris" that included the line "And the world's most lonely hookers are as sad as they can be, because he's not in Paris, France."

Other people who participated included Howard Keel, who sang "Dean hates Paris in the Springtime," Jeanne's friends Gloria Cahn, Jackie Gershwin, and Eddie Fisher sang a song to the tune of "Love and Marriage." Sammy even dragged Mack Gray up onto the stage and had him do a turn with Frank Sinatra and Howard Keel. Frank sang too, an honor Dad reciprocated at Frank's forty-second birthday party at the Villa Capri in 1957, when he sang a version of "He's the Top" with the words "He's the Wop." They would continue to bat different versions of that song back and forth at each other over the years. On Dad's post-Paris night, however, he and Jeanne sat back and enjoyed what proved to be an extraordinarily memorable evening. Looking around the room that night, having just successfully completed his first serious movie role, with his stunning wife by his side and his glamorous friends paying him the ultimate tribute in one of Hollywood's finest restaurants, Dad knew he'd finally arrived.

◆◆◆

ONE AFTERNOON in November 1957, shortly after Dad had returned from Paris, Mother took Claudia, Gail, and me to stay with our aunt. Anne was pregnant with her fourth child and living with her husband, Dale, in a two-bedroom house in North Hollywood. We had overstayed our welcome at Jackie Garcia's bungalow and had to go. There was nowhere for us to play, apart from a square patch of grass in front of the building, and Mother had to take us out for meals because there was no room for us all in the little dinette.

This particular afternoon was no different from any other. Mother bundled us all in the car with a smile and told us, "Okay, kids, let's go and see Aunt Anne for a bit. I think Jackie needs some space."

As we pulled up outside Aunt Anne's, I remember thinking, *Oh, so we're going to stay here for the afternoon.* Mother made it seem fun. None of us realized the significance of that day. None of us knew, when Mother drove off in her car, waving and smiling, promising to be back in three hours, that we'd never live with her again.

After three days she still hadn't returned. Without a change of clothing, we had only the clothes on our backs—matching brown and white checked shirts, blue jeans, and saddle shoes. Anne washed them and slipped us into some of her maternity tops as makeshift dresses while they dried. Exhausted and unable to find Mother in any of her usual haunts, she eventually contacted a mutual friend, a prominent attorney with a Southern accent known as Blossom, to ask her advice.

"I still have Betty's kids and I'm running out of money fast," Anne told her. "Dale only earns sixty dollars a week. I can't find Betty anywhere, and I don't know what to do."

Blossom was adamant. "Well, Anne," she said, "their father's living over there in Beverly Hills and he's got more money than God. Just take them over there and drop them off. You put them in the car right now, you hear?"

After leaving a note for my mother on her front door, she drove us to my father's house at 601 Mountain Drive, crying all the way. She didn't know she was followed by a private detective Dad had hired to keep tabs on us.

My father had just arrived home from recording his first NBC special, *The Dean Martin Show*, a one-time production he had been somewhat reluctantly persuaded to do, for which he was paid almost a quarter of a million dollars. He opened the big wooden front door as Anne rang the bell. Jeanne welcomed us and tried to make us feel at home. "Hi, kids! Anyone for hearts?" she asked, knowing how much we loved the game and trying to defuse the situation.

Dad and Anne stepped into his den. My aunt was nervous and upset, feeling she was betraying Mother, but she didn't know what else to do.

Dad made it easy for her. "I've been half expecting you," he said, smiling. "The private eye who's been watching the kids called."

"You mean you've had these kids followed, and you didn't intervene before now?" Anne cried, her face flushed with anger. "Do you have any idea what it took for me to bring them here, Dean?" Anne said. "And how upset Betty will be about all this?"

"Don't worry," Dad told her, drawing on a cigarette in his usual laid-back way. "Tell Betty she can have the kids back any time she wants."

Anne hit the roof. "And why would you do that, Dean? Do you have any idea what's been going on? They're not going to school, they're sitting in Barney's Beanery all day and they don't have a life. They're here now, and this is where they must stay." While a concerned Jeanne played cards with us outside, Dad and Anne decided our fate.

Within days, Mother's name and ours were splattered all over the gossip columns. DEAN MARTIN SNATCHES HIS KIDS BACK, ran one headline. Mother saw the reports on a newsstand, and rushed over to see Anne.

"What the hell's going on?" she said, confronting her baby sister. "I came to pick up the kids and you weren't here, and now Dean's taken them."

"You couldn't have come for the kids, Betty," Anne told her, as calmly as she could. "I left a note for you on the door, and it was still here when I got back."

"There was no note!" Mother cried, panicking.

"Yes, there was," her sister told her, retrieving it from a drawer. "Here it is."

Mother blushed. "Someone else must have taken it," she said.

"Taken it and put it back?" Anne said, arching an eyebrow.

Mother slumped. "Oh, all right," she conceded, "I didn't come for them, but I was planning to just as soon as I'd had some time to think." Looking up at Anne, she knew she was kidding no one. Heartbroken, Mother admitted herself to a clinic for the first of three unsuccessful sessions of rehabilitation, paid for by her friend Blossom.

Two weeks later, on November 17, 1957, Dad and Jeanne filed a suit at the Santa Monica Superior Court asking for custody of his children and declaring Mother unfit. They claimed that we'd been neglected, that we did not have a proper home, and that Mother had not made financial provision in terms of property or savings for our future, despite having been paid almost $350,000 in alimony and child support since her divorce from Dad. Jeanne swore, in an affidavit, that she was willing to have us live with her. "I wish to accept them into our home and treat them as if they were my children," she affirmed.

Mother didn't bother to show up for the hearing on December 10, and Judge Allen T. Lynch granted custody of us to Dad by default. None of us realized it at the time, but that was the day we lost her forever.

Six

A FEW DAYS AFTER ARRIVING AT MOUNTAIN DRIVE, three packing cases of our clothes and belongings turned up from nowhere. We'd last seen them at the house on Horseshoe Canyon, and they appeared in the foyer along with our little suitcases from Jackie Garcia's.

Seeing our belongings made us realize that we were going to be staying for a while. Watching Jeanne pick over them, I came to understand that she was now in charge. She told me years later that I was always in my own silent world as a little girl, lost in my thoughts. I didn't know why I was living in my father's house, and I just wanted Mother to come back and take us home.

The new house was enormous, five thousand square feet, set in its own orange groves with a stream. Our next-door neighbors were Tony Curtis and Janet Leigh. My two younger brothers, Dino and Ricci, were there, and my new baby sister, Gina. Mother had always taught me only to speak when I was spoken to, so I remained stoically silent. Meals were now prepared for me by servants, and served in a much more formal setting than I was used to. There was no paper-wrapped chicken to burn my fingers on, no burgers from Barney's Beanery. Intimidated and afraid, I lost my appetite completely.

Dad's dressing room became my temporary bedroom. Gail and Claudia moved in with Gina in her bedroom. For the first time in my life, I was sleeping apart from my sisters. Worse still, I was sent to bed a few hours before them. When I was supposed to be in bed, I would sit at the top of the stairs, peering through the banisters, listening for their voices, crying silent tears. Claudia and Gail were equally unsettled at first. Fourteen-year-old Claudia developed a nervous cough that strangely returned every year on the anniversary of our arrival at Dad's house. Gail took to comfort eating so much that Jeanne ended up putting her on a liquid diet in a Beverly Hills hospital. No sooner had we come to terms with our strange new surroundings than Dad and Jeanne told us we were moving again.

"We need to remodel the house, kids, to fit you all in, so we're sending you to boarding school until it's finished," Dad told us one night over dinner. "We're building a new wing over the garage for you. It'll be great."

Glancing at my sisters anxiously, I felt that it would be all right as long as I could just stay with them.

Dad saw our glum faces and tried to make light of it, adding, "Ain't no big deal, kids. I have over two hundred dollars in four different banks."

Later that night, Gail reassured me. "Did you hear what he said, Deana? They're building a wing for us. That must mean we're staying." Overwhelmed by the concept of remaining in one place, I slept better that night.

We were sent to Chadwick, an exclusive school in Rolling Hills, Palos Verdes, two hours' drive away. I hated everything about it. Gail and Claudia were placed in a separate dormitory in the high school, and I had to stay with the younger kids in grade school. I'd only get to see my sisters at mealtimes. The food was lousy, and I especially hated the chicken chow mein with slimy noodles. Every night I cried myself to sleep. I broke out in terrible hives, and was sent to the school nurse, who applied huge amounts of calamine lotion. I didn't eat. I didn't talk to anyone and couldn't concentrate on my studies. I was so far behind the other kids of my age, I didn't understand half of what was being taught and was put in third grade again. Then my leg became infected after I scratched it on a rusty nail.

After a few weeks the school called Dad and Jeanne, and someone came to collect me. I was relieved to be back at Mountain Drive, but also lonely. Gail and Claudia came home every other weekend, and I missed them terribly. I slept on a foldout sofa in Dad's wood-paneled dressing room every night, surrounded by his tailored clothes, handmade DiFabrizio shoes, and artifacts from his favorite westerns. I'd never had to go to bed alone in my life before. My sisters had always been near. Now here I was, in this rambling house, too terrified to voice my fears. I would watch as Dad would come into my room at night and collect his clothes, meticulously laying them out for the morning so as not to disturb me too early. He usually left around six A.M.

The house was still under construction, with workmen everywhere, creating the new wing. Jeanne was firmly in charge, somehow finding time for me, too, between choosing carpets, curtains, and color schemes. Her mother, Peggy, known to us as "Gams" because of her fabulous legs, helped out with everything, including fittings for school uniforms, trips to the dentist, and arrangements for my baptism.

Mother had never gotten around to getting me baptized. We never even went to church. Gail, Claudia, and Craig had all been christened in the days when Mother was still holding things together, but I was somehow overlooked. Jeanne and Dad wanted to send me to the Beverly Hills Catholic School with my new brothers, and when they asked for my records, the school discovered I hadn't been baptized. Jeanne took me to a little store in Westwood called Dina, where she bought me a beautiful white dress. Grandma Peggy stood up as my godmother and the songwriter Jimmy McHugh as my godfather at the Good Shepherd Church in Beverly Hills.

I liked my new school. It reminded me of a school I'd previously attended, Bel-Air Town & Country, with its structure and uniforms. I wore a gray plaid skirt and a white blouse. My fellow pupils included Desi Arnaz Jr., Dinah Shore's daughter Melissa Montgomery, and Danny Thomas's son Tony. Suddenly I wasn't so different. Other kids had famous parents, too.

Dad was away a lot, promoting his latest hit single, "Return to Me," and playing engagements as far away as Miami Beach. The only familiar face was that of my grandmother Angela, who'd regularly visited us with Craig when we lived with Mother. She was a remarkable woman, a very old soul, who never seemed fazed by anything. She'd arrive at the house to prepare huge amounts of gnocchi or pasta. I can remember great sheets of it laid out onto cooking trays in the kitchen and Grandma calmly and painstakingly making each piece.

When my sisters came home for the Christmas break, I began to accept that 601 Mountain Drive was my home and a place I was going to be staying for a while. The stability and the routines, dinner with the family, new clothes and warm beds soon soothed me. My friend Lorna Luft started coming over, enjoying the family life we had, never letting on that hers was slowly falling apart. Her mother, Judy Garland, had become increasingly troubled. Little by little, Jeanne made me feel more at home. Little by little, as I started to make friends at school for the first time, I began to speak.

Gail, on the other hand, who was thirteen, couldn't stop talking. She kept repeating over and over, "Why didn't we come and live here sooner?"

The home Dad called "the Big House" boasted a tennis court, a swimming pool, and hot and cold running maids. There was Alma, the live-in housekeeper, her giant of a husband, Freddy, who was our driver and handyman, and their daughter Sandra. There was Irma the maid, who was German, a cook called Fladia, who was Watusi, six feet tall and incredibly thin, a nanny named Maria who cared for Gina (until Dino and Ricci scared her off), and a laundress named Claudy, who spent her entire day washing and ironing.

The new wing was eventually completed, while Dad joked to friends and onstage that he had to eat standing up "because I screwed myself out of a seat." When asked how many kids he had, he'd say, "I think it's seven but I can't count that high." His father, Pop, when shown along the seemingly endless corridor that led to the new wing, quipped, "What's my room number?"

My brother Craig, then sixteen, came to live with us for a while. But he never seemed completely at ease in the Big House, and not long afterward he returned to our grandparents. Without my big brother, I gradually came to know my new little brothers and my sister Gina, who was nine years younger than I, and in a bassinette. Ricci was a cute toddler whom Jeanne doted on. Dean Paul, known to all as Dino, was three years younger than me, and a bit of a spoiled brat. He answered back all the time, giving the staff a hard time. Gail soon whipped him into shape, enforcing Mother Betty's strict rules and regulations and insisting that he and his brother behave. Once she'd taught him a few manners, Dino was fine and we soon became best friends. We were the closest in age, too young to do things with our older siblings, and too old for the younger kids. We went to the same school and hung out together, playing tennis and swimming in the pool.

Dino was gorgeous to look at, with Jeanne's blond hair and blue eyes. Like Craig, he loved everything to do with the military— guns, tanks, and especially airplanes. I can remember helping him make countless models, sticking them together with Duco cement, while he added the details and paint. He also loved go-karts and motorcycles—*The Great Escape* was his favorite film. We all rode Honda motorcycles around a specially built track that ran around the property. As a special treat, Jeanne had Steve McQueen come by the house and take Dino for a ride on the back of his bike and give him a few much-needed safety tips. Dino was in heaven. He dressed just like Steve, in a sweatshirt with the sleeves cut off and a pair of khaki trousers. Now, riding with his hero, he imagined himself tearing through the German countryside on his own great escape.

JEANNE TOOK us in with good grace, and I never once heard her complain. In fact, I later learned that it was she who persuaded Dad to have us followed by private detectives. All I knew, as a child, was that this gorgeous twenty-nine-year-old blonde, with her big blue eyes, was now my new mother. She filled our home with love and laughter, fun and games. She decorated it beautifully and spent thousands of dollars on antique furniture and paintings.

Dad, whose latest single, "Volare," had just gone gold, used to joke about the antiques, saying, "It's okay, honey, I earn enough, why don't you buy new furniture?"

Jeanne inherited her classic style from Grandma Peggy, who dressed impeccably and took us shopping at Saks Fifth Avenue. It was Peggy who made us wear gloves to church on Sunday and Peggy who chauffeured us around. She set an example for us with her pearls and spectator shoes, hat, and gloves. Dad adored Peggy almost as much as his own mother, and invited her to move in with us, although he ribbed her mercilessly in his stage act.

"My mother-in-law doesn't need glasses," he'd tell his audience. "She drinks right out of the bottle."

Peggy was always a good sport. With Jeanne's fine features, she was elegant, beautiful, and easy to please. Best of all, she had a gambling streak that Dad thought was wonderful. She loved to bet on the horses, especially gray ones, and had her own little bookie whom she'd call every day.

Jeanne's daily uniform was Jax pants and tops, white tennis shoes, always whiter than white, with her hair pulled back into a ponytail and her fingernails painted pink. She had a perfect figure and gorgeous eyelashes that curled naturally. We'd come into her bedroom in the morning to kiss her good-bye before school, and she'd lift her head from the pillow and look as if she'd just emerged from Hair and Makeup. She was an absolute doll. She had a toaster installed in her bedroom so that she could heat her crustless toast from her breakfast tray. Eggs over easy and crispy bacon. The breakfast of champions.

Jeanne was a lot like my mother in many ways. They shared the same sense of humor and a determination to remain optimistic against all odds. She filled our days. Our schedules were packed with school and swimming, tennis, dance classes, bike riding, ice skating, and horseback riding. As with Mother, there was never any time to dwell. We hadn't seen or heard from Mother since she dropped us at Aunt Anne's. Later I learned that she was in rehab during this time. Our overwhelming emotion was of huge relief that we were now somewhere so wonderful, without having to eat leftovers out of the refrigerator or spend the evening with her in bars. If ever I missed her, the cuddles and the kisses, the familiar scent of whiskey on her breath, I retreated to my own silent place within myself until some member of my new extended family dragged me out.

One day Jeanne took me to a recording studio at Capitol Records in Hollywood to watch Dad record "Memories Are Made of This." It was one of her favorite songs of his because of the lines "One house where lovers dwell, three little kids for the flavor. Stir carefully through the days, see how the flavor stays." Although the later song, "Everybody Loves Somebody," was the hit Dad was most frequently asked to sing, "Memories" was a favorite of Dad's, too, and his public seemed to agree with him. It was his first number-one hit.

I remember sitting next to Jeanne in the front row of hard metal seats at the studio that memorable day. I was so small that my feet didn't even touch the ground. Halfway through the recording, with my father standing in front of me, singing with that voice that always seemed to reverberate around my heart, I felt immensely comforted. Without even thinking, I slipped my little arm around my new mother's tiny waist and leaned against her for a cuddle.

"From now on, Deana," Jeanne told me with a surprised smile, returning my squeeze, "everything will be just fine."

HAVING SORTED out his personal life to everyone's satisfaction, except perhaps Mother's, once again Dad concentrated on his Hollywood career.

The Young Lions opened in New York and was a triumph. It was described by many as one of the best films about World War II ever made. Based on the novel by Irwin Shaw, it was nominated for two Academy Awards. Playing a character who begins as a weak man but who finds hidden strengths in himself and others, Dad showed the world that he was a great actor.

The same year *The Young Lions* was made, Dad—as an added insurance policy—launched the first of the NBC television specials he had been working on the day we went to live with him. The show featured guests James Mason and Louis Prima and was a ratings success. For his second show, his guest was Frank Sinatra. It was to become a pilot for something bigger than even he could have imagined. That year he also recorded no less than twenty-seven singles, three of which became best-sellers: "Return to Me," "Angel Baby," and "Volare," which sold over three million copies.

He followed up *The Young Lions* with a critically acclaimed non-singing role as a gambler in the film *Some Came Running*, directed by Mother's old friend Vincente Minnelli, which was nominated for six Oscars. Dad loved making that movie. He once told me he had more fun on that set in Madison, Indiana, than on any other film he ever made. He got the part through his friend Frank Sinatra.

"I'd read in the paper that Frank was looking for a guy to play a blackjack dealer," he said. "So I walked over to him and said, 'You're looking for a guy who smokes, drinks, and plays cards. You're looking at him.' Frank laughed and said, 'What do you know? You're right.' He hired me on the spot."

His co-star was Shirley MacLaine, who became a good friend to them both. Dad and Frank shared a house and played cards late into the night with Frank's assorted associates. For Dad and Shirley, this was their second movie together—she'd starred as a dancer in *Artists and Models*. She had an enormous crush on Dad and was more than happy to be working with him. *Some Came Running* was well received by the critics, and after his success in *The Young Lions*, Dad suddenly found himself with starring roles in two of the hit movies of the year.

Shirley told me years later that Vincente was a very demanding director. In one scene, set in an amusement park, Dad, Shirley, and Frank all had to run toward a giant Ferris wheel. The scene took an age to set up, and just as they were about to start filming, Vincente looked through his viewfinder, shook his head, and yelled, "Move the Ferris wheel ten feet to the left!"

"Your Dad and Frank took one look at each other, jumped into a limousine, and didn't come back for a week," Shirley said. "They had some other place to be and came back when they were good and ready."

At The Sands, where Dad was now booked in twice a year, he started to invite some of his pallies. Frank Sinatra and Sammy Davis Jr. began as members of the audience, sitting at the front tables, making wisecracks. Dad would tell Sammy, "Keep smiling, Smokey, so the spotlight can find you." Dad loved Sammy. When Sammy lost an eye in a car accident, Dad and Frank both wore eye patches to give him moral support.

Then one night in 1959, Frank, who wasn't content with his slot over at the Desert Inn, invited himself onto the stage for a couple of numbers and to crack a few jokes.

"He's only got a tan because he found a bar with a skylight," Frank quipped of Dad, who gave back as good as he got.

"Don't believe it when they say carrots are good for your eyes," he told Frank. "I stuck one in mine last night and it hurt." If he stumbled over a word, he'd add, "I got my nose fixed and now my mouth don't work."

"Water?" he told Sammy, "That stuff'll make you rust."

Another favorite was "If you drink, don't drive. In fact, don't even putt."

The audience, sensing they were witnessing something unique and completely off the cuff, cried for more. Before Dad knew it, Frank had cajoled the rest of their friends on stage, too. This disorganized, unpredictable, and self-indulgent shambles of a boys' night out kept the participants, and those watching, on the very edge of their seats.

Dad always joked, "It's Frank's world. We're just living in it."

Before long, Dad's billing under The Sands's famous flashing neon sign with the slogan A PLACE IN THE SUN read PRESENTS DEAN MARTIN, adding enticingly, MAYBE FRANK. MAYBE SAMMY. Soon the English actor Peter Lawford would be invited to join them. Joey Bishop (who didn't drink) was brought in by the management to try to keep the whole thing together. The ensuing gang were collectively to become known as the Rat Pack (after the Holmby Hills Rat Pack, a tag given to a group headed by Judy Garland, Humphrey Bogart, and Lauren Bacall). They squeezed their shows between mammoth poker games and endless rounds of golf. Regardless of who was holding the kite strings, Dad was truly flying high.

Seven

MOTHER CAME TO VISIT US ONCE OR TWICE FROM THE house she was now staying in on Lookout Mountain with a friend, Georgia Sarkisian. Georgia had a daughter, Cherilyn, who was a few years older than me. Cherilyn was at the same school as Claudia and incredibly tall next to a petite girl like me. She was shy and struck me as being rather lonely. The only time she came out of herself was when she started singing. Her voice was a surprise, low and sexy for such a young woman. The moment she opened her mouth, we knew she was going places. Later she would become known to the world as Cher.

Mother's appearances in my life were brief, arranged visits, during which she'd arrive in a haze of perfume that suddenly seemed unfamiliar.

"Baby!" she'd cry, and run to me, her arms open.

I felt so awkward; I didn't know whether to run from her or toward her. Seeing her here, in this place, our new home, was deeply unsettling. Part of me didn't want her there at all. Part of me wanted to go home with her. To try to compensate for her absence, she'd shower us with expensive gifts, just as Dad had done when he was in the same situation. When Jeanne told her that we were going to Mammoth with Gams to learn how to ski, she arrived with a huge box of Bogner ski pants, ten pairs, all different sizes and none of them small enough to fit us.

Occasionally we'd be allowed to visit her. These were trips we soon came to dread, because Mother seemed to be living in small, dark places.

"Where's the pool?" Claudia asked her once, as we wandered into the yard behind a little house where she was staying with friends.

"There isn't one," she replied brightly. "Now who'd like to come inside and make green potatoes?"

Our recent outings organized by Dad and Jeanne had included a magical visit to the newly opened Disneyland, in the company of Walt Disney himself. We'd explored the castlelike Greystone Mansion a few blocks from our house, seen Dad in Vegas, and attended a ceremony to present him with his latest gold records. With Mother's offer of boiled potatoes, we wondered what on earth we were going to do for the rest of the afternoon.

Without a pool to keep us amused, Mother came up with another idea, a cup of coffee in her hand. "Turn on the sprinklers, Gail," she said. "Now you kids run around." It was clear to Claudia and Gail that she was trying to stay sober after rehab. Watching the clock, anxious about getting us home on time, keen to be on her best behavior, she seemed a little nervous. Returning us to Mountain Drive in time for dinner, she refused to allow us to feel sad at saying good-bye. Clapping her hands together, she said, "Well, kids, that was fun, wasn't it? We'll do it again soon, maybe go ice skating. We'll think of something."

We stood there, unsure what to say. "What's the matter, aren't you going to ask me what time it is?" she cried, her eyes brimming over.

"What time is it, Mother?" Gail said, her voice small.

"Time for all you little doggies to be dead. Don't you feel sick?" With that, she turned on her heel and was gone.

When Craig came to live with us, about a year after we'd moved in with Dad and Jeanne, he looked like the Fonz. He wore loafers and a blue shirt, and sported a smart haircut. He always had a cool car, and sometimes he'd pick me up from school and drive me home. His girlfriends were usually the prettiest in the neighborhood. They seemed to like the quiet, handsome young man I was so proud to call my big brother. One day Craig drove us over to see Aunt Anne at her house in North Hollywood. He had never lost contact with her. This was the first time we'd seen Aunt Anne since the day she'd driven us to Mountain Drive. She looked just the same, as did I, but she hardly recognized Claudia and Gail, with their eye makeup, trendy clothes, and hair back-combed into a beehive.

"Oh my goodness!" she cried, her hands to her face. "Look at you two! You're so grown up!" Delighted that they'd made the desired impact, my sisters relaxed and set about enjoying their visit with someone to whom we all owed a great deal.

Dear Craig, who'd seemed on the periphery of my life for so long, decided to join the army. Dad didn't want him to, so he went to see Mother and persuaded her to sign the relevant release papers. Dad could do nothing to stop him, and so his firstborn son went off to serve in Germany. That is where he met his wife, Sandy, who was the commanding officer's daughter. I remember when Craig telephoned to tell Dad that he was getting married.

"Your father's not happy," Jeanne told us afterward.

Jeanne was always telling us what Dad was thinking, although how she knew, we never really understood. "He's only fifty. He's far too young to be a grandfather," she explained. "Didn't Craig think what this might mean for your father's career?" Nonetheless, she and Dad threw Craig a big wedding reception, which Mother Betty didn't attend, and we all fell in love with Sandy.

GRADUALLY, MOTHER'S contacts with us became less and less frequent. On the few occasions we did see her, her hair seemed grayer, her clothes shabbier, and her cars more unreliable. We didn't want to go and stay with her anymore, in a place with no tennis or swimming or any of the creature comforts we'd grown accustomed to. Perhaps sensing our disapproval, she started taking us to restaurants, bars, and motels instead, hoping that we'd be better impressed with our surroundings. Emerging gradually into womanhood, we felt awkward and vulnerable in these dimly lit places populated largely by men. Gail had to rescue Claudia from a corridor of the Villa Frascati on Sunset, where one of Mother's male friends had her pinned up against the wall. In another dive of a place in Malibu, Gail called a cab when one of Mother's friends started pounding on our bedroom door.

"Never ask me to go and see Mother again!" Gail pleaded with Jeanne as the cab eventually deposited us back in Beverly Hills and Dad had to pick up the tab.

Ashamed and embarrassed by such incidents, Mother gradually withdrew from us too, accepting that we were probably better off where we were.

Aunt Anne told me years later that Mother never fought to get us back because she knew Dad would take better care of us, and she had nothing left to give. "She'd hit bottom," Anne said. "She knew your Dad would look after you, but it broke her heart to lose you. She never intended to hurt anyone, things just got out of her control. She certainly never stopped loving you."

I was so confused about who my mother was, I didn't know which way to turn. Dino and Ricci and Gina called Jeanne "Mom," and so did Gail and Claudia. I did too, but at first it just didn't feel right for someone I barely knew and who had hardly registered a presence in my nine short years. But, in truth, I did have a new mom now, someone who was young and glamorous and—perhaps most important of all—married to my father, so we were something I'd never previously known, a real and complete family.

That was never brought home to Mother Betty more than the time when she read in a newspaper that we were to attend the premiere of Dad's latest film, *Rio Bravo*, in which he'd beaten out Sinatra, James Cagney, and Richard Widmark for the role of Dude, a drunken deputy to John Wayne's sheriff, and Angie Dickinson's girl on the run.

It was one of his best and favorite roles, not least because the director, Howard Hawks, apparently spotted Dad sitting in character at a bar on the set in Tucson, Arizona, and told his producer, "I thought we were going to get Dean Martin." When he was told that the scruffy, unshaven man slumped over a card table ready to start filming *was* Dean Martin, he could hardly believe his eyes. Dad loved that story. Better still, he got rave reviews and the film grossed nearly $6 million. A phenomenal success, when you consider the price of a movie ticket was only a dime. Critics said he'd "come of age." Others said he was hardly recognizable as the drunken derelict and added, "Martin commands unprecedented respect in a difficult characterization."

Hoping to catch a glimpse of us all in our finery, Mother Betty took the bus to Grauman's Chinese Theater and waited outside in the cold night air with the other hopeful fans. There were dozens of teenage girls there, anxiously waiting for Dad and his co-star, the handsome young Ricky Nelson, who had a number-one hit with "Poor Little Fool." When the limousine arrived, we emerged as a family onto the sidewalk, with flashbulbs popping all around us. As Dad and Jeanne smiled and posed with us for the cameras, Mother pushed herself to the front of the crowd and, waving madly, started screaming our names.

"Claudia! Gail! Deana, baby!"

I never saw her, nor did I hear her above the screams of the fans. If I had, I'm not sure what I would have done.

Dad at one year old, 1918.

Dad grew up loving horses.

A young and dapper
Guy (Pop) Crocetti.

Dad with a leg up
on the Crocetti boys.

Mom and Dad—
an evening at the Copa.

Dad and Mom
as newlyweds, 1941.

Mother Betty.

Mother and me
at age three months.

Jerry, Patti, Mom, and Dad—a night on the town.

Dad and Jeanne's
wedding, 1949.

My favorite photo—
Mommy and me.

Mother Jeanne.

New York, 1948—
Dad and Jerry arrive
at the train station.

Soon to be the greatest
comedy team in history
—Dad and Jerry, 1948.

Dad, Jerry, and Frank—
young and cute.

Claudia, me, and Gail—on the set visiting Dad.

Dino, me, Gail, Dad, and Claudia on John Wayne's boat.

My sisters and me with Elvis, the King of Rock 'n' Roll.

Dad and me—
playing in the pool at
601 Mountain Drive.

Our first family trip.

Dad's perfect
swan dive.

Mack Gray with his envelope,
as always with Dad.

Uncle Frank, Dad, and Peter
Lawford—style personified.

Dad and Marilyn in her last movie
—they were great together.

Dad's new solo career—opening night at the Sands.

My sisters did. Spotting her suddenly in the crowd, in that sur-real setting where they were being greeted and fêted as young women from one of Hollywood's most glamorous families, they pre-tended that they didn't see the dowdy, gray-haired woman.

Placing their hands on my shoulders and turning me toward the door so that I wouldn't see our real mother, Gail and Claudia fol-lowed the glittering Mr. and Mrs. Dean Martin into the movie the-ater without even a backward glance.

MY FATHER was, truly, the sweetest man in the world. He had a unique aura and was brilliant at making everyone around him feel good. When people speak to me of meeting him, they don't talk about what he did or even what songs he sang, but about how he made them feel. Just being in his presence was enough. He was generous with his humor and his smile and could almost literally light up a room. His mystique was intangible, but it was there and nobody in his presence could escape it. He was surprisingly tactile. He touched people, hugged them, squeezed their shoulders, and allowed them to touch him in return. With his relaxed manner, he had the ability to set people immediately at ease. He was undoubtedly a complicated man, a Gemini with two distinct facets to his personality, and some-times he would say or do hurtful things without realizing it. There must have been a mass of emotions going on beneath the surface that we didn't know about, but Dad never revealed them. Instead, he made it his business to present the image of a sweet guy who was everybody's pallie. Shirley MacLaine said of Dad "he was nice to everyone, he just didn't want nice to go on too long." When asked once what he'd like written about him by way of an obituary, he replied, " 'Dean Martin? He was a Good Guy.' That'll do just fine."

To know him was to love him, everyone agrees, although it was not always so easy to accept some of the choices he made. Warm, gener-ous, and kind, he loved his family, golf, and women with a passion, but sometimes forgot that he wasn't meant to love them all at once. If he had one fault, it was that he was too trusting. He believed people when they told him they would take care of his money; he believed women when they told him they adored him; he followed his agents' advice and listened to friends in the business, some of whom were bad guys.

Every day he woke up and counted his blessings; every night before he went to bed he said his prayers and thanked God for his good fortune. He wouldn't walk in the front door without kissing the gold Saint Christopher medal Claudia had bought him and which he wore around his neck. He finally had more money than he could possibly spend, a beautiful wife who adored him, seven kids, a palatial home, and a glittering career. He was admired by presidents, movie stars, and the Mafia. Pop singers like the Beatles clamored to meet him. Elvis Presley idolized him and drove past our house on his motorcycle at night, agog that his childhood hero was inside.

A few years later in Las Vegas, I had the pleasure of speaking candidly with Elvis. As a young lady, I was thrilled when he told me: "I love your Dad. You know, they call me the King of Rock 'n' Roll,

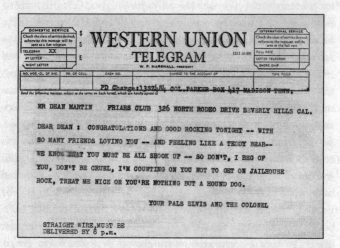

but your dad . . . he's the King of Cool." Some of the most precious mementos are the cute telegrams and letters that Elvis sent to Dad.

Dad had success, wealth, and happiness, yet sometimes he was happiest when left alone. Everybody wanted a piece of him, just a few minutes of his time—Jeanne, his children, his fans, his agent, the studio, even Rocky the miniature poodle. He realized early on that unless he was going to lose himself under an overwhelming mountain of demands, he was going to have to become very self-contained and, occasionally, selfish about what he did and when.

Not that he was heedless of the needs of others. He did things for people all the time, privately, quietly, helping friends and family when they needed him. When someone was in need back in Steubenville, he'd wire a cash order. When a club owner he knew was jailed, he sent his wife and child money. When Freddy the houseman died of a heart attack, Dad took care of everything, and attended the funeral in Watts. He made sure Freddy's daughter, Sandra, and his wife, Alma, had everything they needed and remained part of our family. Alma worked for us for twenty-five years.

When Dino was old enough to join Little League, Dad would show up at as many of the games as he could and yell encouragement from the sidelines like any proud father. When Craig moved to Germany with the army, Dad gave him the surprise of his life by turning up with Frank Sinatra and the entire band to perform a private show for him and his fellow soldiers. Craig never forgot that particular kindness, arranged by Dad as an unscheduled stop during a tour of Europe. "Nobody could believe it," he said. "Frank Sinatra and Dean Martin playing just for us. All of my buddies were absolutely amazed. It was one of the best things he ever did for me."

Dad never expected thanks for what he did, and he never saw the need to get too close to people. He didn't need to do so for himself, and he didn't understand that need in others. Dad lent new meaning to the expression "emotional detachment." Of course, given a choice, I would have preferred it otherwise. We all would. It would have been great if, along with that legendary charm that he could turn on like a lightbulb, he'd had the gushing warmth of Frank Sinatra or Sammy Davis Jr. I would have loved to sit with him and listen to him talk to me freely about his own life and his choices and his loves.

I would have relished his advice peppered with anecdotes from his own experiences. But Dad was simply not the type of man who was able to express himself, and we were never given that choice. With Dad, it was take it or leave it. And allowing that fact to ruin the enjoyment of even the briefest of moments with him would have been far worse. Dad was pure gold. Rare. Expensive sometimes, emotionally. But worth every single ounce.

STILL STRUGGLING with the confusing events of my own short life, I had little or no understanding of the pressures Dad was under. He worked relentlessly to pay for his lifestyle and to support his many dependents, and could often only sleep at night by taking a pill. He'd awaken at dawn and leave for the studio after enjoying his toast and coffee in the quiet of the house at 6:00 a.m. At the studio, everyone said he was a delight to work with, courteous, punctual to the point of obsession, and amenable to script changes. But he was a stickler for finishing on time, and every night he'd come home by six o'clock and we would have dinner by seven o'clock. If there was one thing Dad insisted on, it was a routine. Only by organizing his life into very specific, designated segments of time was he able to keep his cool about the numerous demands made upon him. Mack Gray was his chief timekeeper, and it was his job to keep everything running smoothly.

When I was eleven years old, we went on our first family vacation together, a five-day cruise to Hawaii, where we sat at the captain's table and people lined up for Dad's autograph. That, and the times my classmates applauded me for being his daughter, were the first occasions when I realized that people felt great love for my father, even though they'd never met him. On the cruise ship we took hula lessons and played deck games, and when we reached our destination, we took an entire floor of the Royal Hawaiian Hotel. We had to, because there were so many of us, including Grandma Peggy and Jeanne's brother and sister-in-law, Jack and Shirley Biegger.

The only times I thought of Mother Betty at all were during the evening luaus, complete with tiki torches and exotic cocktails. I couldn't help wondering where she was and what she was doing.

APART FROM when he was away, doing his biannual six-week stints at The Sands, you could set your clock by Dad as he came home from the studio, got out of his car, and walked into the kitchen with that easy, rolling gait of his. As one of our friends once commented, "Your Dad walks like he's conserving energy."

He had taps on the heels of his shoes, and we could hear them clicking as he came into the kitchen. He'd take a piece of Wonder Bread, smear it with butter, fold it over, and carry it into the living room, where he'd turn on the TV, eat his little sandwich, and sometimes fall asleep on the couch.

Jeanne, who was always playing music in the house—Tony Bennett, Andy Williams, Frank Sinatra, or Rosemary Clooney—would turn the stereo down and tell us, "Okay, kids, just give me a few minutes alone with your Dad. Don't make too much noise and don't bother him with anything." When he was ready, they'd go into the bar, where she'd fix them a martini or a J&B (he claimed the initials stood for "Just Booze"), and have some time alone together. That was the precious time he allotted his "Little Jeanne" each day, and we made sure that no one interrupted them.

When cocktails were over, we were allowed half an hour with him before dinner. He'd rarely change clothes and was usually dressed in smart slacks and a V-necked sweater or a polo shirt, but we'd play roughhouse and climb all over him, which he never seemed to mind. Whenever the play-fights got a bit out of hand, he'd yell jokingly, "Not the nose!" or "Not the throat! Remember, the throat pays for everything!"

If any of us had a sandwich, he'd ask for a bite, but always take such a huge mouthful that we'd be left holding just the crusts and complaining bitterly. Learning fast, we took to carefully placing the sandwich between our fingers so that only an ordinary mouthful was permitted. Feigning disappointment, Dad would munch playfully on our fingers as if he were going to eat those as well, until we reluctantly relinquished our prize.

We'd play all sorts of games, like Monopoly, or turn out the lights and play sardines. We'd set up a little stage and perform spoof versions of Dad's movies, with Dino or Ricci pretending to be him. A favorite game was making up words for his ubiquitous Lucky Strike cigarettes. The packet had the slogan "LS/MFT" on it, which stood for "Lucky Strike Means Fine Tobacco." But we'd invent new words for it, like "Let's Suck Mom's Front Tooth" or "Lazy Susans Meet For Tea." We'd go into hysterics over them.

Often Dad would ask me to massage his neck and shoulders, which were tense after a day's filming. "Hey, Deana, baby, rub my neck," he'd say. I'd jump at the chance, sitting on the couch behind him. When I was finished, he'd give me five dollars, although I'd have gladly done it for free.

We had our own projection room, complete with a union-provided projectionist named Lowell. Dad would be given all the latest movies and we would often watch them after dinner. "Roll 'em, Lowell," he'd say, while we snuggled up beside him with popcorn and watched epics like *Ben-Hur* or musicals like *Gigi*.

The hall carpet was bright green, just like a fairway, and one of my fondest memories is of Dad standing at the foot of the stairs with his golf club, night after night, practicing his beautiful swing.

"Fore!" he'd cry, and some missile, anything from a bread roll to a scrunched-up ball of paper, would come flying out of the front door.

When dinner was ready, Dad would take his place at the head of the table. The rest of us sat on either side of him, eating the wonderful meals Fladia or Alma would prepare. We'd have pork chops, potatoes, and vegetables. Grandma Angela made us Italian food like pasta fagioli and Gams melted dark chocolate and poured it over vanilla ice cream.

Grandma Angela gave me the secret recipe for pasta fagioli, immortalized in Dad's hit song "That's Amore": "When the stars make you drool just like pasta fagioli, that's amore." I remember vividly her taking me into the kitchen and tying an apron around me. "I'm going to teach you something very special, Deana—your father's favorite dish, which was given to me by my grandmother," she told me. "I'm not going to write it down. You'll have to remember it and the secret ingredient, and you must not tell anyone, not even your sisters. One day, when I'm gone, you can make it for your Dad and you will make him very happy." I thought immediately of my mother Betty and her meat loaf with onion soup mix, and I fought a sudden desire to cry.

Jeanne would ring a bell on the table to indicate a change of course halfway through dinner, and the boys would try to ambush Fladia as she came in with a new tray. Later, when the house grew bigger, Jeanne had a little buzzer installed under the table to sound in the kitchen. The noise and the humor and the general hubbub at dinner each night was incredible. I'd sit laughing until my stomach ached as Dad and the rest of us cracked jokes and fooled around with each other.

"Don't bite your nails," he'd tell Claudia. "Look what happened to Venus de Milo."

We all had braces on our teeth at various times, and if we smiled at Dad, he'd hold his hands to his face in mock horror and cry, "Oh my God, it looks like a train coming at me." If you asked him to pass the bread, Dad would hurl a roll at you from the far end of the table. He'd pick up the salt and pepper shakers, hold them to his eyes like binoculars, and give a racing commentary: "They're coming around the track, folks, they're coming around."

If he arrived for dinner with even the merest shadow of a beard, he'd tell us, "Don't worry, kids, I'm making a western."

He constantly teased Jeanne about her German ancestry, which she had in common with Irma, our German housekeeper. "Be careful," he'd tell us, "watch those Aryan blue eyes. Next thing we know she'll be holding Bund meetings Thursday nights with Irma behind the pool house."

And when he lit a cigarette after he'd eaten, he'd often joke, "My doctor told me to quit smoking, so I changed doctors."

In such a freewheeling environment, my brothers and sisters and I quickly rose to the challenge and joked with Dad and each other. He was constantly testing out new material on us, and many of the gags that were born around the family table ended up in his stage act. Spontaneously humorous, he was a much funnier man to be with than Jerry Lewis, Danny Thomas, or so many of his comedian friends. He was also inherently kind, feeding his young children the best lines so they could finish the joke, making sure no one was left out or ignored. When he was at home, he enjoyed spending quality time with us, swimming and barbecuing or roughhousing with us and the dog. He was a big kid at heart, and was one of the most playful men I have ever met, enjoying with childlike wonder a simple practical joke like a pratfall, and encouraging us to do likewise. He had a heart the size of Ohio and an uncanny knack for defusing a tricky situation and for bringing out the best in a person. It's his playfulness I miss the most.

Violet Crocetti was a dear and wonderful relative of ours from Steubenville, and she told me a story that just about sums him up. She'd arrived at a party at the Fort Steuben Hotel to celebrate Dad's return to his hometown with Jeanne and Craig, and made a grand entrance in high-heeled shoes and a strapless black taffeta gown. As she walked in, all heads turned and, momentarily distracted, she stumbled and fell head over heels in the middle of the foyer. Everyone gasped with embarrassment as she plunged to the floor and landed in an ungainly heap. No one tried to help her up.

Suddenly, Dad stepped forward, applauding enthusiastically, and picked her up. "Well done, Vi," he said with a smile. "That was exactly as we rehearsed it!" He made everybody believe the whole thing was staged and that she'd done a brilliant pratfall. She was so grateful, she never forgot his kindness.

◆◆◆

DAD HATED confrontation more than anything else in the world. If we'd done something terrible, Jeanne would threaten us with Dad's wrath. "You just wait until your father gets home," she'd say. "You're going to the den." We'd literally quake with fear at the idea, and I did everything I could to avoid going there, because I'd heard Dino and Ricci weep and holler from behind its locked door. It was years later that I discovered the truth. Dad would arrive home and Jeanne would tell him about the misdemeanor that had been committed and duly send the culprit to Dad's den.

Once behind closed doors, Dad would say, "Listen, pally, I don't want to be in here any more than you do, so let's give your mom an Oscar-winning performance and then we can call it a night. Whaddaya say?" Whereupon he would speak in a very persistent and stern manner, never raising his voice, however, and whichever child was in the den would cry and squeal and whimper and we'd be outside, listening in abject horror, imagining the most terrible punishments. The mere threat of being summoned to the den after that was petrifying.

The only time I was ever summoned there was when I was a little older. I had no idea that I'd done anything wrong and was quaking as I went in with Dad, and he shut the door.

"Now, Deana, baby," he said, looking at me sternly as he perched on the edge of his desk, "I understand you've been hanging around State Beach with a boy named Jay Rossi."

"Yes, we're dating," I said, smiling and showing him the gold signet ring my new beau had given me, with the initial R carved on it.

"Well, you're not dating him anymore," he said.

Confused, I looked up at Dad and followed his gaze to a file on his desk. It was from the Beverly Hills Police Department and had Jay's name emblazoned across the front. Inside was a photo of Jay and a record of his fingerprints and a reference to some minor crime he'd committed on a dare.

Swallowing hard, and wondering if Dad still had private detectives following us, I nodded. "Okay, Dad," I said, "I won't see him anymore."

To spend time alone with Dad was a rare treat for any of us, including Jeanne (who I now called Mom). There were so many people demanding his time that he regularly sought solitude on the golf course or in his dressing room, just to get away from everyone.

Some of my most special memories are of the times he'd allow me to accompany him after dinner to the driving range on Wilshire Boulevard between Veteran and Sepulveda, across from the Veterans' Cemetery. Usually we'd be alone, but occasionally we'd be joined by one of Dad's friends. One of these was Stewart Granger, who was tall and handsome and had a wonderful voice. Stewart always wore an ascot and smelled heavenly.

Dad loved to play golf. He'd first learned in New York, at a course on Long Island, and had been bitten by the golf bug. It was the perfect game for someone who liked to be alone and not chatter much. He could be in the company of men whose friendship he cared for, but if he didn't want to say anything, he didn't have to. He didn't use a cart, preferring to walk around in often stifling heat. "I don't need a gym or a sun bed when I'm playing golf," he'd tell me. "I get to do almost all my favorite things in one fell swoop."

I'd spend literally hours sitting on a bench, watching Dad hitting balls out of a bucket into a huge net at the end of the driving range. Silhouetted in the floodlights, he'd stand there silently hitting ball after ball, only talking every now and again to explain his swing or to teach me a few tricks. Dad always said that if he hadn't been an entertainer, he'd have loved to be a professional golfer. He was certainly good enough.

Some people said of Dad that he gave the absolute minimum, but I didn't see it that way at all. Happy with his own company and entirely self-contained, he didn't feel the need, as most of us do, to fill a gap in a conversation with chitchat. In fact, unless he had something important or funny to say, he'd prefer to be silent. I learned that early on, and knew that if I wanted to spend time with him, I'd have to do things his way.

"Why should he always have his own way?" some of my brothers and sisters would complain. "Why can't he just give more of himself and keep everyone happy?" I didn't argue and I didn't try to explain.

I was just grateful for whatever time I had with him, and I learned to savor each moment.

Jerry Lewis once told an interviewer just how it was with Dad. "He let people know right up front, 'This is who I am, and here's how you gotta take me. I'm taking you, whatever your foibles are, whatever the good and the bad, and I'm asking you to do the same with me.' That was what I loved about Dean." Despite their many differences, I sometimes think Jerry knew Dad better than anyone else in the world.

"Follow through, Deana," Dad would say, holding my hands in his as he gave me a personal lesson on how to play golf at the driving range, "Keep your head down, don't bend your elbow, swing through the ball. That's it."

I'd inhale his cologne and love the feel of him standing so close behind me, my little hands in his, never caring whether I hit the ball or not. After years without a father, I was spending time alone with Dad at last, and that, to me, was the greatest prize of all.

Eight

DAD HAD BECOME A MAJOR STAR IN THE HOLLYWOOD firmament. He, Frank Sinatra, Sammy Davis Jr., and Peter Lawford, the Rat Pack, were the toast of the town. And that wasn't all. His movie career was going strong, as well as his radio, nightclub, and television shows, and his record company wanted more.

He'd made another film with Shirley MacLaine, *Career*, in which he played a theater director who helps a determined young actor make it to Broadway. His presence on the set guaranteed fun for everyone. He also had a lot of laughs making the lighthearted caper

Who Was That Lady? with Tony Curtis and Janet Leigh. Next he starred in *Bells Are Ringing*, directed by Vincente Minnelli with the Oscar-winning Judy Holliday. This would be her last film before she died.

Dad had never been busier. He averaged two movies a year, but in the sixties he managed twice that number. Between recording a new album of Italian love songs, he set up his own film company, and named it Claude Productions—named after my sister Claudia. He also signed a new recording contract with Frank Sinatra's Reprise Records, in which Dad was an investor and partner. Dad was also in Las Vegas making *Ocean's Eleven* with the rest of the Rat Pack and their friends Shirley MacLaine and Angie Dickinson. In his spare time between family and golf, he was helping Frank Sinatra campaign for presidential candidate John F. Kennedy. This eclectic group became known as the "Jack Pack." Uncle Frank was mixing with all the right people. Dad knew Jack Kennedy from his Martin & Lewis days, and when Frank asked for his help with the campaign, he was happy to oblige.

"If Kennedy ever makes president," he joked, "he's gonna appoint me Secretary of Liquor."

Jeanne took us to see Dad performing at The Sands, where he and his pallies were putting on a show every night after filming all day. Las Vegas was buzzing with excitement at their presence. Frank called it, a "Summit of Cool," parodying international summits being arranged elsewhere between Khrushchev and Eisenhower. Dad was clearly in his element. "The satisfaction I get from working with these two bums," he said of Frank and Sammy, "is that we have more laughs than the audience."

The cast started work at lunchtime and finished in time for cocktails, before doing a couple of shows each and playing all night. They became increasingly unpredictable, lightheartedly interrupting each other's shows and trying to crack each other up. Dad would rarely complete an entire song, stopping halfway through and telling the audience, "If you want to hear the whole song, buy the record."

"Come on now, dago," Dad would say, strolling onto the stage halfway through Frank's performance, "it's time for bed." The newspaper headlines screamed about how Frank's drunken pack was out of control, when in reality it was all staged in advance. Those boys were wild.

Jeanne took us to Las Vegas occasionally and allowed us to be a part of show-biz history in the making. Even at our tender ages, we realized how truly magical the occasion was. We sat at a ringside seat dressed in our best outfits, and watched excitedly as Dad came on and introduced us.

"I have my lovely family here tonight," he'd say, as the spotlight swiveled around to where we were sitting. When it was my turn, he'd say, "Here's Deana. Stand up, baby, let everyone see how pretty you are." I'd proudly stand up and smile in my pretty new dress and throw Dad a kiss as the audience cheered.

I was always thrilled to watch him perform. He was spellbinding. What was most amazing to me was that he was my father.

"Last night a showgirl was banging on my door for forty-five minutes," he told the audience, winking at Jeanne, "but I wouldn't let her out." Everyone, including Jeanne, laughed.

"If you've seen one topless dancer, you've seen them both," he'd joke. "When Frank dies, they're gonna give his zipper to the Smithsonian."

Glaring at someone in the audience, he said, "What did you think this was? *The Andy Williams Show*? There ain't no ice cream or cookies around here. This is a show about booze and broads."

He sang a few numbers, or rather parodies of a few numbers, with lines such as, "I looked over Jordan and what did I see . . . Mrs. Jordan." "You are too beautiful for one man alone . . . so I brought along my brother." "You made me love you . . . you woke me up to do it."

Later he boasted, "I'm such a ham, last night the refrigerator light came on when I opened the door, and I did four songs."

Illuminated by the spotlight in his tuxedo, his shiny hair glistening like a halo, he sang, he smoked, he drank, he slipped colorful lines into his songs, and he cracked jokes about the family. It was still Dad, but not the Dad we knew at home. This was an entirely different person, and one by whom I was increasingly captivated.

The Sands was one of the first great hotels and casinos on the Strip before Las Vegas became a city with an ever-changing skyline. Mainly low-rise, it began life as a casino with a few rooms and became a Las Vegas legend, a place where careers and memories were made. Dad and Frank both owned stock in it. The central gaming hall was packed with poker tables, wheels of fortune, slot machines, and the sound of money. Just walking in, there was an air of excitement. Players would scream if they won, and people would gather around to see how much. Everyone, including the pit bosses who stood in the middle, surrounded by security, dressed beautifully and smelled gorgeous. Men wore tuxedos with gold cuff links, and ladies wore pastel chiffon gowns that seemed to float on air. It was truly an age of elegance.

Dad had become known as the King of Las Vegas, outstripping Frank and Elvis Presley in ticket sales and popularity. His suite was the best in town, and was situated by the pool. They would drive us there in a golf cart, and there was plenty of room in the suite for all of us. We would phone room service and order anything our hearts desired.

"Five club sandwiches and french fries, followed by ice cream," Gail would say, and we'd love it when the tray came with the sandwiches cut into little triangles.

Dad spent his free time playing golf, or dealing at the card tables. It was a throwback to his youth, when he dealt cards in the back of the Rex Cigar Store. When he wasn't singing in the Copa Room, he'd wander around the casino, gambling a little here and there. He drew a crowd wherever he went, and the casino management was happy to have him around.

He'd often take over from a dealer at one of the blackjack tables, much to the surprise of the players, who never in a million years expected to be dealt cards by Dean Martin. I loved watching their faces as Dad stepped in and took over. After a few minutes, someone would usually work up the courage to ask, "Hey, aren't you Dean Martin?" To which Dad would reply, "No," and the game would continue. You could tell it was something they'd talk about for the rest of their lives, especially when one of the players would bust and Dad would yell "Blackjack!" It was sheer pandemonium as he paid them and the crowd erupted in laughter.

I loved to watch him work the tables, a cigarette in his mouth, his eyes half closed from the smoke curling upward, and the women clamoring for his attention. The pit bosses loved him, as did the dealers, for whom he once bought a new television set to watch the World Series when theirs broke down. He had no ego, they said, and was accomplished at the fine art of dealing. A lot of the best dealers came from Steubenville, Ohio. They respected Dad for many things, especially because he once publicly said, "Anyone who says acting is hard has never had to stand on his feet all day dealing blackjack."

I remember the card tricks he'd teach us at home, his huge hands hiding the cards from us. He joked once about beating Shirley MacLaine at poker chiefly because she'd had a hangover and he could see her cards in the reflection of her sunglasses.

When Dad had enjoyed his fill of dealing to an astonished public, he'd signal to the pit bosses, and another dealer would step in. Despite who he was, he'd back away from the table, his huge hands in the air to show they were "clean," just like the real dealers. I was coming to know yet another side of my father. He seemed as relaxed in a casino as he did at home, watching television and eating a Wonder Bread sandwich.

THE TUXEDO became synonymous with Dad and the Rat Pack. In Dad's day, the tux was the uniform of choice in nightclubs, casinos, and bars where he entertained. Dad's was divine and elegantly tailored by Sy Devore, the Beverly Hills tailor to the stars. Dad used Sy well before the rest of the pack followed.

"I only ever wear one tux at a time," he'd joke. "What do I need two for?"

One day in Beverly Hills, I came home to find three tuxedos hanging in the powder room. They were exquisite—one labeled for Dad, one for Frank, and one for Sammy—who were performing at a benefit for Senator Kennedy later that night.

Sammy was five feet three inches tall, not much bigger than I was. As I held his sweet little tux up in front of me before the mirror, I was entranced. It was perfect in every way. With the finest hand-embroidered black satin on the lapels, it was made for him by Sy Devore. Checking that Alma and Jeanne weren't around, I slipped off my slacks and shirt and carefully buttoned myself into Sammy's tux. It was a perfect fit.

Standing in front of the mirror, I had a few delicious moments to myself, imagining what it would be like to be onstage alongside Dad in this suit. The soft black fabric seemed somehow empowering; it made me feel older and more confident than I really was. I put on a little show for nobody but me, feigning Sammy's song-and-dance routine, beaming back at my own reflection. Then I carefully replaced the suit on its hanger and switched off the light.

One night a few months later, when Dad was filming *All in a Night's Work* with his friend Shirley MacLaine, he came home and told us girls, "Put something nice on tomorrow, you're coming to the studio with me. Elvis Presley wants to meet you." Gail and Claudia and I looked at each other in disbelief.

Off we went to Paramount the next day, so excited we could barely speak. Elvis was utterly charming, and even more handsome than in his movies. He came riding toward us on a bicycle, dismounted, and said "Hey, Dean," in his melodic Memphis accent. "Now these beautiful girls can't all be your daughters." Blushing, giggling, we were each introduced to him as someone took photographs and recorded the moment for history. It is one of my most cherished pictures.

Whenever asked, Elvis always cited Dad as his favorite singer. He claimed that it was Dad's easy singing style that made him want

to emulate him. He presented a cake to Dad on his forty-third birthday on behalf of the studio, and sang him "Happy Birthday."

"Your father is the King of Cool, not me," Elvis told us, as we
posed for pictures and the flashbulbs popped. "He's the greatest."
We already knew that, but coming from Elvis, now that was cool.

JEANNE LOVED to socialize almost as much as my mother Betty
did. She would throw parties at the house, or drag Dad out to daz-
zling events. It was always an exciting time for us girls, waiting at
the bottom of the stairs, to see which beautiful gown she would be
wearing and how she'd styled her hair. Dad, who hated to be kept
waiting almost more than anything in the world, would sit fuming
on the couch, quite literally, lighting one cigarette after another in
between yelling up the stairs at her to hurry up. "Come on, honey,"
he'd call, "I'm dying of old age."

It was always worth the wait when she descended the grand
staircase. Jeanne was a gorgeous creature, immaculately dressed,
and everyone agreed that she and my father made an extraordinarily handsome couple. Their mere arrival at an event guaranteed its
success. The paparazzi would wait outside for them with their cameras and, ever gracious, Dad would always stop and smile. If they
were going out for dinner or to a nightclub, their destination would
be Jack's at the Beach, The Daisy, Chasen's, Villa Capri, or Dominic's
on Beverly Boulevard, so exclusive that it had an unlisted phone
number. Dad and Jeanne were definitely A-list.

Dad didn't like parties because he didn't like the chitchat. He'd
walk in, pay his respects, find someone he knew and say, "Listen,
pally, you've seen me, okay. Tell everyone I was here," before trying
to slip away. He had no interest in talking politics or gossiping about
his co-stars or discussing who was sleeping with whom. He'd stick
around just long enough to be polite, and then he'd slide off home to
bed or into a side room to watch a western. Dad loved his westerns.

Usually he'd make a joke about leaving. "I have to go home and lie on a sponge," he'd say, getting mileage out of his pretense at being a lush.

He also loved to shoot pool, but Jeanne would hide the balls at home so that if he disappeared for a game halfway through a party, he couldn't play. Undaunted, Dad secretly bought another set and simply hid them. Often people would ask, "Where's Dean?" and Jeanne would smile and reply, "Asleep. Now let me fix you another drink." People just accepted it. He didn't give them much choice.

Jeanne wanted us to appreciate the extraordinary life we were part of. It was she who adorned the walls with Dad's growing collection of gold and platinum albums and dozens of photographs of him on his movie sets or with us at home. It was Jeanne who'd patiently line us up in her dressing room to teach us how to meet people. "I want you to stand up straight, extend your hand, have a firm handshake, make direct eye contact, and most important . . . smile," she'd coach. It was also Jeanne who ensured that we were given every opportunity to see sell-out concerts, receive invitations to the most exclusive parties, and visit the biggest movies in the making.

Just as Mother Betty had encouraged us to study ballet, tap, and jazz dance, so Jeanne followed suit. I was signed up for the Paul Henreid cotillion at the Beverly Hills Wilshire Hotel, to learn how to dance everything from the Viennese waltz to the tango and cha-cha. Each girl in the class was paired up with a boy, and if they danced well together, they became partners and entered competitions.

My partner was a handsome young man by the name of Jeff Bridges, whose father, Lloyd, was starring in the television series *Sea Hunt*. Jeff was divine. He was so cute and a great person to dance with. That gave me confidence and brought out the best in me. I wore pink Jax shoes with a kitten heel and a little bow on top, which I adored. Jeff and I would often go over to his house in Westwood to rehearse, and we won trophy after trophy. I was twelve years old and I never wanted to dance with anyone else for the rest of my life. But, sadly, by thirteen we'd outgrown our class and we went our separate ways. I've never had a chance to dance with him since.

Jeanne took us to the set of *Spartacus,* which was really cool. We already knew Tony Curtis, both as a friend of Mother's and as our next-door neighbor. Kirk Douglas was like Superman with a sword, very handsome. I thought Jean Simmons was gorgeous. Kirk kindly posed with us for photographs in his leather slave outfit, and it is another favorite picture. He was a lovely man and soon became a regular visitor to our home.

We were too young to appreciate some of the people who'd drop by. We could walk into the living room at any one time and bump into the biggest stars in Hollywood. There was Judy Garland, Lauren Bacall, Gary Cooper, Rosalind Russell, Janet Leigh and Tony Curtis, Rosemary Clooney, Andy Williams, Cyd Charisse, Doris Day, Natalie Wood, Debbie Reynolds, Gene Kelly, and Peter Sellers, who was hysterical. Tony Bennett and his wife, Sandy, were also frequent callers, as were Milton and Ruth Berle and the list goes on.

Jimmy McHugh, the songwriter who wrote the music for "On the Sunny Side of the Street," was my godfather. He and his friend Louella Parsons, the gossip columnist, were also regulars at our house. Louella was the first reporter to break the news about Dad leaving Mother. The Swiss-born actress Ursula Andress became a close family friend and enjoyed spending time with us. She had this funny expression every time something amused her. She'd say "Oopla!" and we all mimicked her. She was great fun, and her boyfriend, Alain Delon, was just about the sexiest thing on legs I'd ever seen. I'd blush every time he even spoke to me. They certainly made a stunning couple.

The painfully shy Montgomery (Monty) Clift came over a few times and my father enjoyed his company. Ever since *The Young Lions,* Dad had admired his acting skills and his cool demeanor. For a time there was a controversy about Monty being gay, but Dad liked Monty for who he was. He didn't give a hoot whether he was gay or not; Dad was not influenced by such things. Always protecting the underdog, Dad used to take him to dinner in the best restaurants in L.A. to show his public support. Dad was devastated when Monty died of a heart attack, at the young age of forty-six.

DAD CONTINUED to make movies with astonishing speed. There was *Ada* with Susan Hayward, *Sergeants 3* with the Rat Pack, and *Who's Got the Action?* with Lana Turner. He was working with some of Hollywood's most glamorous female stars.

Marilyn Monroe was also a very dear friend, so when she suggested they make a picture together, Dad agreed. The film was about a man who remarries years after his wife is lost at sea, only for her to turn up again and try to win him back. Marilyn was hoping to make this her comeback film after a two-year break, but ill health and personal demons would continue to plague her. The movie was aptly entitled *Something's Got to Give*.

One night she came to the house, arriving with Dad from the set. I remember that evening vividly. She had sunglasses on and a scarf wrapped around her head, and she never took either one off. I remember thinking how beautiful she looked. We were in the living room, the jukebox was playing "Up a Lazy River," and Dino and I did the twist for her. The fragile movie star smiled shyly, applauded, and thanked us. She was very sweet and extremely polite. It was only a few months before she died.

Working with her was not easy. Marilyn was at a crisis point in her life, relying on tranquilizers and sleeping pills that affected her ability to perform. As she famously said after arriving late on the set, "I may be on a calendar, but I'm never on time." Simple shots required dozens of takes, and rehearsals dragged. At one point she disappeared completely and no one knew where she was. She turned up on national television in a skin-tight rhinestone dress, singing that breathless rendition of "Happy Birthday, Mr. President" to JFK. This caused the studio, 20th Century–Fox, to spit bullets. Dad had been invited to perform at the tribute as well, but would not go because the film was so far behind schedule.

Dad was incredibly faithful to Marilyn and never once complained. He even threw a thirty-sixth birthday party for her on the set. In return, she arrived at our house in a stretch limo and took my brother Dino as her date to a Dodgers game, where he sat beside her as the fans screamed and she signed autographs. In the end, the studio threatened to fire her, and Dad quit when they tried to replace her with Lee Remick. One headline read, NO MM, NO MARTIN. The movie was put on hold, and the studio ended up suing Dad for over $3 million for breach of contract. He countersued, claiming they'd damaged his career. The lawsuits came to nothing when the studio agreed to take Marilyn back. Dad agreed to return to the set when he'd finished his next film, *Toys in the Attic*. Sadly, in the end, it was not to be. The film, however, was successfully remade as *Move Over, Darling*, with James Garner and Doris Day.

Little did we know at the time that Marilyn was having affairs with John and Bobby Kennedy. I was in the choir of the Good Shepherd Catholic Church in Beverly Hills and had sung for the president and his wife, Jackie, when they came to California. I'd never personally met them. I recall Jackie wore a turquoise suit and a pillbox hat, and the security was intense. The church was packed, and we sang "Ave Maria," and "The Lord Is My Shepherd."

It was Uncle Frank who'd once again persuaded Dad and Sammy to join him campaigning for Kennedy. Frank was comfortable mixing with influential politicians and studio executives like Hal Wallis, and Jack Warner. He always wanted to learn more and be more. Bettering himself was important to him, and I've always admired that.

When JFK revoked his invitation to Sammy to attend his presidential inauguration ceremony, upset by his controversial plans to marry the Swedish actress May Britt at a time of racial sensitivity, Dad was furious. "If Sammy can't go, I won't go," he announced. Despite the lighthearted ribbing he gave Sammy onstage, he loved him and was always trying to look out for him. He especially tried to lead him away from the drugs that were gradually taking over his life.

We were vacationing at the ten-thousand-acre Alisal Dude Ranch in the Santa Ynez Valley, near Santa Barbara. It was the place where Clark Gable had married Lady Ashley. It was August 5,

1962, when our vacation was suddenly cut short. We received the news that Marilyn Monroe had died. Poor Marilyn. She didn't know what she was getting into with the Kennedys. We drove the 150 miles home, as Dad was originally asked to be a pallbearer. In the end, Marilyn's husband, Joe DiMaggio, banned the entire Hollywood clan from the funeral. Dad and Frank tried to get into the ceremony, but they were barred entry by unsympathetic guards.

I can remember feeling real shock and sadness at Marilyn's death. She was so beautiful and kind; it didn't seem possible that she was gone. Dad was shattered, and I don't think Peter Lawford—who'd first introduced her to the Kennedys—ever really recovered.

Then, a year later, JFK was shot. I remember that day clearly. I was in school and on my way to Spanish class when someone came running down the corridor shouting, "The president's been shot, the president's been shot!" I ran to my class in a daze, only for the teacher to confirm the news. The school was closed and we were sent home for the rest of the afternoon.

Dad was filming his second Rat Pack movie, *Robin and the 7 Hoods*, at the time. He teamed up with Bing Crosby, the singer he'd admired as a boy and whose voice his had often been compared with. The film was a Sinatra production, set in gangland Chicago but minus Peter Lawford.

Dad arrived home from the studio just after I did. He and Jeanne sat with us, watching the television news in complete silence.

"Jack was one of the boys," he told me. "He was just like us." Thinking of Pat Lawford, Peter's wife, who was a Kennedy, he added, "Poor Pat's lost another brother."

Dad may not have agreed with all of the Kennedys' political policies, but he knew the president well and was devastated at his death. It felt like the end of an era, and in many ways it was.

Nine

THE SINATRAS WERE A BIG PART OF OUR LIVES, AND the kids from the two families were great pals. Tina was my best friend at Marymount School in Brentwood. Tina was beautiful and just like her father, tough, strong, and opinionated. He was always just Uncle Frank to me. It was he who dubbed me the Social Butterfly, because I'd flit in, kiss everybody hello, and then rush out again. Tina and I hung out together all the time. At their house in Palm Springs, known as the Compound, we'd spend hours listening to her favorite Johnny Mathis albums, sitting out by the pool with reflectors, trying to get an even suntan. Her older sister, Nancy, named for her mother, was a sweetheart, and her brother, Frank junior, was a quieter version of his father.

I loved to go to the Sinatra home on Nimes Road in Bel-Air after school. Tina's mother, Nancy, would be in the kitchen preparing dinner. We always looked forward to her snack of Italian bread and her homemade marinara sauce, and two big bottles of Pepsi. I'd pull the soft center out of the bread and only eat the crust. It's something I do to this day because Dad once told me, "If you don't eat the middle of the bread, you won't get fat."

Frank adored my father. He and Jerry Lewis had that in common. Frank was called the Chairman of the Board, a name he was given by William B. Williams, a New York disc jockey, by the time they were performing together and holding court in the steam room at The Sands. Dad and Frank loved hanging out together. They were more than friends, they were brothers. They worked hard and they played hard. The difference between them was that Uncle Frank came alive at night and loved to party "into the wee small hours of the morning." Dad, on the other hand, loved to get up "in the wee small hours of the morning" to play golf.

Dad used to joke, "Frank was the rat, I was the pack." The white terry-cloth robe Dad wore in the steam room had the word "Dag," short for "Il Dago," embroidered on the left breast pocket. It was the affectionate name they called each other. Uncle Frank's robe bore his moniker, "Leader," while Sammy's robe, which was brown, had the name "Smokey."

In *Ocean's Eleven* they seemed like teenage boys on the loose, though they were all in their mid-forties. That film was a great success and became a cult favorite, not least for the glimpse it offered of the inner workings of the Rat Pack.

Frank had matching pinkie rings made up for him and Dad, each with an emerald-cut diamond in it. Dad never took his off. The legendary Hollywood photographer Sid Avery, who took the beautiful black-and-white stills of the cast of *Ocean's Eleven,* once said of Dad and Frank, "They'd have killed for each other," adding wryly, "I'm not altogether sure they didn't."

Whenever the two of them performed together, Dad would get the laughs. One day Frank told Dad, "I'm fed up with being the straight guy, I want to do the funny lines."

My father shrugged. "Okay," he said. "Shoot."

That night at The Sands, they switched roles and Dad spoke all Frank's lines, while Frank cracked the jokes. The only trouble was, everyone laughed at Dad being the straight man.

"How come no one's laughing at me?" a dismayed Frank asked my father onstage.

"Because you're just not funny," came the reply, a simple sentence that reduced the audience to hysterics. The truth was, Frank was very funny, but Dad was a natural.

When Dad and Frank were performing in Florida, despite Frank's protests Dad went to bed as usual because he wanted to play golf early the next morning. Taking Dad's exit as a cue, the comedian Tom Dreesen, who was opening for Frank, Dad, and Sammy, also decided to turn in. He'd just taken off his clothes when there was a knock on his door. It was a bellman who looked like a fullback. "Mr. Dreesen," he said, "Mr. Sinatra requests your company in the lounge."

"Here," said Tom, reaching for his wallet and pulling out a twenty-dollar bill. "Please tell Mr. Sinatra you couldn't find me."

"I'm sorry, sir," said the bellman. "Mr. Sinatra said you would say that and gave me fifty bucks to come and find you."

"Okay, then," said Tom, peeling off another thirty. "Here, now please go and find Mr. Sinatra and tell him you couldn't find me."

"Ah, I'm sorry, Mr. Dreesen," the bellman replied. "You see, Mr. Sinatra promised me yet another fifty when I delivered you downstairs."

Tom had no choice but to get dressed and go back down to the lounge. When he met Dad on the fairway the next morning and wearily told him the story, Dad just smiled. He had obviously heard it before.

"It's easy, pally," he said, selecting a nine-iron. "Offer someone else your deluxe suite and take their regular room. They'll only be too delighted, until Frank starts calling."

⧫⧫⧫

I WAS fourteen and feeling safe and secure in my world when Frank Sinatra Jr. was kidnapped. Five years older than I, he was in Lake Tahoe, about to perform with the Tommy Dorsey Band, bringing the extraordinary Sinatra talent to a younger generation. Two men burst in and grabbed him at gunpoint. In their ill-fated get-rich-quick scheme, they'd thought of everything from a getaway car to a rental house in the San Fernando Valley in which to stash their intended victim. All Frank senior had to do was pay them a $240,000 ransom.

But they didn't count on Uncle Frank, who was not the sort of man to cross. Frank had connections from the president down. Frank knew people. Robert Kennedy, the U.S. attorney general, offered his personal support. J. Edgar Hoover alerted his entire FBI organization, and the Mafia pledged to find Frank's boy. Three high school buddies from California were never going to outsmart the might of the nation's top investigators. The story broke internationally; roadblocks were set up and everyone was on the lookout for Frankie.

For the fifty-eight hours that Frank junior was missing, we all held our collective breath, not least because we knew it could so easily have been one of us. The kidnappers might well have considered taking one of Dean Martin's kids instead. Dad's only comment to the press was "The whole world's gone nuts."

As a family, we sat around and waited, too, watching the television news and expecting a call. I rang Tina a few times to offer my support, but the line was always busy. Dinner that night was unusually quiet. It sent cold chills down my spine when Jeanne, being especially protective, told us, "Don't stray too far from the house."

Uncle Frank said later that he was suspended between "anger and anxiety," wanting to "hang somebody by the neck." For the sake of his wife and daughters, he had to stay calm. Dad telephoned him and asked if there was anything he could do, but Frank demurred. "Thanks, Dago," he said. "I'll keep you posted."

The ransom was left for the kidnappers at a gas station on Sunset Boulevard. The FBI sting operation to catch them went wrong and they fled, dumping Frank junior at the edge of a freeway. Shaken by his ordeal, the teenage Frank wandered to a nearby house and asked someone to take him home. Thank God he was safe.

The "gang" was rounded up days later and tried within a month. They were sentenced to seventy-five years plus life, later reduced to twenty-five, and then to twelve. Most of the money was recovered. The ringleader, Barry Keenan, claimed in his defense that the kidnapping had been a put-up job, masterminded by the victim to give a much-needed boost to his faltering singing career. Uncle Frank countered, "This family needs publicity like it needs peritonitis."

Even though Keenan publicly recanted his claim afterward, his story stuck, and Frank junior has fought to shake the stigma ever since. Reserved and always smartly dressed in a tie, he was cursed with sounding and looking exactly like his father. This was a very difficult obstacle to overcome even before he was tainted by the kidnapper's lie. Although he wasn't physically injured by his experiences, he was undoubtedly emotionally and psychologically scarred. He said that the kidnappers didn't steal him as much as they stole his life.

To a certain extent they stole ours, too. From that day on we had twenty-four-hour security guards around us and new measures that seemed like a harsh restriction on our young lives. We were no longer allowed to answer the front door. Our lives were drastically changed forever.

❖❖❖

UNCLE FRANK shocked us all by leaving his beautiful wife, Nancy, for Ava Gardner. Ava was a lot of fun, and a little explosive. She once told me that the secret of her beauty was using Vaseline around her eyes every night, and ... it really works. But it is Nancy—now in her eighties and still looking fabulous—with whom I've stayed close friends. She's a remarkable lady and I cherish the times we spend together.

Tina was unhappy when her father announced, after breaking up with Ava, that he was dating Mia Farrow. She wouldn't speak to him. Dad always joked about Mia, telling Frank he had scotch older than she was, but I do remember Dad trying to help.

The day Frank married Mia in Las Vegas, Dad took Tina into his den and broke the news to her.

"You gotta be kidding," she cried. "It can't possibly be!"

"Go home and tell your mom," he told her gently. "The story's going to break any second."

Tina and Mia ended up being good friends, despite her early apprehension. Tina is someone who feels very passionately about things but she isn't so inflexible that she can't see the other side. It took her a while with Mia, but she came to realize that they both just loved her dad. Tina has been a strong influence on my life, even from those early days. We were great pals, a couple of fearless teenagers hanging out and getting into mischief.

One night Tina and I decided to sneak into the Brentwood hotel where the UCLA basketball team was sequestered. We innocently wanted to see the college basketball star Lou Alcindor, who later changed his name to Kareem Abdul-Jabbar. We made it all the way to the room where Lou and his roommate Mike Warren were watching TV and eating box dinners. We knocked on the door, and, seeing who we were, they let us in. Tina had just taken a bite of one of their sandwiches when coach John Wooden knocked on the door, sending us into a blind panic.

Tina, her mouth full of food, grabbed me and hid us behind the shower curtain. In the next room, we could hear the coach telling the guys dirty jokes. We smothered our giggles while he told Mike he seemed a little tense and offered him a rubdown. I was panicking big-time by now, terrified that we'd be caught and it would make the news. Dad would have been furious. Luckily the coach left and so did we, fleeing giggling into the night.

DAD'S NEXT film, *Toys in the Attic*, with Geraldine Page and Wendy Hiller, was based on a Broadway play and set in New Orleans. It was one of his finest dramatic roles. He starred as a ne'er-do-well brother who returns home to his spinster sisters with a sudden fortune and a new wife. Walter Mirisch, the film's producer, described Dad's performance as "Outstanding." I know Dad was always very proud of his contribution.

"I've done some serious acting," he told me years later, when I was just starting out as an actress. "It wasn't always fooling around, you know." It was completely unlike his next movie, a comedy called *Who's Been Sleeping in My Bed?*, with Jill St. John and Carol Burnett, in which he played an actor and critics described him as "amiable."

Dad and Uncle Frank had been performing at The Sands together as "Dean Martin and Friend" when Frank came up with the idea for yet another movie together, only this time without the rest of the pack. It was a western with a farcical twist called *4 for Texas*, with Frank, Ursula Andress, Anita Ekberg, and Charles Bronson.

No sooner had they finished than Dad began filming the successful light romantic comedy *What a Way to Go!* with Shirley MacLaine, Paul Newman, Gene Kelly, and Robert Mitchum. During production on that movie, in March 1964, Dad was given the great honor of being asked to put his hand- and footprints in front of Grauman's Chinese Theatre in Hollywood. Dad always ribbed Uncle Frank that he was given this honor a full year before him. When they each received a coveted star on the Hollywood Walk of Fame on Hollywood and Vine, they were placed side by side, simultaneously, and each ended up receiving three stars, for their extraordinary achievements in motion pictures, television, and recording.

For Dad's official dedication ceremony outside the most famous moviehouse in the world, we all went along and enjoyed a fabulous afternoon. We kids had to hold Dad steady as he laid his huge hands in wet cement, and then we had to grip his arms as he stepped in with his feet.

"Doesn't Mr. Hoover already have my fingerprints?" he joked to one of the policemen holding back the crowds. Using a long wooden stick, he wrote his name, the date, and—in Dad's typical fashion—the word "Thanks."

There were crowds of people and photographers everywhere. It was a major media event, and we were appropriately dressed. Grandma Angela had made a beautiful shift dress in red for me, with an embroidered white blouse, and Dad said I looked fabulous. Craig, Claudia, Ricci, Gina, and Dino were all there and Dad took us to dinner at Sorrentino's to celebrate. It was an exciting and happy night. On his road trip to California in 1939, he had visited Grauman's and placed his own hands on the imprints made by the likes of Humphrey Bogart, Clark Gable, and James Cagney. It meant more to him as a career milestone than almost any other accolade he had received. Dino Crocetti from Steubenville, Ohio, was immortalized forever in the very fabric of Hollywood. It was a proud moment for us all.

MY LIFE fell into a regular routine of school and extracurricular activities and vacations. It was a happy time, and I loved being part of our family. Grandma Peggy played an increasing role in my life, and I loved her. It was dear Gams who took us to mass every Sunday in the station wagon and then on to the Beverly Wilshire Hotel for brunch of Monte Cristo sandwiches. It was she who took us to Santa Anita during the racing season and whose bookie knew our names; Gams who made me hot chocolate and sang "Mr. Sandman" as a lullaby each night. And it was Gams who rubbed my back or told me a bedtime story until I fell asleep.

Dad was home a lot, and we had dinner together as a family almost every night. To us it was the norm, having our father sitting at the head of the table each night, asking us about our day and cracking jokes. He seemed to enjoy this time with the family, sharing a meal and playing the patriarch. I guess it was the Italian in him. Then, as an investment, he bought a restaurant on Sunset Boulevard and named it Dino's Lodge. Occasionally, when he appeared on television, he would cross his legs to show the words EAT AT DINO'S printed on the sole of his shoe. It was pretty cool, going to dinner at a restaurant Dad owned. We didn't go there very often because it attracted too many fans and Dad would spend the entire evening signing autographs and posing for photographs.

What was even cooler was that the restaurant was featured regularly in the hit television show *77 Sunset Strip*, starring Edd Byrnes as Kookie, the parking lot attendant, whom everyone loved. I still smile when I think of the line from the song, "Kookie, Kookie, lend me your comb." We would sit and watch the program at home as a family and we enjoyed seeing Dad's face on the marquee. Dad put his brother Bill in charge of the restaurant but, sadly, the entire venture ended badly. The inevitable lawsuits followed; Dad and Bill sued for mismanagement and won, but lost the fight to have Dad's name removed from the marquee. And so it stayed for years afterward, although we never went there again.

Dad hit a home run with the success of his song "Everybody Loves Somebody Sometime." Written by Ken Lane, his friend and accompanist, it had been recorded years earlier by Frank Sinatra but it didn't do anything. Looking for a twelfth number for a new album, Ken suddenly suggested, "Hey, Dean, what about my song?"

It went straight to the top of the charts, knocking the Beatles' "A Hard Day's Night" off the number-one slot. When Dad heard the news of its success, he sent Elvis Presley a telegram that read, "If you can't handle the Beatles, I'll do it for you, pally."

Only very rarely would Dad travel outside the United States. Las Vegas was about as far as he cared to go. He would visit the family house in Palm Springs for weekends and holidays or to play golf. Once he went to London, for a performance for the Queen. He had a private audience with her after the show.

"What was she like, Dad?" we asked, excitedly, on his return.

"Terribly nice, but for such a rich woman, she doesn't dress very well," came the reply.

"And what about the rest of the royals?"

"They were just fine," he said. "But then, the only royalty I knew before was Frank."

Dad went on to star in Billy Wilder's film *Kiss Me, Stupid*, with Kim Novak and the wonderful Peter Sellers, who ultimately had to drop out because of a series of heart attacks. Dad claimed Sellers almost gave *him* a heart attack, he made him laugh so much. That movie, above all others, sealed Dad's image as a hard-drinking, womanizing singer who developed a headache unless he had sex every night. In it, he uttered his immortal line about the Beatles: "I sing better than all of them put together, and I'm older . . . than all of them put together." He'd first tested the line on us at home. The movie was filmed with two different endings (one for American tastes and one for European). *Kiss Me, Stupid* attracted censure from the Catholic Legion of Decency for its alleged vulgarity, but was nonetheless considered a success and has become a cult classic for Wilder fans.

Ignoring the critics, Dad was wooed by ABC to occasionally emcee a new TV series called *The Hollywood Palace*, which featured different hosts and guests every week. They'd seen him host NBC specials and knew he would be great at it. Jerry Lewis, whose own show had been canceled, had recently vacated the prime-time slot Dad would be filling. Watching that first night in 1964 were executives from NBC who were reminded of how much they liked Dad's nonchalant style and the lighthearted way he interacted with his guests. Approaching him through his agent, Mort Viner, NBC offered him a small fortune to join their network permanently and present his own weekly variety show. Dad, reluctant to leave the highly profitable and high-profile movie industry where he could fit in golf between takes, turned them down—but not for long.

CHRISTMAS AT 601 Mountain Drive was something to behold. Just decorating the tree was an event. Jeanne would order a giant fir from the Beverly Hills Christmas tree lot, and when Dad came home from work, he'd go down into the basement and get out the lights. We would string them from the living room through the dining room and beyond. It seemed like thousands of red, green, blue, and yellow lights glowed throughout the house. Once the strings were untangled and any broken bulbs had been replaced, we'd help Dad wrap them around the tree's prickly branches as he stood on a ladder high above us, humming quietly to himself all the while.

Only when the lights were in place and the presents were underneath the tree would Jeanne allow friends and neighbors in for the tree trimming. Everyone would help decorate the tree with ornaments, tinsel, and baubles, at a party that featured eggnog, Christmas carols, and deep banks of poinsettias at every window. We'd invite friends like my neighbor Jolene Wagner, Desi and Lucie Arnaz, or Burt Lancaster's son Billy, with whom I went to school. Lucille Ball would come over, with her gravelly voice, deep from smoking. She was an amazing woman, awe-inspiring and intense, not at all like her flighty television persona. I remembered as a very young girl watching *I Love Lucy* cuddled up with Mother and my sisters and laughing so hard that tears streamed down our faces.

Christmas was always at least one time of year when we were guaranteed to see Mother. Time would be set aside for her to come over with her gifts. Dad would make himself scarce if he was in the house. Without the child support, she didn't have much money and her presents were usually clothes. Gail used to joke that they "fell off the back of a truck." More often than not, they just seemed to be a random selection of items that didn't necessarily fit. We gave her gifts Jeanne had bought for us, and spent an hour in her company, before she said her good-byes. Jeanne did her best to make Mother comfortable, but she never lingered long.

"What are you doing this holiday, Mother?" we'd ask.

"Oh, I've been invited to a couple of parties," she'd reply brightly. "I just haven't yet decided which invitation to accept."

Awkward and uncomfortable, we'd sit on the edge of our seats making small talk while Ricci and Dino and Gina waited on the periphery, unsure what to say. Mother tried to keep the conversation light, and Jeanne did, too, but it was never easy. When she eventually went home, we were left with a confused mix of emotions, empty and sad. My head would spin that night in bed with memories of my early childhood, of making green potatoes, and of her tiki-torch parties with all their glamour and glitz. But the memories became increasingly hazy and their quality more and more dreamlike. The mother who came to visit now looked completely different from the mother in my dreams, and I began to wonder if the dream mother ever existed. Seeing her in the flesh only troubled me further. It was agonizing and confusing, yet still a strange relief when, after a while, she stopped coming altogether.

Jeanne would soon turn the mood around. At her Christmas parties there would be tennis and swimming and games and an unlimited supply of snacks and soft drinks. A fire would be burning merrily in the fireplace, Christmas carols would be playing on the jukebox, and it all felt wonderful. It was as if we were living in the pages of a glossy magazine—and actually, we were.

For Christmas morning there would be seven piles of gifts, stretching from the tree all the way across the living room floor, one for each of us. On Christmas Eve, we would all gather as a family in the living room and be allowed to open one gift each, which we could pick from the pile. One year Dad presented us all with little boxes instead. Inside were gold signet rings embossed with a family crest.

"Is this for me?" I asked, wide-eyed and excited to be receiving something from my father.

"Yes," he replied. "Frank gave me these to give to each of you. I hope you like them."

"Thanks, Dad," I said, placing mine on my middle finger, which was the only one it fit. "Is this the Crocetti family crest?"

Dad laughed. "Well, Frank says so, but if you ask me, it looks suspiciously like his."

Special gifts like bicycles or a doll's house would mysteriously appear on Christmas morning. Goodness knows where Santa hid them. The older children would help the younger children unwrap their presents in a wild frenzy of wrapping paper and ribbon, and Jeanne would film the entire proceedings on a home movie camera. She bought and organized everything. Usually our presents were as much as a surprise to Dad as they were to us.

My hazel eyes wide, I'd never known anything like it. The dolls and the candies, the clothes and toys overwhelmed me. It was magical. My earlier childhood was blurring to the point of invisibility. The contrast with the bleaker moments of my life could not have been greater.

Ten

JEANNE ONCE TOLD ME, "DEANA, IF EVER YOU WANT
anything from your dad, don't just ask for money, ask for something
wonderful. He loves to be generous." One Christmas he bought the family dugout season tickets at Dodgers Stadium, and we sat there every
game along with baseball heroes like Joe DiMaggio, Don Drysdale, and
Sandy Koufax. It was incredible. He even played in the Dodgers charity games, wearing a beautiful custom-made Dodgers uniform with his
name embroidered on the back. He was a natural athlete, and we loved
to watch him play. He was very good, and it made us very proud.

A classic example of Dad's generosity was when he came home with charm bracelets for each of the women in his life—Jeanne, Claudia, Gail, me, and Gina. They were gold chains with a heart and very pretty, and each one had been specially engraved with our names on it.

Mine was misspelled. It read DINA. Had he forgotten that we shared almost the same name, or had he just spoken the name to someone who'd written it down wrong, as the registrar had done at the hospital where I was born? Everyone was thrilled with their gift, as was I, but I couldn't help wishing that my name was spelled correctly. For years after that mistake, Dad always spelled my name differently on every card, present, letter, and gift. It was our private joke and something I came to cherish as a bond between us.

"Sorry, baby," he said, when Jeanne pointed out his mistake. "I'll get it altered if you like."

"Oh no, Dad, that's okay," I lied, not wanting to disappoint him. Secretly I was brokenhearted. But he gave me such a smile of gratitude that I couldn't help but forgive him. He really could be the most charming person in the world.

When I was fifteen and a half years old, I needed a car. I was attending Beverly Hills High School and had completed my Driver's Ed course. At last, a driver's license. I had a summer job at Jax's clothing store, where customers like Jacqueline Kennedy and Natalie Wood were regulars, but I wasn't earning enough to pay for a car. So I asked Dad for one.

"Well, what do you want?" he replied.

I hadn't counted on his agreeing so easily, and couldn't think what to say. "Oh, um, a Volkswagen, I guess," I said, thinking of the cute little Beetles everyone loved at the time. The following morning, Dad walked me out onto our huge circular driveway, and there sat my very own shiny red VW, complete with a little wooden steering wheel. After thanking him profusely, I asked, "If I'd wanted a Mercedes, would I have gotten one?"

"You'll never know," he said with a smile, walking back inside.

A year later I traded the VW for an MGB, and then the MGB for a vintage Jaguar. But the Jag kept breaking down. One evening on Sunset Boulevard, the Jag conked out for the very last time. I'd had enough. Handing the keys to the doorman of the nearby Hyatt Hotel, I told him, "It's yours."

I caught a taxi home, and Dad asked me what was wrong. "I gave away that old Jag," I told him. "It broke down again, and I gave it to a doorman."

Dad smiled. He knew exactly what that felt like. It was just a few months earlier when his brand-new, pea-green XKE Jaguar had sputtered to a halt on Sunset Boulevard for the umpteenth time. He'd gotten out of the car, taken a derringer pistol from his boot, and shot it like a horse with a broken leg from one of his westerns.

Now that my own Jag had died a similar death, I was without a car. "Here," Dad said, tossing me the keys to the brand-new gold Firebird he'd bought on a whim while passing a showroom. "I don't drive this anymore. Everyone tells me it's wrong for my image. Take it. It's yours."

Throwing my arms around his neck, I hugged and kissed him until he'd had enough.

On my sixteenth birthday, Dad asked me what I wanted as a gift. "A coat from Wilson's House of Suede," I replied, citing *the* place in L.A. for leather goods.

"Great," said Dad with a smile. "Go get it."

"No," I said, moving on to what I really wanted. "I want you to come and help me pick it out."

His face fell. I knew that what I was asking for was huge. Dad never went anywhere like that with any of us, not even with Jeanne; he was always too busy. It just wasn't his thing. His nose wrinkled and he shifted uneasily from foot to foot.

"Oh, Deana, baby," he said, "I dunno. Couldn't you just go and pick it out yourself?"

"No," I said, standing my ground. "I want you to pick it out for me, Dad, that's what's important."

"Okay," he said, so I gave him the directions and asked him to meet me there the next afternoon at three-thirty. He was there on time—he was always punctual—but I could tell he was just dying inside. He'd had to leave a game of golf after nine holes, and he was sitting uncomfortably in a chair, smoking a cigarette with a swarm of salesgirls buzzing around. He looked up and I knew he just wanted to run away, but I planned to savor every minute with him.

I picked out a coat, tried it on, and asked, "Well, Dad, what do you think?"

"It's great," he said, and stood as if to go.

"No," I said, studying myself critically in the mirror. "I think I'll try some more."

He sat back down.

"What about this one?"

"That's nice."

"No, it's not quite right. How about this?"

"That one's *really* good."

"Which one do you like better?"

"The one you've got on."

"Okay, now what color shall I get it in?"

His face fell again. "Well, what color do you want?"

The salesgirls brought me a book of swatches, and I asked him, "Do you like this color or that color?"

He said, "I dunno, baby, which one do you like?"

"Well, this one's nice." By now, forty-five minutes had elapsed and he was tapping the floor with his foot.

"Okay," I said, beaming at him. "I'll have this jacket in the black."

He grimaced. "Don't get the black, get the beige. I like beige."

I said, "Do you like this shade of beige, or this one?"

He closed his eyes in despair.

"Okay, now shall I have the buttons covered or uncovered?"

He glared openly at me. "What's the difference?"

"Well, I can have just leather or I can have the buttons covered, but that's more expensive."

"Get them covered," he said. I could see he was losing patience, so, laughing and with a hug and a kiss, I finally let him go. He virtually ran from the store, but, as ever, I was very grateful for this morsel of his time, even though I'd had to work so hard for it. Knowing how difficult it seemed to be for him to give of himself, I realized what a generous thing it was for him to do. He could have just told me, "Go buy the coat," and not have interrupted his golf game. This is the sort of thing he would have normally said to his children, but this time, for me, he didn't. Locking the experience away in my heart, I will relive it over and over for the rest of my life, treasuring every precious moment and only wishing that we could have had more. It was such a sweet thing for him to do.

MY SISTERS and I were crazy about the Beatles. I had the biggest crush on George Harrison, Gail liked John Lennon, and Claudia loved Paul McCartney. Our wing of Mountain Drive was like a shrine to the Beatles, their posters plastering every corridor and wall. In 1964 The Fab Four had their first world tour and on August 23, performed in L.A. at the Hollywood Bowl. We couldn't believe our luck, as we not only had the opportunity to attend, but we sat in box seats near the stage. The next day brought a greater surprise as Jeanne arranged for us to attend a garden party at the Brentwood home of Alan Livingston, the president of Capital Records. It was a benefit for the Hemophilia Foundation. The Beatles arrived, and we all had a chance to line up, say hello, and shake their hands. I didn't wash mine for a week. The British legends seemed a bit bashful, and when they spoke, their Liverpool accents were impenetrable. John did most of the talking and everyone was laughing at what he said, but try as I might, I could barely understand a word.

I chose a beige suit, with a matching scarf. I am forever immortalized in a photograph, standing next to my idols. A photo of me shaking John's hand appeared the next morning on the front page of the *Los Angeles Times*. Jeanne was very proud and I was the happiest sixteen-year-old in America.

Later that same year Dad invited us to a taping of *The Hollywood Palace* television show, where he was master of ceremonies. One of his guests was a group called The Rolling Stones.

"It looks like they just got off the boat. They need to take a shower and wash their hair," he told me on the phone. "I thought you girls might like to meet them." Thanks to him, we had already met the Dave Clark Five, Herman's Hermits, and the Lovin' Spoonful. Jeanne had hired the band Canned Heat to play at my senior prom.

I had recently broken my foot skateboarding on our tennis court and was in a cast. That didn't stop me. Claudia and I went over to the Palace to meet Mick Jagger and his fellow band members. From the wings we watched them perform "All I Want to Do Is Make Love to You." Dad had introduced them as the new singing sensation from England and told the audience, "I've been rolled when I was stoned before. Now ladies and gentlemen, the Rolling Stones." When they'd finished their number, he turned to the camera and said with a wink, "Now, you all come back after this commercial, because you don't want to leave me alone out here with them Rolling Stones."

For reasons I never understood, the band took umbrage at his comments and threatened to leave without performing their second set. Their manager went ballistic. All the British newspapers had headlines like DEAN MARTIN SLAMS THE STONES. Dad was just cracking a joke. He never understood why they made so much fuss. And, frankly, he didn't really care.

♦♦♦

I WAS seventeen when I first realized that Dad and Uncle Frank knew people that some regarded with awe or suspicion. I knew the rumors about Frank and the Mob, but as Dad always told me, their only connection was through the entertainment industry.

"These boys own the nightclubs we play in. Of course we're going to socialize," he'd explain. "It's just the nature of the business."

These were the guys who had first hired Dad and Uncle Frank. They owned the nightclubs, so if you wanted to work, you worked for them. They'd liked Dad and accepted his aloof indifference. They'd given him and Frank work in the East Coast nightclubs, which helped them make a name for themselves. Dad and Frank were honorable men. They grew up with these people and never forgot them.

It was Frank who persuaded Dad to be his partner in the Cal-Neva Lodge at Lake Tahoe, a rustic casino and hotel. One day Dad discovered that Sam "Mo-Mo" Giancana—a Chicago crime boss and a target for the FBI—had been staying there with Phyllis McGuire of the McGuire sisters. Dad expressed his concern to Frank. "We could lose our gambling license," he warned him.

"Don't worry, pally," Frank replied.

"Fine," Dad said, "I want you to buy me out."

Poor Frank later had to go before a Senate committee to explain himself, before being forced to relinquish his license by the Nevada gaming commission. By then Dad was long gone from the partnership.

We knew that we were under FBI surveillance from time to time. Almost every big name in Hollywood was. The FBI was especially interested in us because of Dad and Uncle Frank's connections with people like Mo-Mo, whom they'd known since the 1950s. Then there was Skinny D'Amato, who'd given Dad and Jerry their first break in Atlantic City at the 500 club. Another good friend of Dad's, an Arizona hotelier and keen golfer, was a man named Big Lou Rosanova, who called me "the little black one" because of my dark hair. Years later, I invited him to be the godfather to my son. When the priest asked Lou what he did for a living, he leaned forward and replied with a smile, "I'm a simple tailor."

The FBI must have been very disappointed with their stakeouts of 601 Mountain Drive. You could set your clock by Dad, and his party guests, thanks to Jeanne. We were old Hollywood, not old Palermo. In every investigation the FBI conducted into his so-called Mob connections, Dad came up squeaky clean.

My own involvement with people the FBI might have been interested in was limited. It only really happened when I began a singing career. Gail was already an established singer. She'd had songs arranged for her by Sammy Davis Jr. and Uncle Frank, and she was doing well. I'd just recorded my first single, "Girl of the Month Club," for Reprise Records, and hoped for success as a singer. My song, which was written and produced by Lee Hazlewood, a legend in the industry, did well in Nashville and on the country music scene. I was fortunate enough to have some wonderful musicians to work with, like my guitarist, Glenn Campbell. He was so young and cute, a blond mophead, and everyone assured me he was one of the best.

I was offered the chance to play a gig in Detroit to promote my next single, "When He Remembers Me." On Dad's advice, I'd hired an agent named Jack Gilardi, who arranged for me to stay with a friend in the Motor City. The friend turned out to be Pete Licavoli, the head of the Purple Gang. He had a sixteen-year-old daughter, Kathy, with whom I became friends. Wherever Kathy went, bodyguards followed, so Dad knew I'd be safe. He was correct; I was treated like a princess. When I studied some wedding photos framed on the wall of their basement, I remember saying to Kathy, "Oh my, isn't that Machine Gun Kelly?" and "Surely that's not Al Capone at the back there?" Kathy just smiled and nodded.

To return the favor, I took Kathy with me to Las Vegas to see Dad and Uncle Frank at The Sands. They were wonderful to watch. Dad played the lovable lush to perfection, occasionally tripping on the stage, never spilling a drop of his apple juice. Frank wheeled a little bar out onto the stage with a sign that read, DON'T THINK, DRINK.

"Why don't we mix us a little salad?" Dad would ask Frank.

"Are you drunk, dago?" Frank would retort.

"No," my father would reply, swaying gently. "I've only had tee martoonies."

"I've just found the perfect girl," Dad told Frank.

"Oh yeah?"

"She's deaf, dumb, oversexed, and owns a liquor store," he added with a smirk. Boom, boom, went the drums.

Immediately after the show, Dad and Frank and Kathy and I went to another venue to see the comedian Don Rickles in his lounge act. The place was full, and Don was nervous because he knew Dad and Frank were in the audience, sitting at little tables around the stage. Frank came up with a scheme and sent out for fifty newspapers. Enlisting the audience, we waited until Don came bouncing out onto the stage twenty minutes late, hyped up and ready to perform. Suddenly fifty people, including Dad and Frank and Kathy and I, held up their newspapers as if we were busy reading. The prank made Don, and the entire room, break down in laughter, instantly putting him at ease. He was in rare form that night and gave a great performance.

After that, we went on to see the veteran comedian Shecky Green, whose show was very blue but very funny. When it was over, Dad was still laughing so hard he could barely speak. When he did, he blurted out, "That was the funniest fucking show I've ever seen." I was shocked. That was the first time I'd ever heard my father swear. He never swore in front of us at home, and he hated to hear other people cursing. Kathy was with me, and I was especially aware of what she might think. I looked at Dad that night in a new light. I was in Las Vegas, on his "home turf," and for a moment he'd let his guard down and let me see a glimpse of the man's man he was. Here he was, out with the boys, having a good time, drinking and swearing along with the rest of them.

Whenever Dad and Frank got together, they made their own rules. I know that their practical jokes were wild. Someone who often traveled with them was Michael Romanoff, known as Prince Romanoff, the owner of Romanoff's restaurant on Rodeo Drive. He enjoyed gambling, playing cards, and hanging out with Dad and Frank while they were working. Prince Romanoff used to wear bow ties. He wore them all the time. They were his trademark. Dad and Frank used to get the key to his room, find his bow ties—five or six laid out in a box with tissue paper—and cut them so that they were only being held together by the merest thread. Then they'd put them back in the box and neatly refold the tissue paper. When it came time for Prince Romanoff to get ready for their night out, Dad and Frank would arrange to be in his room, so they could watch him dress. One after another he'd pull out a bow tie and start to tie it and it would fall apart. Dad and Frank tried to hide their laughter, but finally they were rolling on the floor, howling.

They'd sometimes spend over an hour painstakingly removing the cellophane wrapping from the bottom of a box of Romanoff's favorite Dunhill cigarettes, just to sabotage them. They'd poke tiny holes in each cigarette with a pin, so that when he went to light one, it wouldn't draw. Their task complete, they'd methodically return the box to its original condition. All this for a laugh.

"He fell for it every time," Dad told me, grinning at the memory. Prince Romanoff was, it turned out, not a prince and couldn't even stake a claim to the name Romanoff. He was a fraud, someone who'd cleverly reinvented himself to impress others. I only really knew him through our monthly family visits to his restaurant, where I always found him rather quirky, with his sense of dress and flamboyant mannerisms. He was always very polite to me, and he made my Dad and Uncle Frank laugh. Anyone who could do that was all right by me. Even when I found out that he wasn't what he said he was, I thought him a lovely man nevertheless.

Dad had other associates whom some might call questionable. One was Ray Ryan, whom Dad asked to be Ricci's godfather. He was a wealthy Texas gambler who sometimes liked to gamble with other people's money. With William Holden, he started the Kenyan Mountain Safari Club, a game reserve in Africa where everyone used to hang out. Dad liked him because he was fun to be with. He'd also helped set up Dad and Jerry's production company, York Pictures Corporation, years before. Dad was always grateful. Ray used to be in Palm Springs and I loved the way he spoke, with his slow Texas drawl. He was killed some years later, blown up by a car bomb presumably planted by someone who didn't think Ray was as much fun as we did.

THE ONE thing Dad knew how to do was to get people out of scrapes. He had a great relationship with the Beverly Hills police, who were his number one fans. Whenever anyone was in trouble, he seemed able to pull strings. That was especially helpful when Pop was arrested for stealing a pad of prescription forms and trying to pass them off at a pharmacy in Inglewood to feed his growing addiction to sleeping pills. The press never got hold of the story and the police delivered Pop home, eliciting a promise from Dad to do a benefit for them.

Dad's problems were solved by his assistant and friend Mack Gray. Mack remained pivotal in Dad's life, and was always there for him. He'd be over at the house before Dad was up. He carried his cigars, his gum, and his gun in a large manila envelope.

"Why don't you get a briefcase, Mack?" I'd ask.

"I like things just the way they are," he'd say, clutching the envelope to him.

A former boyfriend of Lucille Ball, Mack was constantly on duty, except when Dad was out by the pool. Only then would he relax and attempt to get what became known in my family as a "Mack Gray tan." He'd lie down, unbutton his shirt, and place a sun reflector on his stomach. The rest of him remained lily white, but his face and upper chest would be bronzed. He was such a funny guy.

One of my earliest memories of Mack is at Mountain Drive. He came lumbering toward me, bent down, and held my chin in his huge hand. "Where did you get those eyes?" he said, smiling into my face. "Oh, Deana, you're going to break some hearts with those eyes."

One thing I know for sure about Mack is that my dad loved him. He spent more time with Mack than with any of us. As a young girl, I was aware of the amount of time he was able to spend with my father when I had so little. I sometimes thought Mack Gray was the luckiest man alive.

Eleven

DAD WAS NEVER REALLY INTERESTED IN BECOMING A television star. He was concerned about how it would affect the rest of his career. At that time, people were either movie stars or TV stars, and few crossed the line. He was making movies and recording albums in between golfing and family commitments, and he was happy. After much wining and dining, and lengthy meetings with his agent and advisers, NBC eventually persuaded Dad to accept their offer for a weekly variety show. It was too good to refuse. He only had to work one day a week and be paid forty thousand dollars per episode.

The Dean Martin Show first aired in September 1965, showcasing Dad's music and his laid-back personality. It was such a hit that it ran for nine straight years in prime time, regularly attracting between thirty and forty million viewers at ten o'clock every Thursday night. For years it was the number one rated show on television. They felt comforted by the show's cozy bar and den setting and the ease with which Dad, fooling around, made them laugh. From the minute he slid down the fireman's pole and said hello, to his famous sign-off, "Keep them cards and letters comin' in, folks," they were enthralled. Fans who wanted to come to the studio to watch a taping would often wait up to a year for the privilege. In 1967, Dad won a Golden Globe award for best male television star, and was nominated three years running.

From that time on, our lives changed dramatically. Dad's face was suddenly familiar to every television viewer in America and to millions around the world. A new generation of fans who'd never seen Martin & Lewis perform or bought a single Dean Martin album was born. When Dad sang "Little Jeanne" for Mother Jeanne one night, she became known to audiences as the quintessential celebrity wife. All my friends knew who Dad was; that didn't change. What did change was when I was introduced to strangers.

"Oh my God, you're Dean Martin's daughter! I love him. He's so funny," they'd cry, realizing for the first time what we'd all known for years. Dad was the coolest and funniest man we knew.

Dad would regularly invite us to the NBC studio in Burbank on Sunday afternoons to watch the taping of his show. It was tailor-made for someone who was a successful singer, entertainer, movie star, and comedian. It quickly became a family event. We all appeared on the show from time to time, even a reluctant Jeanne. Later my brother Craig worked his way from production assistant to associate producer. It was there that Craig met his second wife, Kami Stevens. She was one of the "Golddiggers," the beautiful troupe of dancers and singers who gave the show its unique air of glamour.

Not surprisingly, with Dad at the helm, the show was a smash hit, thanks to the great team assembled behind the scenes. It was full of spontaneous humor and segments like the "mystery voice" sketch.

"Come on now, folks," Dad would urge his viewing audience, "this voice has been running for weeks and we've had more than three thousand callers, one of you must be able to get it." Then he'd play the voice and it would be Frank Sinatra singing his bestselling hit "Strangers in the Night."

Dad would roll his eyes when Uncle Frank started to sing and say, "If he does that 'doobedoobedoo' one more time, I'll just die." Right on cue, Frank would start with the "doobedoo."

One of the things the audience enjoyed were the goofs, all of which were kept in, as Dad would feign poor eyesight, unable to read the cue cards, or deliberately fluff his lines. In this modern age full of offbeat, wacky humor, it is hard to imagine how radically original Dad's show was for the time. The competition was offering up carefully staged gags with canned laughter, while Dad and his team of people like Bob Newhart, Dom DeLuise, and Don Rickles were doing pratfalls and ad-libbing mercilessly. It was spontaneous and fresh. No one ever knew what the other was going to say. The viewer felt privileged to be part of this crazy, talented, and unpredictable crowd. It was just like the Rat Pack at The Sands, and Dad could do no wrong.

With incredible ratings, he commanded the finest guests and invited us along to meet everyone from Gene Kelly and Tom Jones to Petula Clarke and Orson Welles. Gene was a lovely guy, very easygoing and happy to fall in with the fun and games. Dad was a good dancer, but he had nothing but respect for the master. Tom Jones was quite a performer, and Dad got a kick out of him, joking about his tight trousers and pelvis-thrusting moves. Tom ended up buying one of Dad's houses years later. Dad and Petula Clarke really clicked. They had a certain chemistry together, and she became a frequent guest. Orson Welles was a very respected actor and Dad was thrilled to have him as a guest. He was huge and always smoking cigars, with such an intelligent sense of humor; Orson was an expert at putting us at ease and making us laugh.

James Stewart was another regular; they made a western together called *Bandolero!*, with Raquel Welch. Dad idolized him. I met him several times, and he was always very sweet and incredibly tall. He stood alongside Dad in his tuxedo and enjoyed the comic departure from his usual dramatic roles. They were brilliant together. Jimmy used to do these appalling impersonations of James Cagney and Bette Davis that always just sounded exactly like Jimmy Stewart, and Dad would tell him, "That was spooky, it was so good."

Watching Dad fool around with his guests was reminiscent of the best moments in his act with Jerry Lewis. There was a time when those two merely made each other laugh, spontaneously, tears streaming from their eyes, and if you happened to be watching, you couldn't help but laugh too. There was a magic between them that their movies were never quite able to capture.

For someone so much in demand, Dad had the most amazing working hours. He would arrive at the studio Sunday afternoons at one o'clock on the dot to record his television show in a one-take, three-hour session. Everyone else would rehearse all week long while Dad played golf. The rest of the cast would rehearse with stand-ins. Lee Hale, the show's musical director, would wear a placard with Dad's name on it (one day Dad surprised Lee by turning up and wearing a placard that read "Lee Hale").

They would send Dad the script and a tape of the songs he had to sing. He would listen to them in his car on the way to the golf course. Having read through the script just prior to the recording, he would watch the rehearsal run through on a television in his dressing room and read through his cue cards. Then, one rehearsal with the entire cast, before changing into his tuxedo for the show. Thank god for the cue cards. The secret of the show was that it stayed fresh and spontaneous. Dad liked it that way and so did the audience. It was something he learned in the early days with Jerry.

"If I tell a joke too often in rehearsal," he told Jerry, "it won't make me laugh anymore."

I remember going to the NBC studio with my grandfather "Pop," the man from whom my father inherited much of his humor. Pop was an extraordinarily theatrical sort of person, always impeccably dressed. He spoka lika thesa with a broad Italian accent and was great fun to be around. It must have been a laugh a minute in his barbershop back in Steubenville. He was five feet six inches tall, and always dressed in a very dapper manner, with a beautiful suit, a cigarette, and a straw hat. He used to take us kids down to Muscle Beach in Venice to watch the acrobats and weightlifters and provide a running commentary that doubled us over with laughter.

Some of the acrobats became his friends, and we were enlisted into their act. They would throw us kids up into the air in their human-triangle routines. Being the smallest, I would have the honor of being placed at the top of the pyramid.

Dad and Jeanne hosted a huge party at the Beverly Wilshire Hotel for Pop and Grandma Angela's fiftieth wedding anniversary. Grandma made me the most beautiful dress for the occasion—red and black with a velvet sash and a little red jacket, the lining of which matched the skirt.

"Why, Deana, baby, you look good in green," Dad told me, pretending to be more color-blind than he was.

"I do?" I said, happy to be part of the joke.

"Yeah, baby, you look fabulous," he replied.

Everyone who knew the Martins was there—the Sinatras, the Curtises, and all of Hollywood's royalty. There was dinner, music, and dancing, followed by a giant cake. The dance floor was the same one Jeff Bridges had twirled me around in the Viennese waltz a few years earlier. Grandma was a little taken aback by all the attention, but Pop loved the limelight.

One night soon afterward, halfway through the live taping of Dad's television show, Pop stood up from our specially reserved seats in the front row, put on his hat and coat, and shuffled onto the stage, as an astonished audience and camera crew looked on.

"I gotta goa homa now, Dino," he said, kissing his son on both cheeks and patting him on the back.

Dad cracked up laughing as his father disappeared stage left. The audience probably thought it was part of the act, but it wasn't. Waving one of his hands, Dad, still grinning, said, "Ladies and gentlemen, I give you my father."

IN 1965, Dad went to a one-horse town in the wilds of the Mexican Sierras to film his second major western, *The Sons of Katie Elder*, with John Wayne. The Duke and he got on famously and became good friends in this, their second film together. John Wayne would lend us his yacht, the *Wild Goose*, which he kept at the Newport Marina. We would use it for family trips to Catalina Island. The boat was enormous, with a crew and a cook, and each of us had our own stateroom. We would take turns piloting the boat and we fished. In the evenings we'd play cards or Monopoly. Dad would show us tricks, in which cards would simply disappear into thin air.

In his new movie, Dad played Tom, one of four sons who came together for their mother's funeral and vowed to avenge their father's death. It was a grueling shoot, made more difficult by the high altitudes. Dad never complained. On the contrary, he said acting was so easy, he couldn't understand those who moaned about it. "Who are they kidding?" he said in an interview at the time. "All you have to do is say a few lines. If you make a mistake, the director tells you to do it over again. What's so tough about that?" He made it look effortless, but I had seen him standing in front of his dressing room mirror, the place where he normally only performed his grooming rituals, practicing his lines until he got the delivery just right.

His only preparation for his latest part, he claimed, was watching other westerns. "All I did was watch those old cowboy films and see what they did wrong," he said. "I noticed how cowboys in the bad ones always pushed up their hats up with their thumbs before they spoke. Me, I pulled mine down."

Dad loved westerns, watching them and starring in them. He relished the rare opportunity to take off his tuxedo and slip into jeans, cowboy boots, and a loose-fitting shirt. He was very comfortable in western garb and on a horse. When he was a kid, he'd sit in the Olympic moviehouse, staring up at the screen, imagining himself in the roles played by the likes of Rocky Lane on his trusty stallion Black Jack, or Tom Mix with his horse Tony. Playing with his friends as a young boy, and horseback riding, it was always cowboys and Indians that Dad enjoyed most. A few of his treasures were memorabilia from a classic western, a rare cowboy hat or a poster from one of the films he'd seen a dozen times as a child. Knowing how much he loved westerns, people gave him these things, most of which he displayed in his pool room. In his fantasy of the Wild West, Dad could ride off into the sunset singing, "My Rifle, My Pony, and Me."

DAD WAS born cool. Even as a child, he had a natural suave elegance about him. He was meticulous, courteous, and polite, and avoided confrontation, preferring to follow his own solitary path. Never taking anything too seriously, he was, as many came to realize, content within himself.

Even the press liked him and rarely said anything bad about him. Despite his onstage persona, when he'd stagger on, asking, "How long have I been on?" or quip after his first song, "Have I got time for one more?" he drank relatively moderately—Martinelli's apple juice filled his scotch bottles on stage, and most nights he went to bed with nothing stronger than a large glass of warm milk.

Uncle Frank, who singlehandedly made Jack Daniel's famous, once confessed, "I spill more than Dean drinks." The two of them were stopped by the police after a night out, and Frank, who assumed Dad was drunk at the wheel, told him to stay silent and look straight ahead while he sweet-talked the cop. But when the officer shone his flash light into Dad's face to see who he was, Dad responded like a pro. Lifting his face to the spotlight, he broke into a rendition of "Everybody Loves Somebody Sometime," while Frank grimaced. To his surprise, however, the policeman allowed

Dad to drive them home. Frank's drinking buddy wasn't half as ine-briated as he thought.

Dad said of Frank, "When I'm drinking with him, every third one goes in the pot." He also said that if he drank as hard as most peo-ple thought he did, he'd have been dead long ago. The actor Henry Silva, a dear friend, shared this story with me. He had watched Dad drinking throughout his Las Vegas act and then had gone backstage to his dressing room. He was concerned. "I noticed bottles of Martinelli's apple juice on the bar. Dean came over and gave me a big hug. 'Hi pallie, how you doin'?' Looking straight into his eyes and smelling the apple juice on his breath, I shouted, 'You son of a bitch! You're stone-cold sober!' "

In an unusually frank interview Dad gave to *The Saturday Evening Post*, he talked the reporter through his drinking day while performing at The Sands. It began at lunchtime after a morning round of golf with a bottle of beer and a sandwich, before he played blackjack until five o'clock, not touching a drop. "Then I go to the health club. I shave, shower, take a two-minute ultraviolet-ray treatment, then I lie down. At six o'clock I call my wife and talk to her for ten minutes. Then a guy gives me a massage and I say 'Wake me at seven-thirty.' I brush my teeth, comb my hair, put on my clothes while I'm having four cups of coffee—black with sugar, no cream—then at 8:10 I walk out. About 8:15 I'm in the casino playing a little more blackjack. Then I walk into the dining room, they announce my name. I get up on the stage and I invariably hear some-body at a ringside table say, 'Look at his eyes! You can see how drunk he is.'

"I'll have a slug of liquid in a glass that looks just like Scotch, but it's really apple juice. Then, in the middle of my act, I have a real drink. When I'm through, I go someplace and eat good Italian food and have a little wine. Then I get back on the stage for the second show. When it's over I have three or four drinks and maybe a sleep-ing pill. So that's your alcoholic for you."

I never saw Dad drunk in those years, and I'm sure that if he drank as heavily as people thought he did, he would never have been able to work so hard or so diligently. When a journalist once asked him how he could work when he drank so much, he replied curtly, "Do you think NBC would give all that money to a drunk?" He didn't like to party, and his ideal night was an evening in front of the television. "Alcoholics don't get up at six in the morning to play golf," he'd say. Goodness only knows when he had time for all the affairs his biographers have since claimed he had during the years he was married to Jeanne. I certainly knew nothing about them at the time, although Jeanne did hint at them later. Given his history, it wouldn't have been surprising, but I often wonder how many of these alleged affairs were genuine and how many simply the product of some fertile, and perhaps hopeful, imaginations.

Dad didn't help, joking about women. "Always pick the ugly girl," he'd tell his audience. "She won't turn you down and she's easy to please."

He used to jest that the real love of his life was his horse called Tops, which he used in just about every western he ever made. He loved that horse. He kept him out at my Uncle Jack's ranch in Northridge, and when he died at the age of eighteen, halfway through a movie, Dad was so upset he took time out from filming to fly home to have Tops cremated.

His women would have been jealous of that much attention. My friend Shirley MacLaine, the fantastic actor, writer, and dancer, shared this wonderful story with me. She was madly in love with Dad and hoped for something more. She came to the house to profess her undying love, saw him happily at home with Jeanne and us kids, and she changed her mind. In another instance, a showgirl sent to Dad's room at The Sands by Frank and Sammy, famously reported that Dad was the perfect gentleman. Arriving at his room, he found her undressed, sitting on his bed. Instead of bedding her, he put his jacket around her, gave her a couple hundred dollars, and told her to run along home.

"By the way," he added, "if you see Frank, tell him I was better in bed than he was."

There were undoubtedly other women in his life, as I discovered much later. There was Petula Clarke, and the Swedish actress Inger

Stevens, who was someone he genuinely cared for. He rented her a house on Benedict Canyon. Gail was with Dad in Las Vegas once, when Inger arrived at their table. Making small talk, Gail admired a beautiful and unusual diamond ring Inger was wearing.

"Thank you," the actress said, beaming across at Dad. Poor Inger had a tragic end. When her relationship with Dad eventually ended, she moved away. A few years later, she killed herself.

At home, however, I was oblivious of it all. I thought Dad and Jeanne were the happiest married couple I knew. They never fought, and they never yelled at each other. When I went to friends' houses and saw their parents argue, I was shocked. That would never happen in my house. Dad and Jeanne went out of their way to be respectful, kind, and courteous to each other, and to set a good example for us kids. Just like some of the characters he played, and many of the songs he sang, Dad was secretly a true romantic at heart. Only once in all the years I lived under the same roof did I hear raised voices coming from their bedroom. I remember waking up, sitting up in bed, and thinking, "What's that?" It was so unusual I assumed at first it was the television, but then I recognized Jeanne's voice and slid back down beneath the covers, afraid to hear any more. I now realize, with the hindsight of adulthood, that there must have been a great deal of anger bubbling away beneath the surface that I never knew about. It wasn't until many years later that I learned the truth. Jeanne told me that whenever she was angry with Dad, or they had a fight, she'd open the door to the master bathroom and hurl a mirror into the tiled shower stall, listening to it shatter into a thousand pieces. Screaming silently inside, she'd wait for the noise to end and then quietly sweep up every tiny piece of broken glass.

I THINK the legacy of the Dean Martin name must have been very tough for Dean Paul. He had inherited Dad's drive and, like him, was good at everything he tried.

He began following in Dad's footsteps at an early age. At the age of fourteen and with Dad and Frank's help, he'd fronted a successful teenage band called Dino, Desi, and Billy—with Desi Arnaz Jr. and Billy Hinsche (later of Beach Boys fame). He made a lot of money as a teen star and appeared on *The Ed Sullivan Show*, singing his Top Twenty hit, "I'm a Fool." He bought his first automobile, a Dino Ferrari, and went out every day to run the engine until he was old enough to drive. After the band, his focus changed to scuba diving, tennis, and flying. It was Dean Paul who first interested me in flying.

For the first part of his life he was known as Dino, but when he grew up, he suddenly announced that he wanted to be called Dean Paul.

"That's my name," he insisted. "Not Dino. And from now on I'll only answer to Dean Paul."

He enjoyed collecting guns and a lot of Dad's friends gave him weapons as gifts. The problem was, he built up such a huge collection that when he eventually tried to get rid of it and put them up for sale, he ended up being arrested for selling large quantities of weapons without a license. It was a scary time. Facing a jail sentence, he pleaded guilty to eleven weapons charges, having been indicted by a federal grand jury. He escaped with a year's probation and a stiff fine. After that, he concentrated solely on his flying and playing tennis.

He was an excellent tennis player and regularly practiced on our court at home with Björn Borg, Arthur Ashe, Jimmy Connors, and Ile Nastase. He even made it to Wimbledon before being knocked out by Ken Rosewall. He was also an actor. He was handsome and looked the part. Because of his acting and tennis abilities, he landed a leading role in a film about tennis called *Players* with Ali MacGraw, part of which was filmed at Wimbledon.

Gail, who'd starred in plays since high school and had a great singing voice, went to England for two years to study drama at the Dartington College of Arts in Devon. It was a great accolade—the college only took one American every year, and she was it. She'd always liked older men, and had a fling with her professor. Gail was still good friends with Liza Minnelli, and saw a lot of her. Gail taught Liza to dance and Liza taught Gail to sing. She had a great Barbra Streisand sort of sound, and perfected it into a successful nightclub act. From opening for Dad in Las Vegas, to traveling the country, she carried on the Martin tradition.

Claudia, who was looking increasingly like Sophia Loren in her chic Jax outfits, spent her time thoroughly enjoying her Beverly Hills lifestyle. Jax was the store on the corner of Bedford and Wilshire, owned by Jack and Sally Hanson. They were enterprising fashion designers who sold their own brand of custom-made slacks, shoes, and sweaters. We also shopped regularly at Saks Fifth Avenue, I. Magnin, and, when we were younger, Pixietown on Beverly Drive. The look was heavy eye makeup. I remember Dad once telling Claudia, "If your car breaks down, dear, you can always walk home on your eyeliner." She'd tell Dad she was going to the library to study, but the only thing she was studying was boys.

Her first serious boyfriend was Terry Melcher, Doris Day's son, who was the record producer for the Byrds. He invited us to a studio in Hollywood one day to watch them record their next single. It was a song called "Mr. Tambourine Man," and I remember sitting in the back of the booth with the engineers, thinking, "The Byrds are recording a Bob Dylan song, how cool."

Years later I dated Terry. He was very good looking, six feet tall, with red hair, freckles, and blue eyes. Even Jeanne wasn't above flirting with him, and he recalls one time when he was looking in the refrigerator at our house and Jeanne came up behind him in a frivolous mood.

"Hey, Terry," she said with a wry smile on her face. "Wanna fuck?"

"Actually, Mrs. Martin, I was just getting some milk," he replied, a little nonplussed.

"Suit yourself," she laughed, and wandered off. I hope she was joking.

At eighteen, Claudia shocked us all by eloping to Las Vegas with Gavin Murrell, a big handsome Italian who Dad thought was just after her (or, rather, his) money. He was an actor, but then Dad asked him, "What films have you been in?"

"None," came the reply.

"Then you're not an actor," Dad stated crisply.

Dad refused to let Claudia marry Gavin, so—as Craig had done with the army—she went to see Mother and persuaded her to sign the relevant parental consent forms. Claudia and Gavin tied the knot at a wedding chapel in Las Vegas. Claudia thought that once they were man and wife, Dad would react differently, but she couldn't have been more incorrect. Dad refused to allow Gavin into the house, so Claudia would come to family events like Thanksgiving dinner alone, or not at all. It was tough on her and on us. Gail and I especially missed her and wanted her to come home. None of us knew much about Gavin, apart from the fact that Dad said he wasn't right for her. Dad was clearly deeply concerned for his eldest daughter, and did all he could to bring her back. Eventually, Claudia saw the light and called Dad. He picked her up with her belongings and brought her home. A few weeks later he had the marriage annulled. We never spoke of Gavin again.

◆◆◆

MY LITTLE brother Ricci was the least affected by our father's fame. In fact, he was the one who usually made a joke out of it, and of life in general. He was always making things, electrical gadgets and rockets; his room was a mess of wires and parts. Just about every Fourth of July he ruined the tennis court with his homemade fireworks.

One morning I was sitting with Dad in the breakfast room overlooking the pool, watching in shock—as I always did—as Dad shoveled five teaspoons of sugar into his coffee. Our Japanese gardener was bending over the flowerbeds outside, doing some weeding. Suddenly there came a series of explosions, with smoke and great clods of earth flying up into the air. All we could hear above the gardener's screams was Ricci yelling, "Remember Pearl Harbor," as he set off the miniature mines and hand grenades he'd secretly planted in the backyard.

After that, Jeanne laid down her most famous rule: "Guns and cherry bombs are fine," she warned, "but I will *not* have hand grenades in this house."

Later, Ricci and Dean Paul bought a Sherman tank and parked it in the garage next to Dad's shiny Dual-Ghia without telling him. Coming home from a weekend away, Dad and Jeanne parked the car, and as Dad walked into the house, he switched off the light and said to Jeanne, "Was that a tank in the garage?"

"Yes, dear, I think so," she replied, and they went to bed without another word.

The next morning, Ricci and Dean Paul dressed up in military uniforms rented from Western Costume and kidnapped a screaming Irma, driving her down Sunset Boulevard in the tank. Our house at 601 Mountain Drive was on a movie star bus route for tourists wanting to see the homes of Hollywood stars. The coaches rolled past every fifteen minutes at peak times. On Sunday afternoons the enterprising Ricci would set up a little stall at the end of the driveway to sell anything from a tin of peas to a roll of toilet paper, all stolen from Alma's pantry.

"Come and buy some genuine Dean Martin sweetcorn," he'd cry as the tourists pulled up, blocking the driveway and offloading their curious cargo. My adorable little sister Gina, so cute she'd have attracted a crowd by herself, was enlisted as his unwitting assistant.

"Come on now, folks, don't be shy here, just five dollars for a can of peaches, direct from the legendary star's pantry." That boy was wild.

Grandma "Gams" had a middle-aged boyfriend named Paul who was just as brash as Ricci. Jeanne and I were sitting out by the pool one day sunbathing, when we spotted the balding Paul leading a group of five strangers from the back door of the house and out across the tennis court.

"What are you doing, Paul?" Jeanne asked, standing up and shielding her eyes from the sun.

"Just showing some nice folks around," he said, smiling and waving at her. We later discovered that he was charging five bucks a head for tours around Dean Martin's house.

It was a different world, the days before stalkers and kidnappers, when we had no need for tight security and locked gates. People could wander up to the front door and knock and say hello. It was a rose-tinted time of trust and friendliness.

Twelve

DATING WAS SCARY ENOUGH WITHOUT HAVING TO INTRO-
duce my boyfriends to my father. He was very cool about it,
although I think sometimes it was just as scary for him.

"Don't drink and you won't get yourself into any awkward situ-
ations," he warned me. He hated to see a lady drunk, I think out of
his old-fashioned sense of morality. To his mind, a lady should always
behave like a lady.

"Okay, Dad," I'd say, smiling. "I'll drink apple juice just like you."

"Wear turtleneck sweaters and long sleeves," he added.

"Why?" I asked, thinking how impractical that would be in California.

"It's very sexy," he replied. "Never let them see what they can't have. Trust me, it's better that way."

My first boyfriend was Tony Thomas, Danny Thomas's son, who took me to the Beverly Hills Movie Theatre to see *Billy Budd*. I loved that film almost as much as *The Nun's Story*, which was my childhood favorite. I saw *Billy Budd* eleven times, and drooled over Terence Stamp, who looked so gorgeous. Tony Thomas tried to put his arm around me halfway through the movie, and I burst out laughing. Lesson number one: Never laugh at your boyfriend during an awkward moment. Tony grew up to be a prominent movie and television producer. He had hit television programs like *The Golden Girls*, *Soap*, and *Benson* and his most recent movie, *Insomnia*, starring Al Pacino and Robin Williams. We're still friends, so he must have forgiven me.

In high school I was crazy about someone else, a guy named Michael Nader. He was *the* heartthrob of Beverly Hills High, and one day he asked me out. Knowing Dad's penchant for practical jokes, I cornered him and begged him not to embarrass me.

"Dad," I said, "a boy's coming to take me out tonight, so please be nice, okay?"

My father looked at me, a smile tugging at the corner of his mouth, and said, "Why, Deana, baby, I don't know what you mean!"

Dad had just returned home from filming *Texas Across the River*, a western comedy. His co-stars were Rosemary Forsyth, Joey Bishop, and the French actor Alain Delon, whom Dad used to greet by saying, "'Allo Alain Delon," in his best French accent. He was about to start his second Matt Helm movie, *Murderers' Row*, with the lovely Ann-Margret. As Matt Helm, Dad was America's answer to James Bond, with all those neat gadgets and cool one-liners, working for ICE, Intelligence Counter Espionage. Bond was never so funny, nor did he earn so much. That year alone, Dad's income was estimated at $5 million.

I was nervous as my date arrived, but I welcomed him and led him down the stairs from the hallway to the curved sunken bar, where I offered him a Coke. Michael was eager to meet Dad. He loved the first Matt Helm movie, which Dad had just finished.

"Is it true you really went to the set of *The Silencers*?" Michael asked.

"Yes," I replied. "It was great fun. Dad did this scene while we were there when his big round bed swiveled around, tipped up, and slid him into a giant bubble bath. He does all his own stunts, you know."

In awe, Michael looked around as if half-expecting Dad to come flying through the window on a rope in a turtleneck, Martini glass in hand. Instead, Dad suddenly appeared in the doorway, wearing his blue pajamas and velvet slippers with an embroidered crest. It was only about seven o'clock at night.

"Good evening," he said, smiling and extending a hand as he walked directly toward us. "I'm Deana's father."

"Good evening, sir," said Michael, standing up and returning his firm handshake. "It's wonderful to meet you."

"It's wonderful to meet you, too," said Dad, grinning broadly. I wondered what he was up to. Without saying a word, he walked around to the back of the bar, pulled an iced mug from the refrigerator, and poured himself a draft beer. "Nice to meet you," he said again to Michael. "Good night, Deana." And he blew me a kiss from across the bar, before walking back up the steps and leaving the room. It was only as he walked away that we could see, for the first time, that he had a roll of toilet paper stuffed down the back of his pajamas. He had left a long trail of white paper down the hall, down the stairs, around the bar, and back out into the hallway. I could have died of embarrassment. There wasn't a straight man in that house.

Another boyfriend was Davey Jones, from the television show and the band of the same name, the Monkees. My agent arranged for us to date, to help publicize my launch as a singer. When Davey came to the house to pick me up, thankfully Dad was well behaved. Davey, who was excited to meet Dad, was wearing tight bell-bottomed pants and high platform boots. We went to dinner and had fun, so we started dating. A few weeks later he came by the house again, when Dad, Claudia, Dino, Ricci, and I were all playing football in the yard.

"Come and join us," Dad called when he saw him. Davey was a good sport, so he took off his boots and joined in. The trouble was, he lost so much height when his boots came off that the hem of his pants trailed along the ground and kept tripping him. Undaunted, he rolled up his trouser legs and helped us win the game.

My television debut was with Davey—a starring role in an episode of *The Monkees*, where I played Daphne, a member of an all-girl band. I remember the director being exasperated with me in one particular scene because I wasn't doing it right.

"Deana, Deana, you're not getting it," he told me. "Imagine you've just made love to Davey, and let your face express the way that feels."

Looking at him blankly, I asked, "Well, how *does* that feel?" I was a virgin, and from the look on the faces of the director and the entire crew, everyone had assumed I was sleeping with Davey when I wasn't. I blushed scarlet and almost ran from the set.

I was in a band called the Chromium Plated Streamline Baby, and we played the famous Whisky à Go Go. Davey and his friends came along to see us, as did Cher, who was really beginning to make a name for herself by then with her singing partner, Sonny Bono. Photographers were lined up outside, and we posed for photos. I didn't see Davey much again after that, and a few months later he secretly married his girlfriend Linda Haines. I will always remember our brief time together fondly.

My next boyfriend was Eddie Garner. He was an actor and surfer in those beach-blanket movies of the time, and drop-dead gorgeous. He was twenty years old, tall, and blond. He made a bit of money doing those movies and bought a house on Benedict Canyon. Jeanne, who had a tremendous sense of style, helped him decorate it, which I thought was kind of her. Poor Eddie fell hard for Jeanne, and even turned up drunk at the house one night to tell Dad that he loved her and wanted to run off with her. Fortunately for everyone, he couldn't get past the security guards.

LEE HAZLEWOOD, the songwriter and record producer I'd worked with previously, was having great success. One of his hits was "These Boots Are Made for Walking," which Nancy Sinatra took to the top of the charts.

"Hey, Deana, 'Boots' would have been great for you," he told me later. I never knew if that was a line he fed everyone, or if he really meant it. His song perfectly captured the mood of women of my generation, feisty and sassy. But, sadly, it wasn't to be. The rest, as they say, is history, and Nancy did a great job.

I once asked Dad if I should take singing lessons. He laughed and shook his head.

"No, baby," he said. "You don't need voice lessons, unless you want to sound like everyone else in the choir. What you have is natural. Individual. If you get to be good enough, you can sing on my show. But no child of mine is going to appear on my show unless they can do it for real." I'm proud to say I sang on the show many times.

Uncle Frank gave me some advice as well. "You have to learn to breathe from your diaphragm," he said. "That's what makes the difference."

"Does Dad do that?" I asked innocently.

Frank nearly spilled his Jack Daniel's. "He doesn't need to, he's a natural," he replied, laughing. "He doesn't even know that's what you're supposed to do. He just does it."

For my eighteenth-birthday party, which I shared with my parents' friend, the actress Jill St. John, we hired the quintessential sixties California pop group, Buffalo Springfield. I loved that band and had a crush on the lead singer, Stephen Stills. Their latest single, "For What It's Worth," had become a soundtrack to an angry generation, protesting against Vietnam and the establishment. Terribly excited, I went to see Buffalo Springfield's manager with the six-hundred-dollar check. Neil Young was sitting in the office, strumming his guitar.

"Hi," I said shyly. "What are you doing?"

"Writing a song," he said, smiling up at me through his hair.

"Oh yeah?" I said brashly. "Well, I'm a singer and I've got a recording contract."

"Really? Then I'll write you a song," he said. . . . I'm still waiting.

The party was fantastic, and the band played brilliantly. Suddenly, shortly after midnight, the police arrived to tell us that someone had called to make an official complaint about the noise. "You'll have to break it up now," they told me, much to everyone's dismay.

The next day I discovered that it was Dad who'd called the police, phoning from his bedroom and complaining, "Those damn Martins are making way too much noise. Can you go over and put a stop to it? I can't get any sleep."

Trouble was, Dad had such a distinctive voice that the police said, "Yes, sir, Mr. Martin, we'll be right over."

◆◆◆

A MONTH after I turned eighteen, I left 601 Mountain Drive for England, and a year at the Dartington College of Arts, which Gail had so loved. The college had accepted me as their only American student just two years after they had done the same for her. It was a great honor, but it would also be the first time in nine years that I would live anywhere other than with my family—nine years since I'd arrived at Mountain Drive, mute and breaking out in hives.

Gail was full of good advice. "You must go to the White Hart Inn and drink the local beer. It's warm, dark, and bitter, but it's terribly cool to drink down a whole pint of it."

"But I don't like beer!" I complained.

"Well, you'll have to acquire a taste for either beer or Scotch," she insisted. I decided Scotch was the lesser of two evils. Little did I know. "And you must smoke European cigarettes," she added.

I'd been smoking ever since Alma caught me puffing on my first cigarette behind the house when I was fourteen. She snitched on me, and at dinner that night, Jeanne suddenly piped up, "Well, everyone, Deana's started smoking, so what do we think about that?" I was so ashamed and embarrassed that I jumped up from the dinner table and left the room.

"Don't slam the door," Dad called after me, and I ran all the way up the stairs, along the corridor, and into my bedroom, slamming the door as hard as I could behind me. Trouble was, the house was so big I doubt if anyone heard my brave act of defiance. Dad grounded me for a week.

Now that I was leaving home for the first time, and traveling to what seemed like the other side of the world, where I could smoke, drink, and do what I liked, I was very torn. Not only was I unsure how I would fare, so far away from my family, but days after I'd heard that I'd been accepted, I was offered a part in a movie.

My agent, Jack Gilardi, had a number of actors on his client list such as Telly Savalas, from *Kojak*. Jack secured a few appearances for me. One was on *The Dating Game*, where I was teamed up for a week in Portofino, Italy, with an unknown comedy writer for the Smothers Brothers named Steve Martin. Steve and I got along fine after I selected him as my "dream date," but there was no spark between us, and we just had fun. The film of our first meeting on that show is often seen on TV, in a "before they were famous" segment, featuring Steve, of course.

My bags were packed for Dartington when Jack rang and asked me read for the leading role in a new movie, starring another relatively unknown actor. "It's a good part," he told me. "This actor's pretty short, and they're looking for someone petite enough to make him look taller."

"I don't know, Jack," I said. "I don't really like the sound of it, and I'm all set for England. I leave in a few days."

"All right," he told me, sighing. "I'll find someone else. Have a good trip."

The film was the Oscar-winning masterpiece *The Graduate*, and the replacement Jack found was Katharine Ross, who played alongside the unknown actor Dustin Hoffman and the brilliant Anne Bancroft.

You can't win them all.

◆◆◆

MY CHAPERONE for the first part of my journey to England was Conrad Hilton Jr., known as Nicky, the playboy son of Conrad senior, and the owner of the Hilton Hotels. Nicky and Dad played golf together almost every day. Dad thought Nicky could be trusted. Claudia escorted me to New York, where we met Nicky at the Waldorf Astoria. We dined with both father and son. Conrad was late for dinner, and when he eventually arrived, his son asked him, "Dad, where have you been?"

"Trying to find a parking place," he said.

"Why didn't you just let the valet park it for you?"

"Too damned expensive," came the reply.

Nicky was a delight to be with. When he was younger, he'd been married to Elizabeth Taylor and was considered quite a catch. I was far too young to appreciate just how fortunate I was. In London we stayed at the Dorchester, and Nicky took me to the Mirabelle and to the Playboy Club to meet Victor Lownes, the owner. A new world was opening for me and life was exciting. I traveled to Totnes in Devon by train to start my first term at Dartington. Nicky waved good-bye, and I thanked him for his kindness. He was such a gentleman. I never saw him again. Two years later, at only forty-two, he died in his sleep of a weak heart.

The year that I was in England was one of the most pivotal of my eighteen years. Until that point I'd just been dealing with my unusual upbringing and the emotional baggage that went with it. In England, away from the rest of the family, I became my own person. I had to think for myself, fend for myself, and learn how to get along with people outside my rarefied world. The drama workshops encouraged me to express myself emotionally, and the unfamiliar surroundings forced me to experience a whole new existence. I made new friends, and even had a boyfriend for a while. I learned to enjoy the pleasures of college life and English pubs. Although I still missed my family terribly, I was growing into a young woman away from their influence. Dad was busy filming his highly successful Matt Helm movies for Columbia Pictures, so I relied on my sisters and Jeanne for information in letters.

"Your father's been playing golf, learning his lines for *The Ambushers*, his latest Matt Helm movie," Jeanne wrote. I knew what that meant—he'd tear all the pages out of the script that didn't have dialogue and concentrate only on the parts he was in. "He's enjoying the filming enormously—well, why wouldn't he? He's surrounded by pretty girls, fast cars, and boats all day long. He gets to sing and play. I'm sure life at Mountain Drive is pretty tame by comparison, especially since you're not here."

Dad was paid a great deal of money to do the Matt Helm movies. Critics panned the films, one describing Dad's performance as "embalmed," and others claiming that he didn't take his role seriously enough. Moviegoers disagreed, and the films were box-office hits. Today they are considered cult classics. The original plots, taken from the Donald Hamilton novels, were unrecognizable. But Dad couldn't have cared less. He'd done his great films like *Rio Bravo*, *Toys in the Attic*, *Some Came Running*, and *The Young Lions*. He'd achieved all the accolades he ever needed as an actor, a singer, a recording artist, and an entertainer. Now he was in his fifties, earning more money than he could spend, playing golf every day, and home every night for dinner cracking jokes.

"I played golf today and hit two great balls—I stepped on a rake" was one favorite.

Another favorite end-of-dinner quip of his was "Well, that's it, I've got to go and iron my hands," which meant nothing unless you'd noticed how wrinkled they were. Half the time it didn't matter if anybody else got his jokes, just that he did.

Dad was also developing investments outside the entertainment industry. He purchased a significant amount of land around Los Angeles. He had plans to develop a $25,000 membership country club where he could play golf all day with his buddies.

DARTINGTON WAS big, old, and drafty, just like I imagined an English castle to be. To keep us from dying of the cold, it seemed that they fed us all day long. We'd get up and have toast and bacon and fabulous butter. Classes would be in a huge old room with a big fireplace, where we would be served morning tea. After a class of modern dance, we'd go into the refectory for afternoon tea, which would be served with Devon clotted cream and scones, cakes and jam. I must have drunk gallons of tea and gained fifteen pounds.

I played the lead in *Romeo and Juliet* and mad Ophelia in *Hamlet.* There was a theater on campus, and we put on shows for the locals. At night we'd go into the town, to High Street and Low Street, and enjoy the pubs and cafés.

In England I was no longer just Dean Martin's daughter, but Deana, an aspiring actress; Deana, the young lady who traveled to London first-class on a train with her friends to go nightclubbing or to a toga party. There I met two young musicians, Eric Clapton and Ginger Baker. Eric picked up his guitar and played us a song. People all around me were taking drugs and dancing and having a good time. To be part of sixties London, even for such a brief time, was quite extraordinary. In England I was Deana, who ate fish and chips out of newspaper; Deana, who drank scotch at the White Hart Inn. Sitting there with my pals, I couldn't help but think of Mother and how much she would have enjoyed the old-fashioned bars with their beamed ceilings and cozy fires. Maybe I could send her a postcard with a picture of one of them on the front, I thought. Then I realized I didn't even have her address.

After a while, though, the novelty of England wore off. I'd played all the major roles I wanted to play within the college curriculum, including my favorite—Juliet. Having eaten so many cream teas and fish and chips, I was gaining too much weight and feeling uncomfortable in my own clothes. Winter came, and with it biting winds and relentless rain. Unaccustomed to the climate, I was cold all the time, shivering in my bed at night. I missed L.A. and the sun and my family. I treasured the experiences I'd had, but I was ready to go home. I hoped not to retain the English accent I'd picked up, remembering how mercilessly Dad teased Gail when she came home from Dartington.

"A ba—a—a—rth?" he'd repeat, when she said she was taking one. "Don't you mean 'bath'?"

And when I returned and, despite my best endeavors, found I'd acquired a new plummy way of speaking, Dad ribbed me relentlessly anyway. "So you've been away to college in England and now you know how to speak good?" he'd say. Seeing the expression on my face, he'd glance behind him and say, with a wink, "What? Am I dangling my participle?"

He always made a joke of his lack of education, and often quoted Uncle Frank as calling him the most ill-informed person he knew. Dad didn't read and he didn't pretend to. He claimed he'd read *Black Beauty* in school, and it made him cry, so he decided never to read another book again. If he met anyone at a party and they told him, "I wrote a book," he'd reply, "Congratulations, I read one."

At the end of a dinner out, he'd stand up and say something like "Well, gotta go and finish my novel. I've only got thirty pages left to write," and unless you really knew him, you didn't know how funny that was. And that was just fine with Dad.

If ever we'd ask for his help with our homework, he'd laugh and say, "Are you kidding? If you can't do it, then I'll try and write you a note to excuse you from it." Craig came home one day with a low mark in woodwork, and he was afraid to show Dad his report card. Dad was fine about it. All he said was, "So . . . you won't be a carpenter."

Shubert
Theatre

under the direction of
Messrs. Shubert

PLAYBILL

the national magazine for theatregoers

THE STAR-SPANGLED GIRL

Thirteen

RETURNING TO L.A. IN 1967, I FELT LIKE A NEW PERSON.
Shy little Deana had grown up. I was determined to be a good
actress and launched myself back into Hollywood society. I frequented clubs like the Daisy on Rodeo Drive, and Pips on
Robertson. I dated Denny Doherty from the Mamas and Papas, and
became lifelong friends with Michelle Phillips. They had a huge success with the song "California Dreamin'." I was also part of a fun
group that included the actors David Hemmings, Peggy Lipton, Sal
Mineo, and a list of others. I went to Hollywood premieres, the

Academy Awards, and all the right functions. Mainly I was having fun and enjoying being back home.

Dad was working hard on his films and his television show and his six-week runs in Las Vegas. Becoming a television star had only enhanced his popularity. He had negotiated even better terms for the show, which he'd discussed with us one night over dinner. "You know, Jeanne, I'm tired of doing this TV show," he said. "It feels like I'm just doing the same thing over and over."

Mom looked up from her meal and said, "But, Dean, it's so popular. Millions of people watch you every week. Everyone wants to be your guest. People have even started asking me to ask you."

"I know," he complained, shaking his head, "but when my contract comes up for renewal, I'm gonna ask for something really ridiculous like thirty million dollars for one day a week. That'll put a stop to it."

He was either being very smart or he didn't know his own worth. Either way, NBC agreed and raised his salary from $40,000 an episode to $285,000—a total of $15 million a year—making him the highest paid television performer in history. So the show went on, and Dad became a national icon.

He once said, "Wanna know why the show's a hit? The reason is that it's the real me up there on the screen. Nothing phony. You take everybody else on TV, they're putting on an act, playin' something they aren't. But when people tune me in, they know they're getting Dean Martin."

We'd still go over most Sundays and watch the show being taped, and sometimes we'd take part. There was always a buffet of Italian rolls, cheese, and prosciutto in Dad's dressing room, which we enjoyed. Dad had two dressing rooms, one we could lounge in and watch the rehearsals on a monitor, and a private one for him. He could rehearse his cue cards, have his makeup applied, and enjoy some time to himself. Mack was always there, as was Jay, his dresser. He called them "Daffy" and "Deefy."

When the show was ready to roll, we'd file out and sit in the front row of the audience among Dad's adoring fans, laughing at his jokes and his ad libs, which were often funnier than the script. Dad had one of those faces that encouraged you to laugh along with him. He would sit there laughing so hard he'd be crying and clutching his sides. Valuable minutes of air time were filled with nothing but hysterical laughter, and those sections are some of the best in the show.

He had a segment where a doorbell would ring and he'd open the door, and a celebrity guest or some other surprise would appear. Dad never knew who would be there until he opened the door. He liked it that way, so that he'd be as surprised as everyone else. Just in case he didn't remember the name of the person standing behind the door, a cue card would be held up, giving their name. Once the name was written across the stomach of one of the Golddiggers.

"The Dean Martin Christmas Show," with the Sinatra family as special guests, was broadcast in December 1967 and attracted a record number of viewers. All the children of both families appeared, singing carols around a tree, joking and dancing with Dad and Uncle Frank. Nancy, Tina, and, Frank Jr. joined in. There were sleigh bells and Christmas trees and we wore fur coats and boots, which was funny because we were in California and it was eighty-five degrees outside.

I sang a couple of songs with Uncle Frank, Dad, and Tina, including a fun version of "Do-Re-Mi" from *The Sound of Music.* Dad really enjoyed having his family around him, and was making us laugh so hard we could barely get through the number. At one point, begging him to stop so I could catch my breath and sing my line, I clapped my hand over his mouth to keep him from telling yet another joke. Gail and Nancy sang solo and then a duet; Dino sang with Frank junior. Ricci, Gina, Craig, Claudia, and Jeanne joined in for the carols.

That summer, while Dad was entertaining in Las Vegas and on a family vacation in Palm Springs, NBC released *The Dean Martin Summer Show,* hosted by our friends Dick Martin and Dan Rowan. The comedy pair was so successful that NBC gave them their own show, *Rowan and Martin's Laugh-In.* The following summer the Golddiggers had their own show and Gail hosted *The Dean Martin Summer Replacement Show.* She and I performed a Roaring

Twenties dance routine with the incredibly tall and phenomenally talented Tommy Tune. A dancer and choreographer with an incredible vision of how a number should be done, he was patient with us and easy to work with.

With more time on his hands, Dad played golf six days a week, hanging out with his friends at the country club. His publicist Warren Cowan once told me that in all the years he worked for Dad, he only ever requested publicity twice.

"Some of my clients hassle me constantly, wanting everything they do to appear in the newspapers. Then there is the bad publicity, and they want that taken out," he explained. "But your father was unbelievable. I was on his payroll for over thirty years, and he never asked for any publicity, nothing. The first time he ever phoned and asked me to put something in the paper was in 1961 when Billy Wilder said all actors are idiots, and it is the director who makes them who they are. Your dad took out a full page in *Variety* magazine and gave his response, which was sweet, to the point, and incredibly cool. The only other time your father had me do anything was when he had an incredible day on the golf course. He was so proud, he stepped out of his jet and held up a newspaper that read, 'Dean Martin got a hole-in-one at the Sands Hotel.' He didn't even ask for publicity when The Sands put just 'Dino' on the marquee, the first time a single name had ever been used like that in the history of Las Vegas. That man was priceless."

◆◆◆

I HADN'T seen Mother in years, and learned from Aunt Anne that she had finally moved to San Francisco, after a year spent with friends in Kentucky. There was little point in her staying in L.A., she reasoned, and she wanted to make a fresh start in a place where nobody knew her. The town only held sad memories, after all, and she no longer felt welcome at 601 Mountain Drive. Furthermore, none of us really knew who she was anymore. Craig saw her occasionally; Gail and Claudia refused to see her if it meant meeting in bars.

As for me, it was a sad fact that Mother was no longer an entity in my life. Jeanne had ably stepped into her shoes and become the only mother I'd known for the last ten years. I now called her Mom. Strange as it may seem, I barely allowed myself to think about the woman who had raised me for the first years of my life. It felt to me now almost as if I never really knew her; she seemed increasingly dreamlike in my mind, a glamorous, ethereal presence who used to make us laugh and took us grunion-running at midnight. To have thought any more deeply about her absence would have been too painful. If I were an angry person, I could have been angry that my mother let her life go to hell. That she found solace in a bottle and that she allowed them to take us away from her. That my father left her. That Jeanne took him away. That I didn't have that perfect storybook life. Not at all. My life is like so many others. Filled with conflicts and serious psychological learning curves. But my reality is different. Whatever the myriad of influences that formulated my life, I found that anger was not my way of dealing with things. Nor was wallowing in the real or imagined turmoil I'd experienced. My sisters would not have permitted it, anyway. Not for a minute. The message was loud and clear . . . I had to get on with my life. Don't dwell. Don't sit still. It was my life and only I could live it. Make my way in the world and do my best.

Claudia was acting, and appeared in a California Beach-Blanket movie with Nancy Sinatra called *The Ghost in the Invisible Bikini*, starring, would you believe, Boris Karloff and Basil Rathbone. Next she was in a movie called *Ski Fever*, which was filmed in Czechoslovakia.

Gail was having continuing success as a singer. She even played the Persian Room at the Plaza in New York. Judy Garland joined Jeanne, Claudia, and me in supporting her on opening night. Dad sent flowers. Judy walked in, wearing an enormous cream hat, and everyone was pleased to see her looking so well after the various scares about her health. Gail did a two-week run at the Plaza, and each afternoon she'd order tea in her room and swipe some small piece of silver from the tray. By the end of the run, she had the complete set. The hotel knew exactly what was going on and added the charge to her bill. When she went to leave, her suitcase was so heavy she could barely lift it, so she had to leave the bigger pieces behind.

Gail was engaged to Paul Polena, an Italian attorney who had a son who was her age, and was excitedly planning their society wedding at Mountain Drive. Dino was acting and taking flying lessons and playing tennis for all he was worth. Ricci was an exuberant teenager, gorgeous to look at and very much his own person. Gina was the perfect baby sister, with her big blue eyes, and I loved having her around. Craig was all grown up, married, a father, and working for Dad.

Movie-wise, Dad was making films like *Rough Night in Jericho* with George Peppard and Jean Simmons, *How to Save a Marriage (And Ruin Your Life)* with Stella Stevens, and *5 Card Stud* with Robert Mitchum and Inger Stevens. In the previous two years he'd sold three million albums and three and a half million singles. He currently had two gold albums out, each earning him over a million dollars in sales, and his television show was at its peak, with fifty million viewers. *Newsweek* dubbed him "King Leer." According to the papers, he earned more money in 1967 from his records, movies, and television shows than anyone in the history of show business. Even Frank Sinatra.

But it wasn't all happiness for Dad. On Christmas Day 1967, at 3:15 a.m., our dear Grandmother Angela passed away at seventy-one. She'd been ill for some time, living in the Sierra Towers off Sunset Boulevard. Eventually she was moved to a hospital, where the bed dwarfed her tiny frame. My father, who hated hospitals and elevators with equal passion, could not bring himself to visit her.

"I'll regret to the day I die that I didn't go," he told me sadly, a long time later. "I should have gone and said good-bye." In her name, he built the Angela Crocetti Cobalt Treatment Center in Steubenville's hospital, only the third cobalt treatment center in the country.

A few months later Pop died. His heart just gave out. We were in Las Vegas when the news came that Pop had finally given up the will to live. Stunned at this further blow, we were sitting in silence around a table in Dad's suite, with a low-hanging lamp, when the double doors were thrown open. Uncle Frank walked in looking like something out of a movie, wearing his sunglasses, a green jacket draped over his shoulders, and an entourage of people behind him. He came to each of us in turn, kissing us on both cheeks and giving us—me, Gail, Claudia, and Dino a hug—and then he hugged my father.

"Anything you need, pallie," he said. "Anything. Just ask." With tears in his eyes, he added, "I miss him too," before turning and leaving the way he'd come in. We all sat there, dazed, staring as he left.

A short time afterwards, Dad did something for Frank that only true friends do. He kept his silence. He was out with Frank, celebrating Dad's birthday at the Polo Lounge, when things got out of hand. The temperature rose and the noise levels soared. Sitting at a nearby table were a middle-aged businessman and his friend having dinner, who made the mistake of complaining. Insults were exchanged, and Frank went over to their table. The businessman ended up unconscious on the floor. The injured man was in critical condition for several days and required cranial surgery. Dad, when questioned later by the police, maintained he hadn't seen a thing.

I remember Dad coming home that night. He walked into the living room, where I was watching television, and sat on the edge of the couch with me for a few moments.

"You're home early," I commented.

"Frank blew a fuse tonight," he said, glumly. "He can't let it go."

"What happened?"

"Some drunk called us wops and Frank got mad," Dad replied. "I told him, 'Frank, just let it go, who cares? I call you wop and dago all the time,' but he got mad anyway."

"Was anyone hurt?" I asked.

"I dunno," Dad said, getting to his feet. "I don't know anything." Kissing me good night, he walked wearily up to bed. The next morning he went to Lake Tahoe until the whole scandal blew over. The injured man's family threatened legal action, but then dropped all charges.

AT HOME, life went on as usual. Dad and Jeanne continued to dance the extraordinary waltz that was their marriage. She ran the house, the kids, and the staff, between playing tennis and taking good care of herself. She made sure we were ferried to and from school, parties, sporting events, and sleepovers. She did a lot of charity work, raising money for SHARE, a worldwide charity for children that she co-founded in 1953 with Janet Leigh and Gloria Cahn, composer Sammy Cahn's wife.

Dad stuck strictly to his routine, turning up on time for drinks and dinner, stepping out with Jeanne for social events and celebrations, all the while working, working, working, and playing golf. There were seldom any variations. Dad and Jeanne rarely went on vacation together, or even away for the weekend. She seldom had more time with him than was allocated on his daily schedule, which was run like clockwork by dear old Mack Gray. If she didn't like it, she never showed it. I guess she just broke another mirror in the privacy of her bathroom.

Jeanne was much sought after by the women's magazines for her personal style and her take on life with Dad. I can remember her being interviewed once, sitting down at the bar with a reporter, talking about her daily routine. Sometimes she was too honest for her own good.

In one unusually blunt interview Jeanne gave that year to the *Ladies' Home Journal*, she described Dad as "cold, calculating, and an impersonal man. He's cool and completely withdrawn." She described their several separations as a question of maintaining her dignity in the face of his "carelessness." When asked if she would accept his affairs to try to keep her marriage, she commented, "I do. I think that speaks for itself.

"I receive a fantastic amount of love from Dean, which balances out our marriage," she said, but then added, "there's an Old Country expression, 'I don't want to know.' And actually, I believe in it. If I do know, it stings like hell. The thing I object to most is that he doesn't give more of himself to me. So when these other things come up, it hurts more because I don't get equal time."

She concluded, "The truth is, I bore the hell out of Dean. I always bored him. Most women do. He's not a ladies' man. He's a man's man and I like that about him. More than anything else, he prefers to be alone . . . Being with the children for more than ten minutes bores him too . . . The point is, Dean was not and is not nor will he ever be the ideal husband . . . he gives the minimum amount."

I thought her interview, though truthful, was rather harsh. I wondered if she gave it to stir him up a little. Like most women, Jeanne was not above a little clever manipulation. Dad didn't seem to take offense. I'm not even sure he noticed. With him, no attempt to attract his attention ever seemed to make a difference. Hoping to spend a little more time with him than the bare minimum, Jeanne flew in a private jet to Lake Powell, Utah, to the set of the film *Bandolero!*, which Dad was making with Jimmy Stewart and Raquel Welch. She took me along. One of Dad's co-stars was a twenty-eight-year-old actor by the name of Andrew Prine, who'd also been in *Texas Across the River*. I had a big crush on Andy, but he was far too old for me.

Raquel Welch was beautiful, wearing knee-high socks over her stockings as she accompanied us on the trip. We played our favorite card game, hearts, and she was a lot of fun to be with. She joked about how the directors were making a big deal of her learning a Spanish accent for the movie, when in reality she was half Spanish, and her father's surname was Tejada.

Jimmy Stewart was as adorable as ever, such a sweet man, and he and Dad got along tremendously. There was one scene where Dad's character, Dee, an outlaw, was shot and dying, and Raquel had to press him to her heaving bosom for several minutes while Jimmy delivered his lines.

"Listen, pallie," Dad said, taking Jimmy aside before the shoot, "if you flub your lines a few times with that famous stammer of yours, then I get to stay in the clinch with Raquel longer and they'll just keep reshooting the scene. I'll do the same for you one day. Whaddaya say?"

Jimmy looked at Dad and smiled. "Sure," he replied.

When it came to the shoot, Jimmy recited his three pages of dialogue word-perfect, without a stutter, and gave such a strong delivery that the director was more than happy.

"Cut!" he yelled. "That's a wrap."

Jimmy winked at Dad before walking away.

MY AGENT arranged an audition for me, and I landed my first national theatrical role. I played a blond Olympic swimmer named Sophie Rauschmeyer in the National Touring Company's production of Neil Simon's *The Star-Spangled Girl*, directed by Neil's brother, Danny. The show was a hit on Broadway with Anthony Perkins and Connie Stevens, and this was the first touring production. I had the starring role, and my co-star was a handsome young actor by the name of George Hamilton. I had to have a Southern accent, and when I read for the part, they gave it to me immediately. I was thrilled.

We started off rehearsing in a basement beneath the Greek Theater, but George suggested we move to his mother's beautiful mansion on Carolwood in Beverly Hills. He took all the furniture out of the ballroom, and we used that for our rehearsals. It was April 1968, and I'll remember forever the moment when George's mother burst into the ballroom mid-rehearsal in tears and told us, "Martin Luther King's been shot." We were so shaken. It seemed surreal. We stopped work immediately and went quietly home, too overwhelmed to continue.

The show received outstanding reviews and toured all over the country. Walking up to the theater that first night, I looked up at the marquee and saw my name in letters two feet high, and spotlit. It took me straight back to the Westwood Theatre when I was five years old and the first time I saw Dad's name in lights. That was the first time I understood the connection between us. Here I was, his namesake, taking my first steps to make my own way in the world.

I sent home some clippings, which Jeanne kept, but she and Dad were both too busy to come and lend their support in person. I understood how full their schedules were, but it would have been nice if they had taken the time. Dad told me how much he appreciated having Grandma and Pop around in the early days when he was onstage singing and performing with Jerry Lewis. I had hoped he would remember how wonderful that felt and jump at the chance to do the same for me. But that did not happen. I was very proud of my performance, and I think they would have enjoyed it. To have had Dad sitting in the audience watching my performance, would have meant the world to me.

I wasn't the only one who wished he was around more. Gail would have loved to have him watch her sing in her early engagements too. And Claudia would have been over the moon if he'd taken time to visit her on the set of one of her movies. I guess Dad felt that with so many children, if he did it for one, he would have spent his whole life doing it for the others. The trade-off we had to be content with was that our dad was Dean Martin.

Gail met me in St. Louis, where I was playing at the Schubert Theater and she was singing in a club nearby. We had a great evening. She shared my hotel room, and when I was changing, she noticed the all-over tan I needed for my role.

"You look really tanned," she commented. "Have you been on a sun bed?"

"No," I replied, "it's a cream that comes in a tube. I slather myself with it every other day."

Squeezing some into the palms of her hands, Gail smeared it all over her legs. It was late at night and she was tired, so she did it quickly and without much thought. In the morning, when she pulled back the bedclothes and stepped out of bed, we both gasped. Her lower legs were bright orange, while her thighs, which she hadn't covered, were white. Worse still, the palms of her hands were orange. I laughed so hard I almost fell out of bed.

DECIDING I needed my own space when I returned from the tour, I made the huge decision to leave Mountain Drive. It felt like a giant leap, emotionally, and one I wasn't entirely sure I was ready for. But I left the house full of younger children all going through the pains of teenage life, and found myself an apartment at the Barrington Plaza in Westwood, which Dad helped me pay for. Packing up my belongings and a few extra things Jeanne had bought for me, I kissed her good-bye and climbed into my tiny overloaded car. "Tell Dad I'll call," I told her, wishing he were there to wave me off, too. But the studio or the golf course beckoned, and I knew he wouldn't be home for hours.

I started dating Terry Melcher, one of Claudia's old flames. Through him, I came into contact with someone who would haunt my dreams for the rest of my life—Charles Manson. Terry was by then an independent producer for Apple Records, and Manson fancied himself a singer and guitarist. To woo Terry into considering him for a recording contract, he had a mutual friend, Dennis Wilson of the Beach Boys, introduce them. We met up at Terry's house at 10050 Cielo Drive in Benedict Canyon, above Beverly Hills. Manson's friend Charles "Tex" Watson accompanied him on the first occasion, and later he showed up with a couple of girls. Tex talked about music and what he wanted to do with his life. Manson, on the other hand, who liked to be called Charlie, was very small and looked like every other hippie on Sunset with his guitar.

Sitting on the floor one day and listening to him sing and play, my eyes were drawn to a ring he was wearing on his little finger.

"Here," he told me, sliding it off and handing it to me. "I want you to have this." Before I could object, he pressed it into my hand, adding, "You're Dean Martin's daughter, aren't you?"

I looked down at the flat silver band with unusual Indian symbols engraved on it, and nodded. "Thank you," I said, and slipped the ring on.

◆◆◆

MY NEXT role was in *Young Billy Young*, starring Robert Mitchum and Dad's dear friend Angie Dickinson. It was a western, filmed in Tucson, Arizona, and it also starred David Carradine and Robert Walker Jr. The credits said, "Introducing Deana Martin." I played Evie Cushman, the doctor's daughter, and kept my hair dyed blond so as not to clash with red-haired Angie. We had a great time on that set. Robert Mitchum, whom everyone called "Momma Mitch," was gorgeous and great fun, as was Angie Dickinson.

I fell in love with acting. I also fell for Momma Mitch. He was fifty-two years old, exactly the same age as my father, and just as cool. He was the laid-back star of *The Big Sleep* and *Farewell, My Lovely*. Tucked into every few pages of his script were his "bookmarks," joints, because he constantly smoked pot.

When I arrived home after filming, I really missed him, Angie, and the rest of the crew who were staying on in Tucson. So one night, feeling sorry for myself, I phoned him.

"Hey Momma Mitch," I said, "it's Deana. I'm back in L.A., but I miss you."

"Then come back, baby," he said simply. "You can stay at my place if you like."

I caught the next plane out. Robert was a wonderful guy, and we had a remarkable and fun week together. He was intelligent and articulate. He liked to read, go out to dinner, and play cards until late in the evening. Everyone felt comfortable around him and came to him with their problems. Young and impressionable, I was momentarily smitten at being in the company of such a cool screen legend. I knew it couldn't last, but I enjoyed every minute and am grateful to this day for the brief time I had with him. Goodness knows what Dad would have thought if he'd known about the two of us. He and

Mitch had just worked together on *5 Card Stud* and were good friends.

Jeanne, however, did find out. She tracked me down and called me at his house.

"Deana," she said, "I think you'd better come home, don't you? Now. Before your father finds out."

I felt like I was nine years old again.

Fourteen

SHORTLY AFTER RETURNING TO BEVERLY HILLS, I WAS A bridesmaid at my sister Gail's wedding. It was quite the event, since it was the first time a daughter of Dad's had been properly married (as opposed to Claudia's elopement). The tennis court was tented in white muslin, and Dad proudly gave her away and spoke sweetly of his beautiful daughter. His speech was, as expected, a laugh a minute, with Dad advocating "the power of positive drinking" for the happy couple.

Aunt Anne was invited and came to the house for only the second time. She felt uncomfortable and out of place at first, quelling memories of the last time she'd been there, to hand us over to Dad and Jeanne for good, but she soon relaxed and enjoyed celebrity-watching.

Gail wasn't sure about inviting Mother, but Dad made the decision for her. "There are two people who mustn't be there," he told her. "Betty Martin and Nancy Senior" (Frank's ex-wife). He added, by way of explanation, "It would upset your Uncle Frank." Gail was upset that Nancy couldn't come, but relieved about Mother. She didn't expect Mother to accept, but was afraid she might show up. Gail said, everyone should have an eccentric aunt like Mother, but not as a parent.

It was at Gail's reception, attended by six hundred guests, that I met my future husband, a writer and model named Terry Guerin. He was earning up to two hundred dollars a day modeling, and writing freelance articles and a book at night. He called on me one day soon after the wedding and never left. Within a few days, however, I realized how he managed to stay up all night when I caught him shooting up drugs on the floor of my bathroom.

I confronted him immediately and told him to get out, but he was so contrite, I believed him. "I never wanted you to see this," he told me, angrily discarding his needle. "I have writer's block. This is the only way I can keep going. I promise, as soon as I'm back on track, this will stop."

Foolishly, I believed him. Foolishly, I thought I could save him. I flew to South Africa to make another film, *Strangers at Sunrise*, with George Montgomery, the husband of Dinah Shore. Terry came with me, and when we came back, we got married. It was June 1969, and I was twenty-one years old. All Dad ever said about Terry was "I hope he makes you happy, baby."

"Thanks, Dad," I replied.

Inexplicably, in the days leading up to my wedding, several magazines ran headlines like WHY DEAN DOESN'T WANT DEANA TO MARRY, or DEAN TRIES TO STOP DAUGHTER'S WEDDING. My first reaction was to panic. Did Dad know more about Terry and his drug problems than he was letting on? I needn't have worried. On closer examination, the headlines were just teasers, and the articles themselves went on to say Dad didn't want me to marry because he didn't want his little baby to grow up, or something equally corny. After reading every word, I sighed with relief.

On the big day there was a last-minute problem with the bridesmaids' dresses, which had to be altered. Dad, who hated to be kept waiting above almost anything, paced up and down the hallway, calling up the stairs, "Deana, baby, come on, put some jeans on, let's just get there today, okay?"

When the designer finally arrived and we were all zipped in and ready to go, Dad took one look at her long black hair, which hung down her back, and quipped, "No wonder she took so long, she was drying her hair." His jokes did nothing to soothe my nerves that day. I weighed just ninety-eight pounds and hadn't eaten all morning. Dad walked me down the aisle of the Good Shepherd Church in Beverly Hills, where I'd sung for President Kennedy, but when he let me go, I just toppled over, fainting at the altar. My head was spinning and my heart was pounding and I thought I might be sick. A combination of nerves and hunger overwhelmed me.

All the photographers were there from the national press, and they caught the moment in full Technicolor as Jeanne and Terry helped me outside for some air. Trembling all over, I was embarrassed at having made such a scene and just wanted to get back inside and finish the ceremony. While I was trying to compose myself, Dad stood up and started telling jokes to break the ice. Looking at the altar, he told the congregation, which included Merle Oberon and Rosalind Russell and just about every Sinatra, "Boy, that priest sure keeps a clean bar."

Dino was playing tennis in Wimbledon that year and couldn't make it to the wedding. He phoned me from London the next day to tell me, "Hey, Deana, you're on the front page of all the newspapers here. 'Bride Deana Faints at Altar.' You're upstaging me!"

Soon after my wedding, Dad signed a deal with the newly opened Riviera nightclub and casino in Las Vegas. Uncle Frank had left The Sands two years earlier after a dispute with the management and had signed up with Caesar's Palace. Dad had stayed on, until the Riviera made him an offer he couldn't refuse: $100,000 a week and ten percent. Out of the spoils, he bought Terry and me a house in Mandeville Canyon, on the way to Malibu.

"I own it, but you can live in it," he told me. "If you two ever split up, the house reverts back to me. Okay?"

IN AUGUST 1969, Charles Manson, who'd given me a silver ring I still had, enacted a plan so evil that it shocked the world. Still angry at Terry Melcher for refusing to sign him as a musical artist, he sent several of his followers to the Cielo Drive house that Terry had leased. They brutally slaughtered the five people they found there, including the heavily pregnant Sharon Tate, the wife of film director Roman Polanski. Sharon was a stunning young actress who'd just starred alongside Dad in his third Matt Helm film, *The Wrecking Crew.*

Unknown to Manson, Terry had left the house a few months earlier, and the owner had leased it to Polanski. But for that, Terry might well have been there that night, enjoying the panoramic views and the solitude as the Manson gang crept up on him.

No one knew who was to blame, and none of us suspected Manson or anyone that we knew. Most assumed it was some drug-crazed gang who'd gone berserk when their robbery went wrong. We were chilled by the events, especially when Dad received a horrible letter threatening to kill certain members of our family, which he handed to the FBI. But it wasn't for another year that we would realize how close we'd come to being involved.

I was working for much of that year, and four months after the murders I discovered I was pregnant. The following summer I was booked for a season at Caesar's Palace in Las Vegas in a show called

"The Name's the Same," featuring children of famous parents. There was Gary Lewis, Jerry's son; Maureen Reagan, Ronald's daughter; Mickey Rooney Jr.; Francesca Hilton; Meredith MacRae, daughter of Sheila and Gordon; and a guy who claimed to be Peter Lorre Jr., until we discovered three nights before the show that Peter Lorre did not have a son. Caesar's Palace advertised the show with a giant billboard that read MARTIN & LEWIS. If you looked real hard, you could see the tiny letters spelling DEANA and GARY above our surnames. Five months pregnant, I sang "Stepping Out with My Baby."

Halfway through the run, the Los Angeles Police Department sent two detectives to Las Vegas to interview me about the Manson murders. Sitting me down, they told me, "We believe we know who was responsible for the crimes, and we think you know him. Charles Manson."

I felt the baby kick violently inside me. "Oh my God," I said, shivering. While Manson had given me the creeps, I'd never for one minute suspected that he could be guilty of such a heinous crime. It shook me to the core, to think that I could have been one of his targets. "You're Dean Martin's daughter, aren't you?" officer Gutierez asked with a smile. My mind was racing. Was he planning even then to harm me? Was I an intended victim? Was his goal to secure his place as one of the most notorious murderers in history? Did he expect to find me at Cielo Drive? I would never know.

"But he seemed so ordinary, and he gave me a ring," I told the police.

"We know," they replied. They told me a list had been found, names of people the Manson Family wanted to target next. It included Frank Sinatra, Steve McQueen, Elizabeth Taylor and Richard Burton, Tom Jones, and, among others, Dean Paul Martin.

"Was I on the list?" I asked, trembling.

The two detectives didn't answer.

"We'd like to ask you about these people," one of them said instead, rapidly changing the subject. He threw a batch of crime-scene photographs onto the table in front of me, and I was suddenly confronted with the bloody scenes at Cielo Drive. Feeling faint, I pushed them away.

"I don't think you should be showing me these in my condition," I said, my hand protectively across my stomach.

"How often did you go up to the Manson Family ranch?" they asked.

"Never," I replied.

"Manson said you did, with Sandra Dee."

I looked at them aghast. Me and Sandra Dee? I almost laughed.

"No, I only ever met him at Cielo Drive. Two or three times, with a guy named Tex and a girl named Squeaky."

"Then why did he give you a ring?"

"I guess he thought it was a cool thing to do, seeing who my dad is."

Terry Melcher was horrified that I'd been questioned and cut a deal with the DA, Vincent Bugliosi, so that I wouldn't have to testify at Manson's trial. "Deana had nothing to do with this," he told them. "She's pregnant and shouldn't be upset."

Dad was shocked and disgusted that I'd even met Manson. When he found out, he demanded police protection for all of us. He telephoned me.

"Are you okay, baby?" he asked. I could hear the fear in his voice.

"I'm fine," I replied. "Just a little shaken, that's all."

"I don't understand how you came to be involved," he said. "What were you thinking, getting messed up in all this?"

"Manson was just someone I met at Terry Melcher's house," I told him.

"But this guy could have hurt you," he interrupted. "These people were on drugs. I don't know what you kids are up to these days, but I never expected anything like this."

I knew there was no point in trying to reason with him. Shock and fear had made him suspicious. Yes, most kids had experimented with drugs. Claudia and I once took LSD and went to Disneyland, which was a bad idea—I was so sick, I never tried it again—but we weren't out of control by any means. We were good kids, and our contact with Manson and his followers was purely accidental. I knew that, beneath his anger, Dad was just being a concerned parent. It was the first time I'd seen him be really worried for us, and I was touched by his words.

In the end, I was only asked to give evidence at Charles "Tex" Watson's trial at the superior court. Terrified, I had to stand up in court and identify one of the chief perpetrators of one of the most hideous crimes in America's history.

"He looks kind of different now," I said, speaking so softly they had to ask me to raise my voice. "The man I met over at the house on Cielo Drive had long hair and was much heavier than the man there." As Tex's eyes came up to meet mine, I couldn't help shivering as I thought of the seven people who'd been brutally murdered.

IN DECEMBER 1969, Dad left Jeanne for good. We were all shocked. I had always thought they'd celebrate their golden wedding anniversary together, standing on either side of a huge cake, surrounded by friends and family at the Beverly Wilshire Hotel, just like Grandma and Pop. Separation, divorce, even remarriage had never entered my mind. I realized for the first time that my rose-tinted perceptions of them had been mistaken. My siblings were far more realistic, especially those still living at home. Unknown to me, Dad and Jeanne had been companions rather than lovers for some time, sleeping in separate rooms. All the while I thought they'd stay together forever. They had their differences, of course, like any couple. Jeanne, from Florida, loved the house to be cold, with all the windows and doors thrown open, and Dad, from Ohio, liked it hot, with everything closed. Dad was an early riser, up at six to play golf, and Jeanne was a night owl who liked to sleep in. These may seem like insignificant differences, but I now think they were classic indications of how truly opposite they were. The fact is those differences worked in harmony for twenty years.

Whatever the reasons, at fifty-two, Dad decided he still had some living to do.

The first any of us knew that their marriage was over was when Alma reported, "Your dad left this morning. He had his golf clubs and his bag with him," she told us. "He just came down the stairs, had his breakfast, and walked out the door. I just know he isn't coming back."

He moved into the Beverly Hills Hotel and then into a house on Loma Vista in Trusdale. He wasn't alone. His new roommate was Gail Renshaw, a beautiful blonde and winner of the Miss World U.S.A. beauty contest, whom he'd met in Las Vegas. She was just a year older than I was, at twenty-two, came from Virginia, and spoke with a strong Southern accent. I found the idea of my father being with someone the same age as me a bit discomforting. Some of my siblings felt the same, although others thought it was rather funny. In the end, this was not new territory for us. We had all followed Dad and Jeanne's lead when they were so accepting of Frank's marriage to the young Mia Farrow. After a while, I came to accept it. If Jeanne was okay with it and Dad thought he'd found love again, then good luck to him, I told myself. Although I wasn't sure how I would feel if Gail Renshaw ever asked me to be a bridesmaid.

On his first date with her, at a prearranged dinner at the Riviera, he took my sister Gail along as a chaperone. My poor sister Gail, who was two years older than Dad's date, had no idea she was being used as a foil. She was never needed as a chaperone again. After that, he saw his new girlfriend on his own.

"The first time I met her," he told me with a twinkle, "I just loved the way she said 'Dean.' It's real purty," he said in his best Southern accent.

"Sure, Dad," I told him, wondering how soon the novelty would wear off.

Dad was spotted on the town with his new love, and the press soon jumped on the story. He even took her to see Elvis in Las Vegas. The King, ever the fan of Dad's, sang "Everybody Loves Somebody Sometime" in his honor. It fell upon forty-year-old Jeanne to announce the split in January 1970, which she did with great dignity, I've always felt. Her statement, issued through Mort Viner, said, "It is painfully difficult for me to announce the end of our marriage. My husband informed me several weeks ago that he had met and fallen in love with someone, and he asked me for a divorce. I assured him that I would comply with his wishes. Proceedings will begin immediately. My deepest concern at the present is for our children. It is my hope that all concerned will make every effort to see that their lives are kept within as normal a pattern as the situation will permit. The children have always felt great love for their father, and I fully intend that it remain so."

Jeanne famously added years later, "I married him knowing nothing about him. I divorced him twenty-three years later and I still knew nothing about him." She said, "Now he can hide, which is what he does best."

I went to see Jeanne as soon as I heard and found her surprisingly calm. "Sure, it breaks my heart," she told me, dry-eyed, "but your father's still young and handsome and he wants a last romantic fling, and I'm okay about letting him go. I'm certainly not going to try to keep him with me. It would only make him unhappy."

Dad gave no interviews about the split. He just added a few well-timed lines to his stage act. Commenting that Jeanne would get the house, he said, "That's all right, I could never find it anyway." Joking that he didn't have to pack for his latest show, he quipped, "My clothes were already on the sidewalk." He tried to suggest that the split was caused by his drinking, and he cracked even more drunk-jokes than usual. "I got picked up the other night on suspicion of drunk driving," he said, slurring the word *suspicion*. "The cop asked me to walk a white line and I said, 'Not unless you put a net under it.'"

After some protracted delays, caused by delicate legal negotiations, he and Jeanne were eventually divorced in March 1973. The settlement of $6.5 million made the *Guinness Book of Records* as the most expensive up to that time.

From a personal point of view, Dad and Jeanne's divorce marked the end of an era. The perfect Hollywood family we had been was altered irreparably. Armed with this new information about my father, I began to reexamine the family photograph stored in my memory. I now realized, more than ever, what a great job Dad and Jeanne had done in keeping their personal problems from us. And how oblivious we had all been.

Throughout all the traumas of my life, my brothers and sisters had been there for me. True to our nature, we were there for each other at this unsettling time. If there is one lesson we'd learned, and I think the same can be said for any family, it is that our strength lay in our love for one another. We had a common bond of blood, and it tied us together. Our shared experience of growing up as a family was our foundation, our comfort. We had the happy memories of Mountain Drive, of Dad coming home every night to eat his Wonder Bread sandwich while Jeanne fixed him a drink. The events that had seemed mysterious at the time but now made perfect sense, like the breaking of a mirror in Jeanne's bathroom, or the raised voices from the bedroom, were forgotten and forgiven. In time, circumstances would divide us still further as a family, but at that early, painful stage of our parents' separation, we believed that in unity we had strength.

I HAD no choice but to keep working, even though I was pregnant. I'd spent almost all of the $22,000 I'd made on my last film putting Terry through therapy to get off drugs. His therapist was Dr. Kupper, and I once went to see him myself, to ask him about my own demons. I will always remember his words.

"Deana," he said, taking my hand and smiling, "I could take what's left of your money and put you through hell, but, to be honest, I'm happy if any of my clients emerge from therapy as stable as you are. So keep your money and be proud of what you've achieved. You're just fine."

I never told my father, Jeanne, or even my sisters and brothers what I was going through with Terry. The baby was due in mid-

August, and on July Fourth, Ricci was holding his annual devastation of the tennis court fireworks at Mountain Drive. We were both supposed to attend. But Terry went missing the morning before the event and I could not find him anywhere. He was supposed to be starting a new rehab session the next day, but he disappeared. I went home and found his car in the garage, and a trail of white pills on the floor. Panicking, I finally found him. He was in UCLA Hospital, having taken an overdose. I was three weeks away from giving birth, and my husband was trying to kill himself. I asked Gail to drive me to the hospital, and I sat at his bedside as we waited for him to regain consciousness.

"If you live through this, Terry Guerin," I told him, squeezing his hand as tears streamed down my face, "I'm gonna kill you."

The following day I went to Ricci's party, and pretended that nothing was wrong. "Terry's got the flu," I told Jeanne, smiling. Inside, I was dying.

My wonderful son, Mickey, was born prematurely, a few weeks later on July 24, 1970. Terry drove me to the Cedars of Lebanon Hospital in Hollywood, where leading gynecologist Red Krohn, known as "the doctor to the stars," delivered my baby. Mickey was born with the umbilical cord wrapped around his neck, and for a moment the doctors couldn't hear his heartbeat. Thank God he came out beautifully.

"Is he okay? Does he have everything?" I asked, before passing out. My sisters and their husbands came to see me soon afterward, and to meet their new nephew. Jeanne came, and Dad sent flowers.

The day I sat down with Dad and told him I was getting divorced, Mickey was just six months old. Dad had a cold and was drinking his cure-all remedy, tea with honey. He claimed it was the best thing for his throat. "Do you want to tell me about it, baby?" he asked.

"Not really," I replied.

"Are you okay?"

"I guess."

"Do you want me to send the boys after Terry?" he asked, quite seriously.

"No thanks, Dad," I said, not really surprised by his offer and half-laughing at one of his well-dressed friends paying Terry a visit. "I just want my life back."

Terry went to live in New York shortly afterward, leaving me with a baby, no money, and a truckload of his outstanding parking violations. I was left alone, holding my child, and reflecting on what it meant to be a parent. I was twenty-two years old and just hitting my stride. On the one hand I had a blossoming acting career beckoning me, and a chance to travel and make it in show business just like my father. On the other, I had my son, my only true love.

I remember the moment I made my decision. I was lying in bed, with Mickey in my arms, splashing his little body with my tears.

"I'll never leave you for a life on the road," I told him, as his little hands pulled at my hair. "You and I are in this together."

Dear Dean — Thanks for a truly
happy evening + Warmest Regards
Ron

Fifteen

DAD AND JEANNE BARELY SPOKE TO EACH OTHER FOR
ten years after their divorce. Just as he had with Mother and Jerry
Lewis, Dad cut her completely out of his life. Jeanne was later linked
to Howard Hughes, who sent a plane to fly her to Las Vegas. Actors
William Shatner and Frank Calcagnini were also suitors.

Jeanne was very beautiful, desirable, and a lot of fun. Yet nothing ever came of her subsequent relationships and she never remarried. Jeanne told me, "Deana, it's not like men were beating down
my door. They were too afraid of upsetting your father. The word

was, 'Dean Martin isn't someone whose wife you play around with, even if they are no longer married.' You see, once you've been married to Dean Martin, no one else compares. How do you follow that act?" And she was right, none of Dad's ex-wives ever remarried. They were all happy to remain Mrs. Dean Martin.

All the children except Gina had moved away from home. We had our own lives, filled with careers, marriages, and children. Jeanne did her best at first to gather the family together at holiday dinners and parties. We loved going over there and being together, because we were part of a very funny group. Everybody was hysterical. Whenever I heard friends complain, "Oh God, I have to go to my parents' house for dinner and it will be so dull," I'd feel sorry for them because it was always great fun to visit with my family.

Close as we'd been for so long, things gradually began to change. Jeanne would throw birthday parties and invite only Dino, Ricci, and Gina. Or she'd invite us all to her Christmas Eve party, but only her three children for dinner the following day. Gradually we were excluded from events that involved their side of the family. I'm not sure she even realized what she was doing. It may have just been an instinctive, protective mechanism kicking in—gathering her own children around her. Whatever the case, our close-knit, loving family was being disassembled. I felt as though my heart were being torn from my chest. Anger didn't come into it. I was too hurt to feel rage. I didn't for one minute think Jeanne was doing it in any deliberate, malicious way. But they say blood is thicker than water, and suddenly that rang horribly true among the Martins. Dad had been the common denominator, the glue that bound us all together, and now that he wasn't pivotal to our lives anymore, we were slowly coming unglued.

Dad used his spare time to help Uncle Frank campaign for an old friend of theirs, the former actor turned Governor, Ronald Reagan. Nancy and Ron had been family friends for years, and Ron's daughter by Jane Wyman, Maureen, had been in the Las Vegas show with me. Ron also appeared on Dad's TV show, only this time, as governor of California.

Dad also took on the starring role of a pilot in the screen adaptation of Arthur Hailey's bestselling book *Airport*. It was a good role for him—suave, graying, and cool in a crisis. He was playing himself. He'd been nervous about working with Burt Lancaster and Helen Hayes. He loved Jacqueline Bisset, about whom he said, "She's just gorgeous. Those eyes!" He locked himself away for days to practice his lines. It must have paid off, because the movie was a smash hit and Dad earned a record $7 million from it.

His love affair with Gail Renshaw lasted less than a year. They were engaged, but I guess he tired of her accent sooner than he expected. He'd also met the woman who would become the third Mrs. Dean Martin—a receptionist at a Beverly Hills beauty salon. Her name was Cathy Mae Hawn, a twenty-three-year-old blond divorcée with a four-year-old daughter.

The first I knew about Cathy was when I received an eleven-thousand-dollar bill from Bonwit Teller, a top fashion house on Rodeo Drive, for two fur coats. Knowing I didn't possess a fur coat, I called Dad's business office and asked what it meant.

"Oh, it must be Cathy," came the reply.

"Cathy?" I asked.

"Your dad's new fiancée. She and her mother have been shopping and charging everything to your dad's account. He doesn't have one at Bonwit Teller, but you do, so they charged it all to you instead."

Their first Christmas together, Dad and Cathy gave all of us children a beautiful fluffy white terry-cloth bathrobe with our name embroidered on the pocket. They were just like the ones the Rat Pack wore in the sauna of The Sands. In each pocket was a check for five hundred dollars.

The following year we didn't get a thing. Someone at Dad's business office rang with the message, "Just wanted to let you know, your father isn't exchanging gifts this year."

"What do you mean?" I asked, confused.

"Dean Martin will not be exchanging gifts with his children this year."

"Oh, I see," I said. "Well, you can tell Dad that I'll be dropping his gift over on Christmas morning, as always."

I didn't see much of Dad in the three years that he was with Cathy. He was in New Mexico filming and traveling a lot. I did go and visit them once, not long after Dad had bought her a new car as a surprise. Typical Dad. Always something flashy and expensive. He chose a bright yellow Cadillac.

Cathy hated that car. She kicked the tire and told Dad, "It's an old person's car," before storming off.

Dad and I were left staring at this beautiful Cadillac in stunned silence.

"Since when don't young people like yellow," Dad quipped.

The reason he'd bought her a new car was that she'd crashed his beloved Stutz Blackhawk with his legendary license plate DRUNKY. He loved his funny license plates. He once had a station wagon with the initials BFS on it. Whenever people asked him what the letters stood for, he'd grin and reply, "Big Fucking Star."

MY BROTHERS, sisters, and I were moving on with our lives. Craig and Kami moved to Hawaii for a while and bought a liquor store. Their marriage didn't last, and Craig returned to the mainland and to television production. He started dating Carol Costello, the stunning daughter of comedian Lou Costello. Carol had been married before and had five kids and Craig happily took them all on as his own. He is such a sweet man.

Dino, who now insisted on being called Dean Paul, was enjoying bachelorhood. Remembering how much I'd enjoyed my dramatic roles at Dartington, I took him and Tina Sinatra to see the Franco Zeffirelli film *Romeo and Juliet*. I'll never forget that day. He sat next to me, staring up at the screen and the vision of loveliness that was Juliet as played by the beautiful young English actress Olivia Hussey. Leaning over to me, he whispered, "I'm going to marry her."

Laughing, I dug him in the ribs and told him not to be silly. "You've got to meet her first," I told him.

Looking at me very strangely, he nodded. "You're right."

Booking a flight to London, he somehow orchestrated a meeting with Olivia, and before we knew it, they were engaged. Persistence was definitely his strong point. After he swept her off her feet, they had a fabulous wedding in 1971, on Olivia's twentieth birthday. Two years later their son, Alexander, was born, the light of Dean Paul's life. Sadly, the marriage ended and they divorced, although Olivia has remained close friends with our whole family.

Along with millions of proud Americans, Dean Paul had watched on television as the twenty-year-old figure skater Dorothy Hamill won a gold medal at the Innsbruck Olympics. When his marriage to Olivia was over, he told us, "I'm going to marry Dorothy Hamill." This time we believed him. Somehow he found out that "America's sweetheart" was training at Lake Placid. He flew there to meet her. Later he proposed and she accepted. They were very much in love, and she was one of the nicest people I have ever had the pleasure of knowing. She became the star of the Ice Capades, and won the World Professional Skating Championships five years in a row.

One of the few additions Dad made in his routine in Las Vegas was in her honor. He'd throw ice from his glass onto the stage and say, "Okay, Dorothy Hamill, let's see you skate on that." Despite being the sweetest girl, her fame and success put pressure on the marriage, and it failed. Dean Paul was too much his own man to be famous for being just Dean Martin's son, and Dorothy Hamill's husband, although—as with Olivia—he never stopped loving her.

Gail's marriage to Paul Polena only lasted a few years, and they had two lovely children, Claudia, known as Cappy, and Liza, named after Liza Minnelli. After two years she married Gus Fisher, a real-estate agent and the ex-husband of Rue McClanahan, who played Blanche in the television show *The Golden Girls*. They had a beautiful daughter whom they named Samantha before their marriage ended. Then Mike Downey, a former award-winning writer for the *Los Angeles Times* and the *Chicago Tribune* came into her life. She'd been reading his column for years and loved his laconic wit. She fell in love with him long before they met. Mike wrote a column about Uncle Frank's funeral mass at the Good Shepherd Church in Beverly Hills. He spoke about the comedian Tom Dreesen and his role in the mass. In his article he mentioned that they were friends from Chicago. Gail immediately called our brother Craig and asked, "Don't you play golf with Tom Dreesen?"

"Yes . . . occasionally. Why?"

"I've been reading Mike Downey's column in the *Los Angeles Times* for twelve years and he just wrote that Tom Dreesen is a friend of his."

"Yeeesss . . . and so?"

"And so I want you to call Tom and set up a dinner for all of us and invite Mike. I would like to meet him."

Twenty minutes later, Craig returned Gail's call and asked, "How's Thursday?"

And so, the rest is history. This sort of thing seems to run in my family. One thing is certain, we are not a shy group. Now they are happily married and commute between L.A. and Chicago, where Mike is the lead sportswriter and still winning awards.

For Ricci's twenty-first birthday, Jeanne threw him a party to remember at Mountain Drive. Elton John and John Lennon were invited, and did a live set in which they performed "Birthday," the Beatles number that begins, "You say it's your birthday . . ." Ricci is such a sweetheart; he contributes so much to our lives. It had to be very difficult for him, growing up in the shadow of Dean Paul, but he developed his own inimitable style. After doing some work as a carpenter and setting up his own band, Ricci lived the playboy lifestyle, dating girls like Melanie Griffith, the daughter of Tippi Hedren, a friend of Jeanne's.

Like all of us, Dad really enjoyed having Ricci around; he was the court jester. There is a lot of Jerry Lewis in him. Ricci is always the bartender, fixing the drinks and cracking jokes. He is one of the funniest people I have ever met. People love to have him at parties because he is so entertaining. He starred in a movie called *Maui* with Lisa Hartman, and was adorable. He married a flight attendant named Annie, and they have three beautiful daughters, Pepper Jazz, Montana Sage, and Rio Dean. Now he runs a recording studio near Salt Lake City and performs "Tribute to Dean Martin" shows across the country.

Gina has always been so adorable, and the baby of our family. It was exciting for me when I first moved to Mountain Drive, because at last I had a little sister to play with. I took her under my wing and looked after her, calling her "Ginakins." I remember taking her to have her ears pierced when she was eight. The following day the nuns sent her home from the Beverly Hills Catholic School, claiming she had "the devil in her ears." She skated in the Ice Capades with Dorothy Hamill, then met and fell in love with Carl Wilson, "the voice of the Beach Boys." We'd known the Beach Boys all our lives, through Terry Melcher and other friends back in the sixties. Having met Carl, Gina toured the world with him. Carl had two sons, Jonah and Justin, from a previous marriage to Annie Hinsche, and we've all stayed close friends.

My sister Claudia married an actor named Kiel Martin, who played J.D. LaRue in the popular television series *Hill Street Blues*. They bought a house in Topanga Canyon, had a beautiful baby daughter named Jesse, and lived the hippie lifestyle. One time out at Claudia's house, they were smoking pot while our Mother Betty was staying on a rare visit. Everyone seemed to be high that day, except Gail and me. I tried it once and it made me hungry, paranoid, and uncomfortable. How attractive is that?

My mother Betty, who thoroughly disapproved of drugs, wandered into the room where Kiel was stoned, and hissed "Junkie!" under her breath. Without missing a beat, Kiel hissed "Drunkie!" back at her. Mother and the rest of us collapsed in hysterics. Oh God, Topanga Canyon, those were very different days.

Claudia's marriage to Kiel ended in divorce. A few years later, while working in Beverly Hills, she met Tom Brown, the director of sales for Bally's casinos in Las Vegas and Reno. They married and relocated to Reno soon afterward. Tom was a charming man and an amazing human being. When he died, people came from far and wide and from all walks of life to pay their respects. One man in coveralls even drove all night from Washington State in his pickup truck, with his dogs in the back. He just wanted to say good-bye before driving home again. Tom inspired that kind of devotion. The governor of Nevada was the next to speak.

Of course, we didn't always get along perfectly. There were the usual rivalries and petty disputes one would expect in any family. Occasionally someone would flare up, vent their feelings, and then calm down. Increasingly, our busy working lives meant that we didn't see each other as often as we would have liked. Children, jobs, travel, and personal commitments conspired to keep us apart. Some kept in contact more than others, visiting when possible and telephoning or writing. Others were more distant, living and working far away, their lives filled with raising kids and earning a living. But when I look back, I can honestly say that as a family we did pretty darn well. We all gathered for Christmas, Thanksgiving, and family celebrations. We do this because we want to be together. We wouldn't have it any other way, because we all love each other.

UNTIL WE married, each of us had an allowance from Dad, and he helped to buy us cars and houses. Dad's business manager would write occasional checks for us, but someone abused the system, so Dad cut us all off for a while. We all knew who was responsible, and at first we were angry. Dad's response was expected. Generous to a fault, he couldn't hold out on us for long. Within a few months of splitting up with Terry, I had no choice but to move out of the house Dad had given us in Mandeville Canyon because I could no longer afford it. Mickey and I moved into a smaller place, an apartment off Rodeo Drive in Beverly Hills.

Dad had an incredible work ethic and always encouraged us to pay our own way. "You've got to find something you enjoy doing and then work at it," he'd tell us.

He'd had to work hard in Steubenville. He'd only rarely talk about how difficult it was, working in the steel mills. "I'd come home filthy dirty, choking from the black soot that filled my lungs. It was in my pores, even under my fingernails," he'd say, with a faraway look in his eyes. I couldn't imagine this meticulous man, whose grooming set was laid out in a precise order on his dressing table, being able to bear such conditions. He clearly didn't want to remember those times. He had escaped that life and was grateful. He always had a deep affection for the people of Steubenville, and he enjoyed it when they called or came to see him in Las Vegas. He gave to many charities in his hometown, paying for school band uniforms and gifts to the children's hospital. He never forgot his roots. As he said in almost every show, and even to the Queen of England, "I'm from Ohio, a town called Steubenville."

Dad's life was work, work, work. There must have been times when he was scared to death, lying awake at night, worrying how he was going to pay for all of us, the house on Mountain Drive, the horse ranch in Ventura, and the business called "Dean Martin." He was a far better actor in real life than people gave him credit for, because we never once had an inkling that his life was anything other than a breeze. His modesty was legendary.

"I'm not a great singer, but I can hold a tune," he would humbly say. Or, "Acting's easy, you just remember your lines and repeat them."

As far back as I remember, he was always working, making movies or recording songs or working on his television show. He made sixty movies and recorded more than a thousand songs, which is phenomenal for someone who started out as a nightclub singer on fifteen dollars a week. He had a career that he loved, and too much was at stake. I'm sure that his rigorous work ethic came from my grandmother.

"You know why I work so hard, Deana?" he'd ask me.

"Yes, Dad," I'd say, echoing his words as he gave me his pat response. "So I can take care of you kids and play golf."

"That's right, baby."

MY CONTACT with Mother Betty was infrequent at best. Usually it came about because she was visiting Claudia or Gail, and they invited me over. Unknown to me, she had religiously followed my every move as a singer and actress, cutting my clippings from *Variety* magazine and the entertainment newspapers. She made up stories for her friends of how she spoke regularly with us and how we told her what we were doing. She would embellish a single telephone call or brief encounter so that it seemed as if she were constantly in touch. She must have been in a lot of pain.

Mother got along famously with Claudia's husband Tom, so she'd sometimes visit them. One morning Claudia was out in the garden, planting some spring bulbs, when Mother came wandering out of the house.

"Listen, dear, the vodka, did you hide it from someone?"

Claudia carried on and, in rhythm with her methodical digging, replied, "I-hid-the-vodka-from-anyone-who-might-need-vodka-at-eight-in-the-morning."

"Oh," came the disappointed reply. Mother wandered back into the house. A while later she returned to ask, plaintively, "And the Tuaca, too?"

The expression "And the Tuaca, too?" became an inside joke in our family after that, and I have never been able to see a bottle of that golden, seventy-proof Italian liqueur without laughing.

Gail would often drop in on Mother when she was in San Francisco. Mornings were the best time to catch her at home. She drank her coffee strong and black, and poured liquor into it. Often, when Mother stayed with Gail or vice versa, Gail would go to bed leaving Mother at the kitchen table with her "coffee" and the newspaper. By the time she would awaken, eight hours later, Mother would have been to bed, gotten up, made a new pot of coffee, fetched the new newspaper, and started the cycle all over again, sitting in exactly the same place.

Once when Gail went to stay with Mother, she was drinking so much that Gail finally persuaded her to go to a clinic and get some help. Six hours after driving her there and dropping her off with her suitcase, Gail was awakened in the middle of the night by banging on the door. Mother had returned.

"Pay the cab, will you?" she said, entering with her suitcase.

"You're receiving money from Dad every month, you pay for the cab," Gail retorted. The Hispanic cabdriver just stood in the doorway.

"Well, how much is it?" Mother asked, rummaging in her big black handbag for a checkbook.

"With the stop at the liquor store, that's fifty-five dollars," the cabdriver replied.

"Okay," said Mother, neatly filling in the amount. "And who do I make it out to?"

"José Xavier De Fernandez," came the reply.

Mother stopped writing and looked up. Her eyes glazed, she said, "I'll just make it out to cash."

Whenever Gail or Claudia telephoned, Mother would usually be out. They had the numbers of all her haunts and would try her at each one until they reached her. Whenever she was home in the evening, Mother would be watching one of her favorite television programs. The phone would ring, one of her daughters would say hello, and Mother would reply, "Oh, hello, dear. How wonderful to hear from you. But listen, I'm just watching *Magnum P.I.* Can I call you back?" She rarely did.

Once, when Mother was due to visit Gail and her daughters in Las Vegas, they all went to the airport to meet her. She didn't show up. The next time she promised to visit, for Easter, Gail told her kids, "Okay, let's go to the airport for breakfast, and if Grandma Betty shows up we can bring her home." They went to the airport and to their surprise, coming toward them on the moving sidewalk was a friend of Mother's named Charley.

"Betty sent me," he said apologetically, holding up armfuls of Easter baskets.

When Mother did make contact, she'd often hang up halfway through a conversation, later blaming everything from a technical fault to birds on the line. More often than not, it was because a favorite program had started on TV. On the rare occasions when she would write, the letterhead from her six-story apartment block just read FIREPROOF BUILDING.

On one such piece of paper, Mother wrote a song provisionally called "I Won't Tell Him," which her sister Anne later found. The words went:

> *Wherever he is, where I look in vain,*
> *his lips I could kiss, but my heart's full of pain,*
> *I could see him today but in my own way, I won't tell him.*
> *If only he knew that it hurts me to say, the words won't*
> *   come out, my eyes give me away.*
> *So what else can I do, he's so stubborn too. He doesn't love*
> *   me at all.*

Across the bottom line, she'd written "Never did, never will" in pencil and scribbled it out. At the end she wrote, "To whom it may concern (up there). Signed, Betty Martin." Anne is having the words and music transferred to CD and calling it "Betty's Song." I look forward to hearing the song. I loved her first song, "For Your Love," which was a huge hit for Ed Townsend.

MAYBE IF I had gone into therapy with Dr. Kupper, I would have been able to feel differently about Mother, even to be angry with her. Even though my sisters were resuming contact with her, it never occurred to me to do the same. I don't think I was punishing her in any way, or even denying myself the opportunity to vent my emotions. It was simpler than that to me. Jeanne was my mother, and had been for more years than Betty. When I saw her at my sisters' houses, I didn't feel any great swell of emotion. I didn't feel anything at all. I am not a judgmental person, and largely accepted her for who she was. Of course there were times when I felt mad at her, mad at the way she was wasting her life, but I accepted and understood that that was who she was, and I didn't beat myself up over it. It was as if she were some distant aunt of whom I had fond childhood memories, but no strong desire to see.

I did go to visit her in San Francisco years later. It had been a few years since I'd seen her at Claudia's house in Reno. I was staying at the Fairmont and told her I'd pick her up.

"I'll be waiting outside my apartment," she said excitedly.

When I arrived, I looked around for her but couldn't see her. My heart sinking, I wondered if she had changed her mind. The only person there was a white-haired lady who kept smiling at me. When I realized who it was, I was shocked. She'd shrunk in height and ballooned in weight. She'd let herself go. There was no resemblance at all to the glamorous woman who'd taken us grunion-hunting by moonlight, clad in a shimmering gown, her head back and laughing as we clawed at the wet sand.

"Deana, baby!" she cried, when she saw me, throwing her arms wide. "Come here my little baby." Holding each other close, we both wept.

She was well known in the local bars and liked to go to the Buena Vista Café for Irish coffee. Her new "living room" was the Castle Bar, her armchair a bar stool for "the Betts," as she'd become known.

"Hey, the Betts is here!" the regulars would cry, and their faces would light up in anticipation of Mother's company.

Looking at me, they'd grin and say, "This must be the baby. This must be little Deana," and she'd nod proudly. They all seemed to know me.

The walls of that bar on Geary Street were plastered with framed newspaper clippings and the glossy Sid Avery photographs taken of us all when we were very small and still part of her world. The jukebox featured Gail's solo recording of "Second Hand Rose," and the wedding photo Gail had sent her was framed on the wall above it. She was very proud of her children and loved to share stories about us with her friends.

Every customer who happened to take a seat at "the Betts's" side was treated to a drink and regaled with tales of her former life, of the people she knew, of a time when she was still Mrs. Dean Martin.

Sixteen

LIKE DAD, I'M A BORN OPTIMIST AND WAKE UP HAPPY each morning, but the 1970s contained some of the lowest moments of my life. Being a single mom and an aspiring actress, taking part-time secretarial jobs and evening acting classes and living in an apartment, all conspired to lower my spirits.

Some of my friends were faring much better than I was. Liza was dating Desi Arnaz Jr. when she won an Academy Award for *Cabaret* in 1972. She did a fabulous job, and the award was well deserved. She and Desi came over to Jeanne's house immediately after the awards ceremony, and we celebrated together. The father of a friend of mine owned a jewelry store in Beverly Hills, and he had given me a tiny gold Oscar on a chain. Intensely proud of Liza, I gave it to her.

Those huge eyes of hers, with those great long lashes, grew even larger, and she shook her head as she looked down at the necklace. "Oh no, Deana," she said, "I can't possibly take this!" Pressing it into her hand, I told her, "Well, you must have it. You got the Oscar before me, so you keep it." As I said earlier . . . always the optimist.

Meanwhile, I was leading a far less glamorous existence. I was caring for my son while I continued to audition for work as an actor. If there was any spare time, I was campaigning for Senator George McGovern in the 1972 presidential race, and organizing rallies. Tina and I even worked up some ideas about producing a movie together. Regrettably, my father was dating someone who I felt had little interest in getting to know me.

One day at Jeanne's house, I saw a note about a surprise birthday party Cathy was arranging for Dad at Chasen's restaurant. I was so excited, I contacted Cathy's assistant and told her I'd love to come.

"No," the assistant said coldly. "You've misunderstood. That invitation was for Gina, not Deana." I was shattered.

One day, at an all-time low, I picked up the phone and called Dad. I hadn't seen him in ages, and I just wanted to hear his voice, to hear him say, "Hi, Deana, baby, how's it going?"

He never personally answered the phone, so I asked the maid to put him on.

"Hi, Dad," I said brightly. "It's Deana."

"What do you want?" he said, his mood evident.

"What do you mean, Dad? I don't want anything," I replied, hurt at the accusation. "I just wanted to talk to you."

"Nobody phones me unless they want something from me," he said gruffly.

My eyes smarting, I yelled, "Well, how about sending me a little love sometime?" and slammed the phone down. I was so mad at him, because I very rarely asked him for anything, and if I did, it was usually for someone else. I cried myself to sleep.

Mad as hell, I had a great idea. I'd write a book. Its provisional title was *Dad's Rich, I'm Not*. I thought it could be a tongue-in-cheek memoir of what it was like to be Dean Martin's daughter and the repercussions of having a famous father. Such as being turned down for acting roles by people who'd tell me, patronizingly, "We liked you better, but we're giving the role to so-and-so because she really needs the work." Even if it was just a line, the truth was that I was struggling as a single parent regardless of who my father was.

The assumption was always that I must be loaded, thanks to Dad, and was only dabbling at acting for fun. My son Mickey, meanwhile, was at school in Beverly Hills with all the kids who lived in huge mansions. Usually he didn't tell anyone who his grandfather was, something he could get away with because of his Guerin surname. It made me so sad that he felt that way about the man he called "Pop," with whom I'd always hoped he'd have a close relationship—but it was not to be. With Claudia away and Gail on the road, for a long time it felt just like Mickey and me against the world.

Bitter and upset, I began putting my feelings on paper, and before I knew it, I had a proposal that was good enough to show a publisher. They liked it and offered me a $10,000 advance. It was just enough money to allow Mickey and me to relax for a while. I was thrilled.

Dad got wind of the book via Mort Viner when news of it hit the trade papers. He called me up, something he rarely did.

"I understand you're writing a book, Deana," he said coldly.

"Yes, Dad, I am," I replied, somewhat warily.

"Burn it," he said.

"What?"

"Burn it."

"What do you mean, 'Burn it'? You don't even know what it's about."

"Just burn it," he insisted.

"But, Dad, it's just a story about what it was like growing up as your daughter and the famous people I grew up with. It's very light-hearted and it'll be fine."

"Burn it," he repeated.

"Well, look, let me finish it first, and then you can read it and see what you think."

"Burn it," he pressed.

Furious, I hung up on him. Pacing the floor, I wondered what to do. Eventually I called him back. "Well, Dad, are you prepared to buy this book from me?" I asked, hoping to shock him into changing his mind.

"What do you mean?" he said.

"I've been offered good money for this book. Are you prepared to buy it from me?"

There was a pause. "How much?"

"Well, how about a new automobile?" I asked, much more boldly than I felt, remembering Jeanne's advice always to ask for something wonderful.

"Okay," he said, and hung up.

I was still mad at him, but decided to shelve the book. Dad's business managers bought me a Firebird. It was a beautiful car, and I persuaded myself that this would have to suffice. A month later the bill for the car was sent to me by mail.

I called up Ellie, Dad's accountant in his business office, to tell her about the mistake. "There seems to be some misunderstanding," I told her. "Dad agreed to buy me this car as a gift."

"But he specifically told us to be sure to send you the bill," she replied.

"He actually told you that?" I asked, my heart racing.

"Yes."

"Then tell him he can keep the darn car," I said, and hung up.

Seething, boiling over with anger and frustration at years of feeling neglected and misunderstood by my father, I decided there and then that Mickey and I would move as far away as we could from

L.A., to New York City. I had some friends there, and I knew I could find work in a town where people wouldn't make so many assumptions because of who my father was. I packed our bags and flew to the East Coast, where we lived, quite meagerly, for a year, in an apartment in Greenwich Village. I went on a television game show and did a couple of plays, one with Danny DeVito, but I was soon fed up with the cold and the snow. The book, needless to say, was never written.

I FLEW home from New York just in time for Dad's wedding to Cathy in April 1973. He was pleased to see me and I was just as happy to see him. During the time that I had been away from his influence, my anger and frustration had abated. I'd missed him and the family more than I cared to admit and was glad to be home. We were like that, as a family. One minute we'd be mad at each other and the next, we'd move on and everything would be fine. It sounds crazy I know, but ultimately, I believe we were healthier and happier because of it. If Cathy made him happy, then I was fine with that too. He was a true romantic underneath that devil-may-care attitude. He loved getting married and he loved having a wife.

The wedding was as lavish as you'd expect it to be, although Dad quipped, "I gave orders that no champagne glass should ever be more than half full." Held in a makeshift chapel at their new red brick Tudor mansion on Copa de Oro in Bel-Air, and then at the Beverly Hills Hotel for the reception, it was a spectacular event that must have cost millions. They rented church props from Warner Brothers, had huge gilt cages filled with white doves, and flew in flowers from Paris. Cathy wore a massive headdress made of lilies of the valley, like a white crown nesting on her red hair. Dad mingled with the crowd, and when he wanted some solitude, he told them, "Pardon me, I have to go and burp my wife." Uncle Frank was best man, and as a thank-you present, Dad bought him a diamond-studded gold cigarette lighter with the inscription FUCK YOU VERY

MUCH. For Cathy he bought a $50,000 sapphire-and-diamond bracelet.

In his mid-fifties and a newlywed for the third time, Dad showed no sign of slowing down. He signed a new deal in Las Vegas, with the MGM Grand, which he always called the "Megum," for $200,000 a week for six weeks a year. That hotel was so big he complained, "I have to leave my dressing room two days before I'm on." He made them build a dressing room for him right next to the stage, and he'd sit in there watching *The Mary Tyler Moore Show* on television until the announcement came, "Direct from the bar, Mr. Dean Martin!" Then he'd literally get up, open his dressing room door, and walk right onto the stage.

He also agreed to a three-picture, three-year deal with MGM. The ratings were down on his television show despite a new name, *The Dean Martin Comedy Hour.* The cue cards had been replaced with a TelePrompTer, and Dad—in the oversized spectacles that were fashionable at the time—relied on it increasingly. The highlight of the show became Dad's "Roast of the Week," in which some star such as Johnny Carson, Bob Hope, or Lucille Ball, was "roasted" instead of toasted by the likes of Don Rickles, Billy Crystal, Rich Little, etc., in a tongue-in-cheek tribute. Dad had been hosting such comic testimonial dinners for years at the exclusive Friars Club (where Uncle Frank was Chief Abbot). Those shows had never been broadcast because the language was too blue. Someone came up with the idea for Dad to clean up the concept and include roasts at the end of his show. They bolstered the ratings.

Dad carried on working. His spectacles became bigger and bigger, until they almost completely covered his face. By 1974 his television show had morphed into *The Dean Martin Celebrity Roasts*, filmed at the Ziegfeld Room of the MGM Grand in front of an audience of nine hundred eager fans. Because Dad was chairman, he was able to invite all sorts of people you'd never normally expect to appear on such a show. There were his old pals Orson Welles and Jimmy Stewart, Gregory Peck, and Ronald Reagan. I attended the one in which my friend Angie Dickinson was in the hot seat. She looked gorgeous with her strapless gown and her beautiful straw-berry blond hair, giggling hysterically.

Dad, inhaling deeply on his Kent cigarette, asked, "What do you get when you take away the body, the hair, the makeup, and the dress from Angie? Ruth Buzzi." And Ruth came out, all made up to look goofy and unattractive, just as she always did on *Rowan & Martin's Laugh-In*, and beat Dad with her purse.

It was a brilliant show and still stands the test of time. Today, the *Dean Martin Celebrity Roasts* are the number one selling videos in history. After nine years, being the nature of television, it ran its course. Dad's trail-blazing television career was nearing an end.

When I would stop by to see him, he was at times moody, mak-ing bitter remarks about Jeanne and the rest of the family for the first time in his life, which took me by surprise. It was as if he sud-denly wanted to distance himself from us and the life we'd once had. I sensed a real change in him. My contact subsequently became lim-ited. Cathy was having a house built for them in Malibu. She liked to keep him to herself, rarely organizing family events or inviting any of us older children over. The only real contact he had with his children was with Sasha, Cathy's daughter, whom he'd adopted.

The contrast between Cathy's and Jeanne's responses to us kids couldn't have been greater. Both Betty and Jeanne had been excited and enthusiastic to have us around. They embraced us into their lives and made it such fun. Cathy was the exact opposite. It seemed to me as if she were trying to build her own little empire with her daughter, Sasha, and was pushing us away. Even at Dad's work, Cathy's influence was felt. She'd arrive on the set of his television show and stick around all day, making sure Dad didn't stray from the marital path. After a while she began to make suggestions about how to produce the show, and it became such a problem that the team had to take Dad to one side and ask him to speak with her.

Dad had always been someone who relied on his wives to orga-nize his life and remember special birthdays and anniversaries. Betty and especially Jeanne had been brilliant at it. Now all that stopped.

To be fair, Cathy was very young and didn't know any better. On the few occasions when I did see her, she was always sweet and polite, but I could sense that she didn't quite know how to respond. The only time I can ever remember her going out of her way to be kind to me was when I dropped in to see Dad one Easter.

Mickey and I took a traditional Easter basket to Sasha, full of chocolates and sweets. In the living room, she was sitting on the floor, seven years old, surrounded by four other baskets. Prompted by me, Mickey went over and handed Sasha ours.

"What? Another one?" was all she said. Mickey was heartbroken.

But the look on Dad's face was of utter disbelief. "We say 'thank you,' " he told his newest daughter. "How could you be so rude?"

Worse still for Mickey, there was no basket for him.

The only grandparents Mickey ever knew were Dad and Jeanne, and now Cathy. My mother, Betty, was no longer part of our lives. But Mickey barely knew "Dad," something that upset me more than anything. I had so longed for them to be close, for Dad to take a part in Mickey's life and be the grandfather to him that he deserved. Dad had been absent from my early childhood because he was working all the time, I had made myself believe. Now there was no excuse. Poor Mickey rarely saw Dad more than three times a year, at Easter, Thanksgiving, and Christmas. The older he grew, the less he felt a part of Dad's life. He even had a recurring nightmare he once shared with me.

"I dreamed that I walked down the road and Pop walked toward me and didn't recognize me," Mickey told me, obviously upset. "He didn't even know who I was."

Trying to defuse the situation with Sasha and the Easter basket, I commented on how nice Cathy smelled.

"What is that?" I asked, inhaling her scent.

"Worth," she replied. "Why don't you come upstairs and I'll give you some."

Up in her dressing room, she opened a cupboard and showed me wall-to-wall Worth products, at least five of each item. "Take one of each," she offered, handing me a bag.

I took it home and splashed some on my chest and neck. Within thirty minutes I broke out in hives, the like of which I hadn't seen since I was nine years old. No perfume before or since has given me that reaction.

It wasn't just Cathy. Dad was as much to blame; he did nothing to bridge the gap I felt she was making between him and us. I don't think he fully appreciated how much he hurt us. Nor did we ever feel able to tell him. He was such a complicated man, and it sometimes seemed to me that we spent our lives tiptoeing around each other, so as not to hurt his feelings.

My sisters and Craig were also excluded from Dad's life, as were their children. Craig no longer worked for him and lived his own life with Carol Costello and her family. Claudia lived in the Nevada desert and rarely saw him. A few years earlier, Dad had suddenly changed the name of Claude Productions, his film production company originally named in her honor, to the Sasha Corporation, a move that hurt Claudia deeply.

Gail lived in Palm Springs and had little or no contact with him after a silly row they had. Once she even went to see him perform in Las Vegas, and when he found out she was in the audience, he refused to come onstage. Poor Gail had to leave.

She once told me, "I don't know why you keep pushing to see Dad, Deana. It's just not worth the heartache."

On that particular point, however, we would always disagree. I wanted him to love me . . . as much as I loved him.

Seventeen

THAT CHRISTMAS, I WANTED TO GET DAD SOMETHING really special, something that could only have come from me. It was difficult enough to buy him a gift, because he was literally a man who had everything. He also preferred his presents to come unwrapped.

Wrapped gifts were stacked, ten deep, in a back room somewhere, because they took too long to open. So, if I bought him a nice picture frame or a cashmere sweater, I'd tie a simple red bow around it that he could just slip off. All the family knew to do that. It was just his way. He could also be extremely blunt about gifts. Once, when he received some new cologne from a niece, he looked at it, and then at her, and said, "But I don't wear this."

"I know, Uncle Dean," she replied, "you only wear Fabergé Woodhue, but I thought it might be nice to try something different every now and again."

"But I don't wear this," he repeated, and put it to one side.

Thinking diligently about something to buy or make for Dad that was completely original, I suddenly remembered Grandma Angela's pasta fagioli.

"I'm going to teach you something very special," she'd told me. "Your father's favorite dish. One day, when I've gone, you can make it for him and he'll be very happy."

I remembered vividly her secret recipe for the thick Italian peasant soup. I spent hours making a big batch, using the correct cannellini beans, onions, extra virgin olive oil, tube pasta, and her secret ingredient. I poured the finished product into a giant Ball Mason glass jar.

I was very pleased with myself. The end result looked just like Grandma's. I tied a red bow around the jar and wrote out a little card. I excitedly drove to Dad's house, rang the bell, and went in. I found him sitting on the couch.

"Merry Christmas," I said, handing him the jar with a kiss.

He took it and his eyes lit up. He looked up at me and said, "Is this what I think it is? Is this pasta fagioli?"

"Yes," I said, smiling.

Dad cradled the jar in his hands and said, "It's still warm."

"Well, that's because I just made it," I said. "Grandma always said to serve it fresh."

"Oh my God," Dad replied. He summoned a housekeeper to heat it up, immediately, and when it was ready, I brought it to him ceremoniously with a little Romano cheese grated on top.

It was perfect; it couldn't have been more so, and he loved it. Watching him enjoy every mouthful was wonderful for me because that's exactly what my grandmother had planned.

A week or so passed and the telephone rang.

"Deana, this is your dad," he said.

"I know your voice, Dad," I told him, laughing, surprised and delighted to hear him on the line.

"Do you think you could make me some pasta fagioli?"

"Yes, Dad, I'd be happy to."

I made another batch, took it over to his house, and dropped it off. There was a little envelope waiting for me, with my name on it, spelled wrong, of course. He never spelled my name the same way twice. The envelope said Deena, and inside were five one-hundred-dollar bills. A note attached to it said, "This is for the work and the beans."

I called him that night. "You know, Dad, you don't have to give me five hundred dollars to make you pasta fagioli," I told him. "Anyway, the beans cost two dollars."

"Well, it's for the work," he said.

Laughing, I told him, "It takes two hours, so I'm being very well paid, but thank you very much."

"You're welcome," he replied.

The following week he called me again, asking for a third batch. There was another envelope waiting for me, with my name spelled differently again, containing another five one-hundred-dollar bills. The note this time said, "Dear Dena, buy a house. Love Dad." I eventually made so much money making that soup for him, I probably could have bought a house. I made it for years, until I was so sick of pasta fagioli that I could never eat it myself. But I didn't mind. It was another special connection with Dad, a gift from my grandmother, and a chance to show him just how much I loved him.

♦♦♦

DAD'S NEXT TV role was as a criminal lawyer, Joe Ricco, in a series set in San Francisco called *Mr. Ricco*, which received reasonable reviews, but didn't last long. He made his final recording for Reprise Records in 1974—after that, there would only be compilations. My friend Tina told me her father was complaining that he was seeing less and less of Dad. He was concerned.

"Is everything all right with Uncle Dean?" she asked me. "I mean, Dad says he seems so different, so aloof these days." It was a question I was asked a great deal, but one I didn't have an answer for. Something wasn't quite right. Was he missing Jeanne and us kids, but didn't know how to resume contact? I wondered if I'd ever know.

Newspaper articles began to appear about how reclusive Dad was becoming. Once *Esquire* was forced to interview his agent, Mort Viner, instead of Dad. "Look," Mort told the interviewer, "Dean doesn't do interviews. Why don't you take me to lunch, ask me any questions you would ask Dean, I'll answer them and you can quote them as if they were Dean. I know him very well. I know all his answers to all the questions you could ask. I do it with other reporters all the time."

When I couldn't reach Dad myself, despite repeated attempts, I rang Mort to see how my father was.

"He's fine," came the breezy reply. "You know your Dad. If he wants company he'll ask for it."

The next thing I knew, I read that Dad had sold his mansion on Copa de Oro for $1.6 million to the singer Tom Jones. He moved out to the house Cathy and he had built in Malibu, which seemed a very unlikely place for Dad to be living. He hated leaving town, apart from his annual trip to Las Vegas or Palm Springs. Malibu was too far from his golf course. I tried to reach him on the telephone, but he, Cathy, and Sasha must have already left.

One day I was watching television absentmindedly while cooking dinner, when a news bulletin interrupted the program, claiming Dad had been shot.

I was so shocked, I didn't know what to do. I stood there staring at the TV screen, wondering whom I should call first. I called Mort Viner.

"Mort, it's Deana," I said, breathlessly. "What's going on?"

"Nothing," he said. "Why?"

"Why?" I shrieked. "The TV news just said that Dad has been shot!"

"Oh, that," he said dismissively. "It was nothing."

"What do you mean, nothing? Was he shot?"

"Yes, but not seriously."

"Oh my God, where is he? Is he all right?"

"He's fine," Mort assured me. "He's at my house. He shot himself in the hand, cleaning his gun. It was a minor flesh wound. They stitched it up and released him."

An alarm bell rang deep inside my head and wouldn't stop. Dad always carried his little pearl-handled derringer in the ankle of his boot. Guns had always been part of our lives. But when he cleaned his gun, he was always so careful. He would never have left it loaded.

"What do you mean? He was cleaning his gun with a bullet in it?" I said, deeply suspicious. Pausing, I asked, "Mort, is everything okay?"

"Yes, it's fine, Deana," he told me, slightly impatiently. "I have to go. Your Dad will call you soon, I promise."

Hanging up, I wondered whether Mort's story was true or not. I never found out. Six days later, though, Dad filed for divorce.

DAD'S DIVORCE took a long time. The negotiations lasted over a year, and Cathy's lawyers had a field day. None of us know exactly how much she got, but it was substantial. The house in Malibu remained hers, there was considerable monthly alimony to pay, and Sasha was taken care of for the rest of her life.

After the divorce, Dad seemed even more unsettled than usual. He moved from house to house, thinking each time that a new environment would make him happy. The trouble was, all the houses were basically the same. He'd have them decorated identically to Jeanne's taste at Mountain Drive, with everything in exactly the same place as it always had been. He'd always been incredibly neat and had an order for everything. Whenever he moved, he'd go away for a few weeks and have someone transfer everything to the new house just as it had been in his previous one, with his toiletries laid out just so. He was color-blind and couldn't tell if his socks were dark blue, black, or brown, so the colors would be written on each dresser drawer. He'd walk into his new home and feel immediately at ease, because it would always be the same.

He started dating Peggy Crosby, the daughter-in-law of Bing, and then a lovely actress named Phyllis Davis, whom we all liked. She was in a TV show called *Vegas* and was funny, beautiful, and down to earth. She and I became good friends, and one day I went back to her house in the Hollywood Hills after lunch. Phyllis had a friend named Char, a psychic, who joined us. Just as we were sitting down, the French doors blew open and a cool breeze filled the room.

Laughing, I said, "Oh, the ghost of Christmas past!"

Char stared at me and beyond me and said, in a strange voice, "Do you know someone whose name has the letters *a-n-g*? It ends with an *a*?"

"Angela?" I said. "My grandmother Angela? Who died on Christmas Day?"

Marlon Brando, Dad, and Montgomery Clift
on a break while filming *The Young Lions*.

Sammy, Frank, and Dad—
he made everything fun.

The two coolest guys
in the business
—Dad and Frank.

Dad,
Jimmy Thompson,
Ben Hogan,
Jerry Lewis,
Byron Nelson,
Sam Snead,
and Julius Boros.

Cary Grant, Prince Charles,
and Dad—very royal, indeed.

Dad, Judy, and Uncle Frank make
beautiful music.

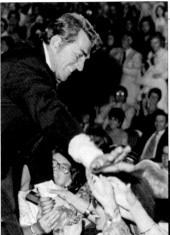

Dad taking
England
by storm.

I'll never forget
the day at Grauman's
Chinese Theater
—we were all so proud.

Me, Dad, Frank, and Tina Sinatra,
singing on the Christmas show.

Dad, Uncle Frank, and the Goose.

Friars Club testimonial for
Dean Martin, 1959—
Larry Sherry, Dean Martin,
Danny Thomas, George Jessell,
Tony Martin, Bill Miller,
George Burns.

Grandma and Pop's fiftieth wedding anniversary
at the Beverly Wilshire Hotel.

Screen Producers Guild Awards—George E. Jessel,
Rosalind Russell, Groucho Marx, Frank Sinatra, Dinah Shore,
Dean Martin, Danny Kaye, Irving Berlin, 1965.

Oh, my God,
I'm with the Beatles!

Mickey's fourteenth birthday
at the Bel-Air Hotel.

Dad and me—going over our lines.

Dad and me at
my wedding, 1990.

Grandma Peggy's eighty-second
birthday party—what fun she was.

Me, Dad, and John
—a little chitchat.

My men and me in
Steubenville, Ohio, 2002.

My handsome husband, John,
and me at the Broadcasting
Hall of Fame Awards.

John, Ricci, David,
Alex, Jason, me,
Olivia, and Gina at
Mom's, 2003.

Mom and me
at Christmas,
1994.

Mickey, Paola, me, John, Hunter, and a brand-new Jagger—March 1, 2003.

"Yes," Char smiled. "She's always with you."

"That's a little too spooky for me, Char."

Sadly, Dad's relationship with Phyllis didn't last, and I lost contact with her and Char.

⟐

I TOOK a series of jobs. I was acting and managing the Maurice Andre beauty salon on Rodeo Drive. I also did a commercial for Firestone Tires. Then I decided to go into real estate, so I went back to school and took the exams needed to get a license. That's when I discovered that being in the real-estate business in L.A. is almost as rough as being in show business. How you looked was as important as the property you were selling. Image was everything. The Thunderbird I'd bought when I came back from New York wasn't making the right impression. Taking my courage in both hands, I went to see Dad at his house on Loma Vista.

"Hi, Dad," I said, when he opened the door. "I have some great news."

"Well, you'd better come on in and tell me," he said.

We went inside, and I sat down and showed him my portfolio of properties. "The new job's going great, and I have all these houses to sell," I beamed.

"That's great, baby," he said, drawing on his cigarette, "but why are you showing me these?"

"Because what I really need in order to sell them, Dad, is a new car." I held my breath as he digested my words.

"And this is good news?" he asked.

"My car just isn't right," I said, my eyes pleading.

"You could try washing it," he said.

"Come on, Dad, you know what I mean. I think one of those new Cadillacs would project just the right image for selling houses, don't you?"

"Again, I say, this is *good* news?"

Throwing my arms around his neck, I kissed his face and told him how much I loved him. My new Cadillac was delivered to my doorstep within the week. This time he didn't send the bill.

Shortly after I took delivery, Mickey and I were driving through Beverly Hills one night when the police stopped us. I had forgotten to affix the new registration sticker to the license plate. It was about six o'clock at night, and the sun roof was open.

Just as the motorcycle cop asked me for my driver's license, Mickey, who was six years old, popped his head out of the sun roof and stared at him. "Do you know who Dean Martin is?" he asked. I was shocked. He wasn't usually a name-dropper.

"Sure," came the reply.

"Well, he's my grandfather and we've just come from his house," he said, waiting for the response.

The cop looked extremely skeptical, but smiled politely. Staring at my driver's license, and my name printed across it, he stopped smiling. "Okay, Miss Martin, well, you just hurry along home now and find that sticker. Good evening to you." With that, he touched his cap and waved me on.

Waiting until we were far enough away for him not to hear us, I let out a squeal of delight and, turning to my beaming son, I cried, "Way to go, Mickey!"

I worked in real estate for four years, selling Dad a house and selling Jeanne's house for her (with disastrous consequences). It was such hard work, and with so little financial reward, that I eventually decided to change professions. I became a fitness instructor instead. I worked out most days, and the owner of the gym I attended suggested I give it a try. At least that way I'd keep fit and be able to work my hours around Mickey's school and extracurricular activities. I turned my back on real estate without a second glance.

◆◆◆

IN SEPTEMBER 1976, in Las Vegas, something remarkable happened. Jerry Lewis, whose career had followed a different path from

Dad's after they split, was the master of ceremonies at an annual telethon for muscular dystrophy, which raised millions of dollars each year and was first started by Dad and Jerry in 1952. On a whim, Frank Sinatra decided to persuade Dad to put in a surprise appearance. Uncle Frank thought it was time for these special friends to reunite. He felt that getting the two of them back together again might be just the right boost Dad needed, so he made the arrangements.

"Come on, Dag," he cajoled, using his affectionate nickname he'd always used for Dad. "It'll be a hoot."

Jerry knew nothing of the planned meeting until Dad was brought onto the stage. Mickey and I watched along with the rest of the country as Uncle Frank suddenly appeared at stage left.

Collaring Jerry, Frank announced, "I have a friend who loves what you do each year and who just wanted to come out and say hello."

Live, in front of an estimated 120 million viewers, Dad walked out into the spotlight as Jerry held his face in his hands and fought back the tears. The comedy partners, who hadn't seen or spoken with each other in years, embraced each other warmly. Jerry told me years later that "I could hardly keep it together when I saw my partner walking toward me." Still full of love and respect, he described to me one of the highlights of his life as "Magic in a Bottle. That's what we had."

"So, have you been working?" Jerry asked Dad, which was hilarious because Dad still dominated the nation's television viewing.

"Not much," Dad replied, as ever rising to the bait.

Their spontaneity was still there, the way they worked the audience and each other, completely unscripted. Frank stood in the middle, little more than a spectator, and watched with the rest of us, in awe. They had so much in common, so much shared experience, so much to talk about. It was a truly historic moment.

❖

DAD HAD been an early riser his entire life. Decades of having to be at the studio at six in the morning or on the golf course for the start of a game, had set his body clock. When he was making movies, he used to be in bed by ten. To guarantee a good night's sleep, he would take a pill.

A pill to sleep or for pain. Jeanne did too. Pharmaceutical-sized jars of pills were locked up along with the cases of wine and liquor in the storeroom. Most of Dad and Jeanne's friends did likewise. It was a socially acceptable part of their Hollywood lives.

Playing golf is a tried-and-true method of getting a bad back, and Dad suffered from a lot of lower-back stiffness caused by his swing. He had endured a hernia for years, and had some serious dental problems from a relatively young age—which can't have been helped by the five teaspoons of sugar he took in his coffee every morning. Despite frequent visits to the dentist, he suffered terribly with his teeth until the day he died. The combination of his various aches and pains conspired against him, and the only way he knew how to alleviate them was by taking Percodan, the same painkillers Mack Gray and Jerry Lewis had been taking for years.

I once had a headache while I was visiting him. I asked him if he had any aspirin.

"No, just Percodan," he said. "They'll do the trick."

I took one and soon started to feel dizzy and fuzzy-headed. "Boy, Dad, these are really strong," I told him, worried about driving home.

"I know," he replied. "That's why I take them. They're the only thing that works."

All the medical literature on Percodan today warns against the dangers of becoming addicted. It is highly habit-forming, causes damage to the liver and kidneys as well as stomach ulcers, and can only be issued by prescription. Dad had no idea of the dangers. The little yellow pills worked for him, so he kept taking them. He would never have believed that Percodan was in the same league as the cocaine Sammy Davis Jr. and Peter Lawford had a penchant for. He would have been appalled if told he was developing an addiction himself, similar to the one Pop had for sleeping pills. All Dad knew was that the drugs he took regularly had a pleasantly numbing effect.

I didn't notice any major changes in Dad to begin with. He had definitely slowed down a lot, and was playing less golf, but I put that down to the fact that he was getting older. He was still working a little. He and Frank played a week-long gig at a club in Chicago for old times' sake and split the fee of $600,000. Strangely, it was only when I saw him on television that I'd notice there was something wrong. He did a series of commercials for AT&T (for a staggering fee of $7 million), which I always thought ironic since he avoided using the telephone.

Six years had passed since his last movie, but he was persuaded into starring in *The Cannonball Run.* It was a wacky coast-to-coast car race. His co-stars were Burt Reynolds, Roger Moore, Farrah Fawcett, Dom DeLuise, Peter Fonda, and Sammy Davis Jr.

"It'll be just like the old Rat Pack days," Sammy told him. "Come on, Dean, it'll be fun." The film was a huge hit and made $175 million at the box office. The film was directed by Hal Needham, a world famous stuntman. Hal had actually doubled for Dad in two movies. "Can you imagine, I was a stunt man one day and directing superstars like your Dad another," he told me. "Ain't life grand?"

In 1981, Mack Gray, Dad's best friend and lifetime companion, died after a short illness. He was seventy-five years old. Dad was devastated, although he pulled himself together to be a pallbearer. Mack and he had been virtually inseparable for thirty years, and Dad wanted to be there for him in the end. Mack had grown especially fond of Gina, my little sister, and remembered her in his will. Life just didn't seem the same without him. Dad withdrew into himself even more without his best buddy around. He attended but was too upset to perform at the inaugural eve gala that year for his old friend the new president, Ronald Reagan.

Dad didn't like to watch his old movies anymore and see how he used to look. I think it was too painful for him to be reminded of his physical decline. It was such a stark contrast from the consummate professional we all knew and loved. He'd struggle with his words. Gone was much of the quick repartee and lucidity. His nightclub show, in which he'd always pretended to be under the influence, suddenly rang true. Years of drinking and taking pills were taking their toll.

"I don't drink any more, and I don't drink any less" was one of his quips.

If someone asked him, "What's in your glass?" he'd look sheepish and swirl it around a little. "Ice?" he'd reply.

Another joke was, "I don't drink any more, I freeze it and have it as a Popsicle."

Suddenly the jokes didn't seem so funny anymore.

Eighteen

DAD WAS A LONER AT HEART, AND ALWAYS HAD BEEN.
Life and work forced him to be with so many people that, in his final
years, he actively relished his solitude. Jeanne and he started talking again in the early 1980s. After more than twelve years apart,
they occasionally got together for dinner or drinks. When he first
went over to the house she'd moved to, on Robert Lane, he looked
around and joked, "So this is where all my money went." I was glad
for them both that they'd buried the hatchet.

Dad was inherently quiet and not very conversational at parties, because he didn't enjoy chitchat. He didn't feel compelled to be the center of attention in a room, even if he always was. But he was never lonely. He'd accomplished everything he'd wanted to and had led a life most people only dreamed of. Now he just wanted a little peace and quiet.

That didn't mean he just wanted to stay at home alone. Every night at seven o'clock, Dad would venture out to his favorite restaurants for dinner. He loved the ambience of places like Carmine's, La Famiglia, and later Da Vinci's. He enjoyed being waited on by devoted staff who knew his every whim.

When La Famiglia was forced to close down because of a smoking ban in Beverly Hills, Dad offered the owner, Joe Patti, money to keep it open just for him, but Joe had had enough. Years later the restaurant became Nic's Restaurant and Martini Bar. The new owner, Larry Nicola, very sweetly installed a booth where Dad's had been, with a photograph of him and a little martini glass and a candle on the shelf next to it. Every day they make a fresh martini in Dad's honor and light the candle. After La Famiglia closed, Dad's new restaurant of choice became Da Vinci's. He ate there every weeknight, and on Sundays, when it was closed, he dined at the Hamburger Hamlet on Sunset.

In Da Vinci's, he'd sit in his regular booth, having been safely and punctually delivered by his driver. Once he was seated, a waiter would bring him his usual "setup," a glass of J&B scotch, a glass of ice, a glass of water, and a big spoon.

"Thanks, pallie," he'd say, without having to place the order.

He'd slip some ice cubes into the scotch and then, using the spoon, add the water himself, very precisely. That way he knew he had just the right mix, and it was just the way he liked it.

He ate the same meal most nights—linguine pomodoro as an appetizer, a piece of whitefish for an entrée, and his favorite tiramisu, which he called "rum cake," for dessert. With dinner he'd drink a glass of red wine, and enjoy a cappuccino with dessert. If someone he knew saw him eating alone, they'd often ask him to join them, but he'd usually decline, saying, "Oh no, thanks, I'm just fine."

When I would join him for dinner, he'd agree with the proviso, "Okay, baby, but let's just eat. Not a lot of chitchat. I might tell you a story." So we'd sit side by side quietly, eat our meal, and say good night. I always enjoyed the precious time we spent together.

Dad had a wonderful prank he would play in the restaurant because he felt so at home there. If the staff was busy, and someone was standing in the doorway waiting for a table, he'd get up from his booth and escort them to theirs.

"This way," he'd say, leading them across the floor and handing them some menus. "This should suit you just fine."

The customers would stare at him and each other, mouths agape, and whisper, "Oh my God, it's Dean Martin!"

Ever the consummate performer, he'd head back to his table, sit down, and finish his meal.

◆◆◆

DAD'S LAST appearance on the big screen came in 1983, when he agreed to star in *Cannonball Run II* with Sammy Davis Jr. and Burt Reynolds. A highlight was working alongside his old pal, Shirley MacLaine, and a cameo appearance by Frank Sinatra, who was not going to be missing all the fun. It was Frank's seventh and final movie with Dad.

Critics were less kind this time around and told Dad, Frank, and Sammy that they should have known better. The movie didn't even break even at the box office a year later, and after sixty pictures and numerous cameo appearances, that was a wrap on Dad's film career.

Turning to his singing career, he recorded his first album in ten years, a collection of country songs called *The Nashville Sessions* for Warner Brothers. He also took a rare trip abroad to London and Paris for some charity shows that were too good to refuse. He signed a deal worth $1.5 million to open the new Golden Nugget casino in Atlantic City.

At a star-studded event at the Waldorf-Astoria in New York, the Friars Club gave him the ultimate accolade of Man of the Year. Uncle Frank was the host and Shirley MacLaine gave a speech. More than a thousand people showed their affection and love for Dad by paying top dollar to be there. It was a fitting tribute.

◆◆◆

DEAN PAUL was getting impatient. He had so many burning ambitions; he was an action hero and sports pro, and he wanted to be taken seriously as an actor. He'd been nominated for a Golden Globe for his 1980 role in *Players* as Best New Male Star in a Motion Picture. Little happened to follow it up. Dean Paul had accepted almost every role that was offered to him, even a part on *The Love Boat*, because his agent once told him, "If you're gonna be in the business, you've gotta be *in* the business." Five years later and he'd landed a part as a doctor in a television series called *The Misfits of Science*, co-starring Courtney Cox. He came to my apartment often to practice his lines and pick up a few tips.

"I know I'm not a great actor, Deana," he'd tell me, "but I'd like not to be a bad one. You've been in plays and films. Will you help me with this?" He was a quick student, and it was always a pleasure to spend time with him. He had also asked Dad for acting tips, and Dad had told him the same thing he'd told me. "Listen to what the other person is saying. Really listen, and then react." It was great advice.

Dean Paul loved to fly. He started taking lessons at the Van Nuys Airport when he was seventeen years old. I remember one time he flew me over to Palm Springs, and I was thrilled. It was scary, exciting, and educational. He walked me through his every maneuver. I read the pre-flight checklist out loud to him as he methodically completed each task. He could see that I loved it.

"Would you like to learn how to fly, Deana?" he asked as we reached altitude.

Looking wide-eyed at all the instruments and gauges, I asked, "Will I be able to learn how all these things work?"

"Of course you can. Anyone who can memorize as much dialogue as you—this will be a snap!"

I was proud that he believed in me. "Okay!" I agreed. "Sounds like fun."

"Let me know when you have the time and I'll get you started."

Looking out the window, I said, "Is that ice on the wing?"

"I hope not," he said. "But why don't you open the POH again (Pilot Operating Handbook) and turn to the page for the 'icing procedures,' and let's run through the list."

We worked through the specific procedures for icing and we landed safely in Palm Springs. I'll never forget his calm and professional demeanor. As we were taxiing to the terminal, my mind was racing. "I'm going to be a pilot," I thought. "How amazing is that?"

Dean Paul had also realized a lifelong dream to be a jet fighter pilot. He'd applied to the California Air National Guard, only to be turned down as too old. Refusing to accept defeat, he went to Washington and pleaded his case personally. They told him they didn't want older married men with children, because they weren't focused enough on their jobs. Dean Paul countered, "I can be more focused than anyone I know. When it comes to doing something I've always wanted, I have tunnel vision." The generals believed him and allowed him to enlist.

Once he'd completed his training in Tennessee, he was put into a uniform and entrusted with the task of keeping the West Coast of America safe from air attack. He used to tell me, "Just look up in the sky, Deana, and I'll be up there somewhere, protecting you."

In 1987 he was thirty-five years old and really achieving all he wanted in life. He'd recovered from the breakup of his second marriage and was getting along famously with both of his ex-wives. He adored his son Alex, whose godparents were Liza Minnelli and Desi Arnaz Jr. Dean Paul was delighted with the way Alex was turning out. He had his mother's spirituality and good looks. He had his father's blond hair and his sense of humor. Dean Paul was determined that he and Alex would have the kind of warm, close relationship that fathers and sons should have.

Asked once what it was like to be Dean Martin's son, he'd said, "There is no way that my father is going to sit down and open up. He doesn't do that for his closest friends. He never really tells you what he feels or what he's thinking. I don't know him very well at all." That was never going to happen with him and Alex.

On an overcast Saturday morning, on March 21, 1987, Dean Paul decided to take Alex along with him to March Air Force Base near Riverside. Alex was going to watch from the runway as his father performed a low-level bombing practice run in an F-4C Phantom jet. Alex was just fourteen years old and as excited as any young boy would be to see his dad in uniform and in action. Waving good-bye as he climbed into the cockpit, Dean Paul smiled and snapped on his helmet. The four jets in his squadron took off in high winds and disappeared into the thick cloud cover that was starting to spit snow. Shortly they began to come back, one by one. But the fourth jet never returned. Dean Paul's plane had disappeared off the radar screens nine minutes after takeoff.

What happened that day is still a mystery. I'd last seen Dean Paul three days earlier, when he'd dropped in for a Coke and to go through a new movie script he'd been offered.

"Have you eaten?" I asked.

"Yes, thanks," he replied, so he sat with me while I nibbled on a salad.

I listened as he read his lines and I offered him some advice. "Don't keep doing that Steve McQueen thing," I told him, laughing. "Be yourself. It's too obvious." His agent had actually advised him to go into therapy, to open up and release some of his emotions. Dean Paul was quite serious, intense, and this role called for someone much lighter.

The night that Dean Paul came over with the movie script was a night like so many others, and we were planning to meet again the following week. He was happy, excited, and keyed up for what lay ahead. "I think this can be really great," he told me, his eyes bright. "Everything's starting to come together."

At the Family Fitness Center on March 21, the television was on at half volume, its flickering images drawing people's eyes as they were on the exercise machines. In my role as director of fitness, I was walking through the club, checking on everyone, when a familiar face flashed on the screen above my head. It was Dean Paul. As I stared openmouthed at the television, I read the words of the scrolling news bulletin underneath. DEAN MARTIN'S SON MISSING.

My heart beat inside my chest like a trapped butterfly. Shaking, I mumbled some excuse to the front desk and made my way to my office, shutting the door behind me. Dialing Jeanne's number, I found myself unable to swallow or muster enough saliva to speak.

"Jeanne? It's Deana," I eventually managed. "I just heard the news on TV. Is it true? What's going on?"

Jeanne's voice was as calm and steady as always. "We're still waiting for word. I want to keep this line open. Your dad's fine. He's here with me and the rest of the family—Ricci, Gina, and Alex. We'll call when we hear anything." With that, she put down the phone and her words, like a dagger, cut me off physically and figuratively. Suddenly our family was divided. I had no choice but to sit by the phone and the television, waiting for news about my brother, along with the rest of the nation.

Gail was trying to be positive. "Oh, Dino will be fine," she told me on the telephone. "He'll have ejected at the last minute, lost the plane, and be cursing his way around in the desert somewhere, just itching to get back into the pilot's seat."

"You're right," I said. "Think how many close shaves he's already had racing around in cars and motorcycles. I'm sure he'll be fine."

Mickey, who adored his uncle Dean Paul, was sixteen at the time and devastated by the news. Driving himself over to Jeanne's house, he knocked on the door to offer "Pop" and Grandma Jeanne his love and support. She opened the door, peered at him over her glasses, and listened to what he had to say.

"Thank you, Mickey," she said. "I appreciate that and I'll pass your message on, but I'm afraid I can't invite you in. It's just family, you see." Still in shock, she closed the door, something Mickey has never quite been able to forgive her for. Without even realizing it on that most dreadful of days, Jeanne hurt us both very much.

It took four long days to find out what happened. For those four days we held our collective breath and waited for word as the search-and-rescue helicopters swept back and forth across the mountain range between Palm Springs and San Bernardino, a hundred miles east of L.A., looking for wreckage. Dean Paul, as captain, had been in control of his plane in poor visibility, accompanied by a young weapons officer, Ramon Ortiz, whose family was also sitting anxiously by the phone.

Ronald Reagan, now the President of the United States and a family friend, rang to offer his assistance. He even sent up the military's top spy plane to look for Dean Paul's jet. Uncle Frank also called. The news was especially poignant for him. His mother, Dolly, had been killed in a plane crash in the same area on her way to see Frank open at Caesar's Palace in Las Vegas ten years earlier.

"If there's anything I can do, pal," he said, his voice shaking. "Anything at all."

Dad, too numb for conversation, thanked him and put down the receiver. Those who were with him said he sat drinking scotch, lighting one cigarette from another, and staring at the telephone.

Clutching at straws, Ricci and Dean Paul's best friend, Scott Sandler, paid $5,000 to a psychic who, touching Dino's flying suit, told them that he was dead. Shaken, they fled. Jeanne had spoken to their old friend Shirley MacLaine, who'd suggested that a psychic friend of hers try to find Dean Paul. It was Char Margolis, the woman whom I had already met through Phyllis Davis and who had told me my grandmother was always with me.

Char went with Ricci to the air force base and pored over maps of the area. Chartering a private helicopter, they flew toward the region she'd identified as giving off the strongest signals. They went despite the protests of the search-and-rescue pilots who had checked the area several times already. As they approached the range of foothills known as the Little San Gorgonio Mountains, news came across the radio that Dean Paul's jet had been found. It was in the exact area Char had pinpointed.

I first heard the confirmation that my brother was dead on television. I tried to phone Dad, but Jeanne said he wasn't taking any calls. Instead, Claudia flew in from Reno, and Craig and I collected her from the airport and we went over to Gail's house to cling to each other. Gail had been mothering us since we were children, and now she represented the mother figure in this, our separate annex to the Martin family. Betty's kids.

Later that night, a colonel from the base called on Dad and Jeanne. His cap in his hand, he told the assembled family that Dean Paul's Phantom Jet had disintegrated when it crashed into the side of a mountain at 550 miles per hour during a freak blizzard. There were no survivors.

One never knows what tomorrow will bring. Life moves us in many directions. The passion I once had for flying is gone. The sorrow I felt at the loss of my brother stripped the joy away.

♦♦♦

THE FUNERAL took place outside on a beautiful day at the Veterans' Memorial in the Los Angeles National Cemetery in Westwood. Dad had never looked older or more tired. His health hadn't been very good, and this took the wind out of his sails.

Jeanne, who arrived with Alex on Ricci's arm wearing a bright floral skirt, white boots, and a pink denim jacket, somehow managed to remain calm behind her enormous blue-tinted sunglasses. She said firmly afterward, "I know what Dean Paul would have wanted, and he wouldn't have wanted black."

The actor James Woods, a close friend of Dean Paul's, took the podium and read the eulogy, which had just the right mix of humor and sadness as he spoke of their great friendship. Uncle Frank couldn't face the funeral, but Tina came with Nancy, and they were completely distraught. I sat, trembling, next to Mickey, a few seats behind Dad and Alex, wondering how much pain a human heart could withstand.

Just as the service was drawing to an end, the air was suddenly filled with the growl of jets overhead and we all looked up into the bright blue sky. I had no idea what was going to happen, but I watched, amazed, as the Air National Guard performed its "Missing Man" maneuver. The squadron kept in perfect diamond formation, until one lone jet peeled off and disappeared into the clouds, leaving only a curling trail of white smoke. It was so unbearably poignant, so true to the circumstances of Dean Paul's death, that I don't know how we got through it. That was the only time I ever saw my father cry. His shoulders shook violently as he collapsed into himself, unable to take any more.

Afterward, we all went back to Dad's house on Loma Vista and tried to gather ourselves together. It was the first time I'd been able to speak directly with Dad since the accident, and I held him close to me, alarmed at how frail he felt. In the end, neither of us was able to say a word. Sammy Davis Jr. hugged him next and started crying, and he had to be led away.

Mort Viner was there, and he told Dad, "You know, Jerry was there today."

"Jerry?" Dad asked, his eyes not his own.

"Jerry Lewis."

"Really?"

"Yes, he slipped in at the back and didn't let anyone know he was coming."

"Well, why didn't he say hello?"

"I guess he didn't want to bother you."

Drawing deeply on a cigarette, Dad said, "Get him on the phone." Going to his den, he spoke privately with Jerry for almost two hours, the first time they'd talked like that in years. At the end of the call, Jerry told Dad, "You know I love you, Dean."

"I know," Dad said. "I love you too, Jerry."

Dean Paul would, I know, have been delighted that he was the one who brought Martin & Lewis together after so many years of silence and bitter recrimination. It was one of his greatest legacies.

My big brother, Craig, suffered a double blow that dreadful week. A few days after Dean Paul's remains were found, Craig's beautiful fiancée, Carol Costello, a forty-eight-year-old mother of five, suffered a brain hemorrhage and died. Craig came home and found her lying on the floor. The funeral was held on the same day as Dean Paul's. Craig, his face pale with sadness, came to the reception at Dad's house, having just buried the woman he loved.

♦♦♦

JEANNE ALWAYS felt that after Dean Paul's death, Dad couldn't bear to handle his feelings of grief. He "closed up on life," she told everyone.

My perspective is different. Losing Dean Paul was one of the most difficult things we had to encounter as a family. When a tragedy happens, people strive to make sense of it, to find a reason for the inexplicable. But it doesn't make sense. Dad, like the rest of us, was devastated. He was seventy years old and in declining health. He had never expected to bury his son. People still wanted him to be the vibrant, handsome entertainer they had always known. Those days were gone.

But that didn't stop him from getting out there and doing what he did best—entertain people. His annual stint in Vegas that year was due to start just a few weeks after Dean Paul died. Initially, Dad canceled, not feeling up to facing his public. But after a few days' thought, he changed his mind.

"Life goes on," he told one interviewer. "It's very hard losing a child, but I have six other beautiful children, and life has to go on for their sake."

Dean Paul's death undoubtedly broke his heart, as it did to all of us. Dad told Ricci that despite all his money and success, he hadn't been able to save his beloved son. We all felt it, that overwhelming void Dean Paul's death had caused. Nothing would ever be the same again for any of us.

Sometimes I drive over to Westwood to spend some time with Dean Paul. His grave is tucked away in a corner, just across from where Dad used to take me to the driving range as a young girl. Every time I go, the grass has grown so high around it, that I can barely find it. Jeanne can't face it, so it is left to me and others who visit to tidy it up. I take some flowers and sit with him for a while, reminiscing about the times we spent together. How much of a brat he was when I first arrived at Mountain Drive. How we grew up together, making model airplanes, playing practical jokes, swimming, riding bikes, and shooting guns.

He'd played tennis ardently, and he'd come off the court, dripping sweat and walking toward me with open arms. "Hey, Deana, come on, give me a hug," he'd grin, as I'd scream and run away. We'd have lunch together at the Hamburger Hamlet when the kids were in school. He would take me out to dinner or to some swanky premiere. The press loved that. "Deana and Dino," the captions would read as we held each other close and smiled for the cameras. Our bond was much stronger than just the name we shared. Dean Paul had an incredible presence and a huge heart. I miss him more than words can say.

The inscription on his simple white tombstone reads DEAN PAUL MARTIN. CPT US AIR FORCE. NOVEMBER 17, 1951–MARCH 21, 1987.

Whenever I'm there, I remember his words, "Just look up in the sky, Deana, and I'll be up there somewhere, protecting you."

Nineteen

EARLY IN 1988, DAD WAS IN PALM SPRINGS WITH UNCLE Frank and Sammy when they came up with the idea of a reunion of the Rat Pack, to rekindle some of the golden days of twenty-five years earlier. Frank and Sammy thought it was just what Dad needed, but Dad wasn't as enthusiastic.

The tour, which would start in Oakland and take in twenty-nine cities, would be called "The Together Again Tour." Frank, Dad, and Sammy would get up on stage and perform the act they knew by heart—the gags, the numbers, and the wisecracks.

"It'll be great," Frank told a deeply reluctant Dad. "You'll see."

"Why don't we find a good bar instead?" Dad replied. This time he was serious.

The idea was exciting in the beginning, and everyone except Dad was behind it. I, however, was concerned for Dad, and worried that he was taking on too much. The differences in the three superstars' lifestyles and tastes could be handled when they were younger, but not now, when they had a collective age of 204 and were very set in their ways. Dad liked to do Las Vegas shows, one a night in his tux, then go directly back to his room to go to sleep. Frank liked stadium concerts and to host big parties back at his hotel. Sammy could perform anywhere and loved the glitz and glamour of show business, the champagne and canapés in his dressing room afterward with people coming backstage.

The tour was sold out months in advance. People lined up around the block for the chance to buy tickets to see these three legends doing their famous act, maybe for the last time. Dad opened the show to 16,000 fans on March 13, 1988, with his trademark "How long have I been on?" and a couple of numbers, "Bourbon from Heaven," adapted from "Pennies from Heaven," and "When you're drinking, you get stinking, and the world looks good to you." The fans loved it, but there was some discomfort about how Dad looked, and drinking was no longer as amusing as it used to be. Dad sang seven songs completing his set. Sammy was next, and Frank came on after the intermission. The three returned to the stage for a twenty-minute medley as a finale. Dad's performance was not up to par, and Uncle Frank spoke to Mort about it, which, of course, went straight back to Dad.

In Chicago, Frank came to Dad's room after the show and insisted he join him in the lounge. "If you don't, I'll set fire to your bed," he said. Dad, knowing he probably would, acquiesced.

The party was in full swing, but Dad was staring off into the distance. "What the hell am I doing here?" he thought. "I'd rather be home in bed watching a western." Later that night, back in his room, he woke Mort with a phone call. "Get a plane," he said, "We're going home." Feeling unwell, he checked himself into a hospital, complaining of an old kidney problem. His involvement was over so quickly that I didn't even get a chance to see him perform. Sammy and Uncle Frank continued with the tour, with Liza Minnelli kindly stepping into Dad's shoes under a new banner, "The Ultimate Event." Only this time, to my mind, the ultimate performer was missing.

"I didn't need the aggravation," Dad told me when he returned home. "It used to be fun. This was too much like hard work." But within a month he was at the Bally Grand in Reno, Nevada, performing solo again, just the way he liked it. For good measure, he opened with a line about his health. "Frank sent me a kidney," he joked, "only I didn't know whose it was." The reviews of his show were less than kind.

A highlight of the Bally concerts came when the management wheeled a surprise seventy-second birthday cake for Dad out onto the stage, pushed by Jerry Lewis. Jerry sang, "Happy birthday to you, from the old Jew." The two men looked at each other, and Jerry said, "Why we broke up I'll never know." Dad said, "I agree," and they embraced.

Dad's next public performance was at a tribute dinner for Sammy at the Shrine, organized by Uncle Frank. Dear Sammy was dying. Cancer had silenced his golden throat. Dad wanted to pay tribute, but his own health wasn't good. He had kidney and prostate problems, and he was to undergo new tests on his liver. In the end, Dad made a brief appearance to read some telegrams before going home. Some reports described him as "frail."

Dad later went to visit Sammy at the Cedars Sinai Hospital, a huge gesture and one I'm sure Sammy appreciated, knowing Dad's fear of hospitals. Dad loved Sammy, as he was so much more than a friend. He was family. They had spent more than half of their lives performing together. Dad had laid his career in Las Vegas on the line for his pallie, and now Sammy was going to leave him. When Sammy passed away, he took part of Dad with him.

♦♦♦

MY FITNESS company, "Bodies by Deana," had taken off. I was also the director of fitness at the Family Fitness Center. I wanted to drum up more business and thought a televised commercial would be perfect. I knew just the man for the job. Ricci was making music videos and had both the expertise and the equipment I needed.

Thinking back to Dad's AT&T ads, I suddenly had an idea.

"Hey, Dad," I said one day when I went to see him, "you're such an old hand at these commercials, how about doing one for me?"

"What do you mean?"

"I mean starring in a commercial for me. I can't pay you the same rate you got from AT&T. In fact, I probably can't pay you at all, but it'll be fun. What do you say?"

To my surprise, he agreed to do it, and we had a lot of laughs making that video. Ricci organized it all. He had Dad sitting in a chair, wearing a tux, reading the comic section of the *L.A. Times*, halfheartedly listening to me as I told him about exercise.

"Guess what I did today Dad?" I asked him, my hand on his shoulder as he read.

"What did you do, honey?"

"I worked out." Cut to a clip of me in a leotard, pumping iron.

"That's good."

"No, I mean, I *really* worked out."

Cut to more images of me sweating and pushing myself to the limit on various fitness machines.

"That's good."

"And you know what else I did? I signed up the whole family." Standing next to me suddenly were Gina, Cappy, Liza, Mickey, and Samantha.

"Then I signed you up too, Dad," I finally said, smiling.

At which point he looked up from his paper and grimaced.

It was cute, and I loved working with him. He was such a pro. There was hardly any need for rehearsals, which, knowing Dad, was probably just as well.

WHEN DAD opened at Bally's, I went along to see him. I wasn't alone. There had been little room in my life for romance in the nearly twenty years since I divorced. I had dated some wonderful men, including some Hollywood names. But I started work early and came home late, and there wasn't time for it. Mickey was eighteen years old, living at home with me, but very much his own man. He had a wide circle of friends and was doing well in high school. For a long time it had been him and me, and there was no space for anyone else. We were just fine together, or so I thought.

Gail had begged me to come to dinner on Valentine's Day because her husband had a client in town. "It'll be fun," she said. The client was a man named John Griffeth.

Individually, neither of us was keen on the idea of a blind date, and each planned on getting through the evening as politely as possible before escaping. We were certainly not looking for a permanent relationship. As he approached, Gail kicked me under the table and said, "He's gorgeous!" And he certainly was . . . tall, dark, and handsome. Then we were introduced. From the minute I saw him, I was a goner. His beautiful face lit up with a huge smile, and he leaned down and took my hand and I melted.

"Good evening," he said. "My name is John Griffeth, and it's a pleasure to meet you."

I loved everything about him, the way he looked, the sound of his voice, and most of all, his sense of humor. John was an entrepreneur and the type not to take prisoners. I know we ordered dinner, we had to, I'm certain. But I can't tell you what we ate, what we drank, or anything about the evening, except this . . . after dinner, he walked me to my car, and we stood under the stars on a perfect night. He held my face in his hands, looked deep into my eyes, and kissed me. Still holding me in his hands, he looked at me, as if to memorize every nuance of my face, then we kissed again. A long, intense, and very passionate kiss. Then, ever so softly, he said, "We should spend the rest of our lives together."

We went to Reno to see Dad with Claudia, Gail, and Craig and their husbands and wives. Sitting in a restaurant before the show, I announced that John and I were getting married.

"We are?" John said, laughing.

"You'd better be good to my baby sister," Claudia told John, "or you'll have me to answer to."

John was a television director and had met Dad years before when televising a PGA golf tournament. Dad, a terrific golfer, was playing as one of the celebrity amateurs. He was a huge fan, but he'd never met him as a prospective son-in-law before. I introduced them, and they got along great. I needn't have worried.

The show was terrific, and the audience appreciated Dad. I was relieved that I didn't have to be nervous about his performance. Afterward, we all piled into his dressing room. As always, there were trays of food and a little bar setup, and Dad had ordered extra chairs.

"Didn't I put out a nice spread?" he said, pointing at the food he'd had the staff prepare.

We laughed and I stepped forward to introduce John.

"Dad, this is John," I said.

"They're getting married," Claudia interrupted. "And it was news to John!"

Dad smiled. "Ain't that a kick in the head," he said. "My baby's getting married. Congratulations." Dad was especially pleased when he learned that John came from Shelby, Ohio. As a fellow Ohioan, he definitely approved.

Gail proposed a champagne toast and we all raised our glasses.

Dad said, "Skoal!"

In unison, the Martin family gave the standard reply: "Sure it's cold, it's got ice in it!"

John must have wondered what he was getting into.

IN MAY 1989, Mother died. Dad hadn't seen her in more than forty years. It had been more than two years since I'd last seen her, on a visit to Claudia in Reno. In all the years since she left us at Aunt Anne's and promised to be back in three hours, I had probably seen her no more than ten times.

I had come to the conclusion that my poor mother was a mess. Complicated? Yes. Flawed? Undoubtedly. And, undeniably, an alcoholic. Her life had fallen apart when Dad left her and she had never been able to pick herself up, dust herself off, and start all over again, even for the sake of her four small children. She had chosen a path that would, inevitably, lead her away from all of us. It would probably take years of therapy for me to come to terms fully with her absence from my life. Sometimes when I think of her—especially how she was toward the end—I suddenly find that I am crying. The tears that spill from my eyes still surprise me, and I feel overwhelming sadness. For a while I retreat into that small, dark place inside me that I created when I was a very young child. It's so much safer there.

But then I think how fortunate I was to have Jeanne step straight into her shoes. To have a beautiful home and everything I could want, with my father and my brothers and sisters around me.

I am glad for Mother, who had all but cut herself off from her friends and family, that she made contact with her old boyfriend Rainbo just before she died. She and Rainbo could have been very happy. He was a kind and loving man who'd always been very good to us. It was her drinking that drove him away. Now, facing his own demise after terminal cancer had been diagnosed, he called and asked if he could visit, something she was unsure of at first.

"Oh, I don't know, Rainbo," she told him. "I'm not so beautiful anymore."

"Neither am I," he said, but he lied. He was still very handsome and had aged well.

Mother gave him a tour of her favorite haunts and they parted with a hug and a kiss. When Anne told me about the visit, I cried. Rainbo had been a big part of my life, too.

Anne was visiting Gail in 1989 when the telephone rang. Because Gail was busy, Anne picked it up and heard a man's voice tell her he was calling from the San Francisco Police Department.

Mother had passed away in her sleep, lying on her couch in her two-bedroom apartment above the Castle Bar in Geary Street, a book on her lap. A lifelong heavy smoker, she'd died of respiratory failure. A friend named Lefty, who ran the market across the street where Mother did her shopping, missed her daily visit and asked the building manager to check on her. The death certificate said she died of heart failure and emphysema on her sixty-fifth birthday, July 14, 1989.

Gail called me and I stood listening to the news, feeling absolute sadness. I remember telling Mickey and thinking, "She died completely alone. How different her life could have been. She'd had so much going for her. Four children and seven gorgeous grandchildren. How I wish her life could have been different. If only I could have made it so."

I called Dad and told him the news.

"I'm very sorry to hear that, honey," he said, with genuine sadness. "She gave me all you beautiful children. You know I really loved Betty. You know why?"

"No, Dad, why?"

"Because she loved me long before I was Dean Martin."

"Do you want to come to the funeral?" I asked.

"No, I'm sorry, I can't," he replied. But he paid for everything.

Mother had told Gail that she wanted to be cremated and have her ashes scattered under the Golden Gate Bridge. Gail, Claudia, and I flew up to make the arrangements, filing into a local funeral home.

"This must be a very hard time for you," the somber-faced funeral director said from behind his desk, and we nodded in unison. "Now tell me, why are you here?"

Claudia said, "We've come to consecrate our mother—I mean *cremate* our mother." We started giggling at Claudia's slip of the tongue, and the man clearly disapproved.

He asked, "Was your mother Hispanic?"

Gail cried, "With a name like Elizabeth MacDonald? Hardly!" We started laughing again, only so hard this time that it was all we could do to make the arrangements. Nerves got the better of us, and our emotions were topsy-turvy. We picked out a beautiful urn for the ashes, and we fled.

We went to Mother's apartment to settle her affairs and were amazed. In her final few years she'd had bookshelves built from floor to ceiling on every wall except where there were windows, and she had lined them, three deep, with books. She had accumulated a massive library, everything from cookbooks and historical biographies to crime novels, and she'd read them all. We took a few for ourselves as mementos and donated the rest to a local library.

Opening her closet doors, we found them filled with shoes, most of which had never been worn, all in their original boxes. I recalled the racks and racks of beautiful shoes she'd had when I was a child, and how we'd loved to put them on and dress up in her fancy clothes. The apartment seemed neat and tidy on the surface but in the drawers and cupboards everything was just thrown in haphazardly. All her worldly goods were there.

After the simple cremation service, we hired a boat, loading it up with champagne and Irish whiskey. We had to scatter her ashes under the Bay Bridge, because for some reason it is against the law to do so under the Golden Gate. All her children were there, with their partners, and dear Aunt Anne. The captain asked, "How many in your party?" to which Gail, quick as a flash, replied, "Ten out, nine back," which seemed entirely appropriate because that was Mother's sense of humor, although the captain looked horrified.

Out in the bay, Craig scattered Mother's ashes and we all sang her "Happy Birthday." We sat around, drinking and laughing and crying, wrapped up against a chill breeze. Each of us told a sweet story about Mother and the fun we'd had. Mine recalled the nights we'd go grunion-hunting. Gail spoke of some of the times Mother made her laugh. John, who'd never met her, recited a poignant Irish prayer, which was just perfect: "May the road rise to meet you, may the wind be always at your back, may the sun shine warm upon your face and the rains fall softly upon your fields. And until we meet again, may God hold you in the hollow of his hand."

Afterward we went to the Buena Vista Café, which Mother so loved, to drink Irish coffee. We each vowed that every time we were in San Francisco we'd stop at the Buena Vista and have one in her memory. Our plan was to commemorate the woman who had brought us into the world while Dad chased his dream; the young mother who'd singlehandedly steered us through the most formative years of our lives and had given us our sense of humor and our good manners. Yes, her problems had eventually overcome her and led her miles from her family and estranged her from the man she loved, but mother's only crime was to fall in love with a nightclub singer in 1941, when she was eighteen years old. Young, athletic, and beautiful, with her whole life ahead of her, she'd sacrificed everything for that love of nearly fifty years. Like Jeanne, she'd never remarried. It was as if once they'd had the best, nothing else would do. I was happy to know that Dad marked the passing of Mrs. Dean Martin, the mother of his first four children, by taking care of her final expenses.

"I think it's only fitting because she took care of me and you for all those years," he said.

God bless you, Betts.

Twenty

JOHN AND I WERE MARRIED ON FEBRUARY 17, 1990, AT
a church on South Beverly Drive, with a reception at the Friars Club
afterwards. Dad was in the hospital having some tests, but he had
assured me there was no way he was going to miss the wedding.
Jeanne was very excited and helped me with all the arrangements. I
was glad to be welcomed back again, after so many years of feeling
shut out. I'm sure she probably didn't even register my previous pain
because now she was once again my loving mother. In her mind there
had never been any change in her attitude toward me. I was still her

baby girl, and she was going to be a part of my big day. That's how crazy our family is sometimes. But I guess it's just how we are.

Shortly before our wedding, Mother Jeanne had to have surgery. We sat in her living room on the couch and she said, "Baby, I'm not sure if I can be at your wedding. The doctor says I have to have some surgery."

"I'll just die if you're not there," I said.

She took me in her arms, held my head to her chest, and said, "Okay, I'll do the best I can." And she did.

Best of all, Jeanne and John got along great, having hit it off one night over martinis at her house, where John and I had gone after an aerobics class, a hard hour and a half workout and no food. He wanted to ask for her personal approval of our marriage and was a little nervous.

Soon after we arrived at her house on Linden, Jeanne asked, "Would you care for something to drink?"

"Yes," we agreed.

"Good, then. I'm going to teach Deana how to make a martini tonight."

John loves martinis and thought this was a great idea. Jeanne went through the ritual of making her favorite drink, chilling the enormous glasses with ice cubes and water. She poured the chilled vodka into the shaker, took a stirrer and touched it into the vermouth and then into the shaker. "That's all the vermouth you need," she said. Retrieving the chilled glasses, she filled them right to the top and served green olives on the side.

We were exhausted and thirsty, and they went down very smoothly.

"This is delicious," John said. "The best martini I've ever had. But I do need to ask you something, Jeanne."

"First I want to try my hand at making a martini," I said. "If John likes martinis, then I should know how to make them for him."

I followed Jeanne's directions to the letter, and poured us all a second martini. And so the evening went on. We still hadn't eaten a thing, and by the third martini we'd forgotten why we came.

"Didn't you want to ask me something, John?" Jeanne asked.

"I dunno," John replied. "What is it you would like to know?"

We had a fabulous night, and I am now an expert martini-maker. John did eventually ask for my hand in marriage. But not that night. A few nights later at La Famiglia, Dad turned to me, "Deana, baby, does he make you happy?"

"Yes, Dad," I replied.

"More important," Jeanne said, "does he make you laugh?"

Grinning, I gave her my answer. "Absolutely."

For the three days before the wedding, I lived in Jeanne's house, making all the last-minute preparations. We dined together every night and had lots of laughs. It was probably the nicest time I have ever spent with her alone, just her and me, being mother and daughter. I remembered the day Jeanne took me to Capitol Records to watch Dad record "Memories Are Made of This." How I slipped my little arm around my new mother's tiny waist and leaned against her for a cuddle. "From now on, Deana," she told me, "everything will be just fine."

The wedding day dawned, and Jeanne and I had breakfast. Gail and Claudia helped me into my dress, which was off-white, lacy, and beaded, with puff sleeves and a fitted skirt. My hair was interwoven with flowers and pearls.

"You look beautiful, Deana," Gail told me. Mother Jeanne gave me a little gold locket on a blue satin string for my "something old, something borrowed, and something blue." All morning I was anxious that Dad might not be able to make it. Even though he had promised me, I feared that something might come up. Little did I know, Dad was still in the hospital. But, true to his word, the day of my wedding he checked himself out, against doctor's wishes, to be there.

Gail was my matron of honor and Samantha, Gail's three-year-old daughter, my flower girl. John's eight-year-old nephew, Trefor, was the ring-bearer, and Mickey proudly walked me down the aisle. I so wanted Mickey to feel a part of this wedding and give me away. Dad wholeheartedly approved. It was a rite of passage for us both.

Feeling very emotional, I arrived at the church to find Dad sitting in the front row, just as he had promised. Craig came with his lovely new wife, Donna, and Claudia and Tom flew in from Reno. Ricci was there, but Gina couldn't make it. She was in China at the time with the Beach Boys, having recently married Carl Wilson. With almost all my family around me, the picture was complete. I couldn't have been happier.

John, on the other hand, normally so calm and collected, was a nervous wreck. He'd already asked the priest to make sure there was some vodka behind the scenes, so that he could have a drink to steady his nerves. Before the ceremony, the priest complied, but he provided brandy instead.

"Brandy?" John said. "I can't drink brandy. Everyone will smell it on my breath."

I didn't publicize the wedding. I invited just family and close friends. The only big star was Dad, sitting in the front row next to Mother, and that was the way I wanted it. He knew he couldn't miss it. He stayed just long enough for some photographs to be taken, and then he went back to his hospital bed. He wasn't at all well, and I was just so grateful that he was there. It wouldn't have been the same without him. When I found out what he had to go through to attend our wedding, I was overwhelmed.

DAD MISSED the days of Mountain Drive, a home he hadn't lived in for more than twenty years, and that had long ago been torn down. He often spoke of how happy we'd all been there. That house above all others, with its pool and tennis court, fabulous grounds, and movie-star neighbors, represented the time of his greatest success, when he could do no wrong and Hollywood was his. "I don't know why we ever left," he'd say wryly, forgetting that we didn't. He did.

Gone were the orange groves and the leafy, magical grounds we'd played in. Gone was the charming stone façade where Hollywood's brightest stars had regularly gathered. In its place was a modern concrete and steel building resembling nothing more than a shopping mall.

Sadly, he also had to give up his lifelong passion—golf. His back was getting worse, and his spirits were getting low. His health was deteriorating, and he was becoming reclusive. Hoping a change of scene might improve his spirits, he moved to 511 North Maple Drive, Beverly Hills.

"I don't want a place that's too big," he said. "It's too far to walk from the kitchen to the pool table with my bread-and-butter sandwich."

Jeanne redecorated the family house out in Palm Springs and decorated a room specially for Dad. John and I, Jeanne, and Gail, and various other family members would make the trek across the desert regularly for our traditional game night, and to partake of Jeanne's legendary hospitality. Dad only used the room she'd prepared for him once.

Uncle Frank, Dad's closest friend, would only see him a few times a year. He would phone Dad and say, "Whassamatter, your phone out of order?" They'd chat for a while and promise to meet for dinner.

Living so close to him, I'd often drop by. The door would open and I'd ask his housekeeper if he wanted visitors.

"Is he up?" I'd ask. "You can always tell me he's sleeping if he doesn't want to see anyone." Usually she'd say yes and I'd be ushered in.

Dad would be lying in bed, in his light blue cotton pajamas, watching television. Everything around him was incredibly neat, as always. A glass of water was on his nightstand next to the rosary he pressed between his fingers every night.

"Hi baby," he'd say, lowering the volume on the television and dragging his eyes from the screen. "Come and sit here." He'd pat the bed next to him and I'd climb up and sit with him for an hour, occasionally talking, but usually just sitting in silence, waiting for him to speak during the commercial breaks.

Then, as I was leaving, I'd kiss him and say, "Okay, Dad, I'll drop by again soon if that's okay, just to see how you're doing."

"Oh, okay," he'd say, "any time, baby. But if I'm sleeping, I'm sure you'll understand."

John and I brought him a huge basket of western movies one Christmas, but I don't think he ever watched them; it was too complicated for him even to put them into the VCR. He just liked to watch TV and flick channels with the remote control. His favorites were game shows where he could try to answer the questions. And he loved football, anything sporty, and, of course, golf.

He got a kick out of *Jeopardy!*, where they give the answers first and you have to figure out the question. One day I was in his kitchen, dropping off some pasta fagioli, when he yelled from the bedroom.

"Hey, Deana, quick, come and see!" he cried. I ran in and saw him smiling and pointing at the screen. The answer being given was "Craig, Claudia, Gail, Deana, Dino, Ricci, and Gina." More animated than I'd seen him in ages, his eyes huge behind his magnified spectacles, Dad coached the female contestant until she came up with the right question: "Who are Dean Martin's children?"

Dad would only get out of bed to play an occasional game of pool or, of course, to go out to dinner. He still ate at Da Vinci's during the week, with Jeanne joining him most Saturdays. On Sundays he would venture to the Hamburger Hamlet on Sunset. There he would sit in his red leather button tufted chair at his usual table and order a "setup" and a chicken pot pie. His cook, Connie, made him sandwiches or pasta for his lunch, and he didn't want for anything, but he was still smoking too much and not taking very good care of himself.

He even stopped using the sun bed, something he'd relied on all his life to keep him looking young and healthy. I'd never forgotten the day I visited him at Paramount studios years earlier, when he and I ran into Cary Grant. Dad turned to me and said, "You know what Cary Grant is without a tan?"

"No," I replied.

"An old man," he said.

Now that Dad's tan was gone, his once-glowing skin seemed to age. He seemed to be shrinking, the spark dimming in his eyes, and his speech was becoming slurred. I was watching him turn into my grandfather "Pop."

◆◆◆

A FEW weeks later, I appeared on the early-morning television show *Geraldo*, along with several other children of famous parents. Sitting next to me were the sons of Mickey Rooney and Jayne Mansfield. When it was my turn, Geraldo asked me how Dad was:

"Well, Deana, we've heard some reports about your Dad and they say he's not well. How is he?"

"I saw him just yesterday and he's good," I replied.

Geraldo surprised me by telling me there was a caller on the line. It was Dad.

"Hello, baby," he said, as I laughed, amazed that he was up so early. Geraldo asked him how he was, and he said he was fine, just not playing golf anymore.

"So what did you want to say to your daughter, Dean?" Geraldo asked.

"Tell her I love my baby. I love all my children," he said, his voice filling the studio. Wiping away the tears, it took me several minutes to recover. I discovered later that it was my dear John who had secretly arranged the whole thing with Dad. Sadly, this was the last time he did anything publicly.

◆◆◆

DAD AND JOHN got along fine. John was the only man who ever stood up to him on my behalf. For my birthday, John asked Dad to join us at Chasen's restaurant for dinner.

"Sure, that would be swell," Dad said.

But on the night of the dinner, Mort Viner rang our home. "I'm sorry, but Dean had another engagement he'd forgotten about. He won't be able to join you after all."

It fell to John to tell me the bad news. I was so upset I burst into tears. John was furious on my behalf, and he picked up the phone and called Dad. When he eventually got through, he spoke to him in a way no one ever did.

"Listen, Dean," he told him, "if you don't want to come to dinner, you call me up and tell me yourself, don't ask Mort to do your dirty work for you."

Dad professed ignorance. "What do you mean?" he asked.

"I mean if you're not coming tonight, then at least have the courtesy to call and tell me yourself."

"I don't know what you're talking about," Dad told him. "Of course I'm coming. You should know by now not to believe a single word Mort Viner tells you. I'm going to be there, it's my baby's birthday. What time do you want me to be ready?"

We arrived outside his house in a limo to pick him up, and he walked out of the door, right on time. We had a lovely dinner, where he was charming, gracious, and funny. Dropping him home again after coffee, I thanked him for coming.

"It was my pleasure, baby," he said, returning my kiss with affection. "I had fun."

I never discovered whether he'd ever really meant to cancel dinner that night. Even in old age, my father's intentions were a mystery to me. I know one thing for sure, and it made me very sad. Soon after that evening, he changed his personal telephone number and we had to go through the service to reach him.

◆◆◆

IN SEPTEMBER 1991, Dad performed his last live shows in Las Vegas. The critics described him as "gaunt" and said he appeared unwell. Dad was terribly tired, and found the daily schedule too grueling. Citing his poor health, he canceled his final engagements and never performed again. He was seventy-four years old, and in over forty-four years of performing in Las Vegas and Reno to capacity crowds, he'd only missed two shows—one when Pop died and one when he had the flu. That's what I call a pro.

"The good Lord gave me a talent," he once said, "and I'll use it until it runs out." I guess that day finally came. The golden age of Dean Martin was passing and, for me, the lights of Las Vegas would never burn as bright.

Not long afterward, he finally acceded to his doctor's advice, and he was admitted to Cedars-Sinai Hospital for further tests. A scan found his lungs riddled with tumors, and the doctors gave him months to live. Typically, Dad brushed their diagnosis aside, not even telling the family. It was left for the newspapers to find out and for us to read about it. Mort Viner was quoted as saying, "It's obvious that Dean has resigned himself to facing death."

He was tired all the time now, and he wanted to be left alone. He became almost completely deaf in his left ear, and always made sure people sat on his right. "Come and sit on this side of me, baby, I can hear you better," he'd say.

One evening around this time, Uncle Frank telephoned Dad and asked if he'd like to go to dinner. Frank was a night owl who, even at his age, liked to stay up late. Dad, however, liked to eat early and be in bed by ten. Tony Oppedisano—Frank's right-hand man "Tony O"—placed the call for Frank and told me years later how it went.

"Hey, Dag, want to get something to eat?"

"Sure. I'll meet you at seven at Da Vinci's."

"What?" Frank cried, "are we meeting for lunch?"

Dad and Frank, escorted by Tony O and Mort, met at Da Vinci's. The two old friends saw each other pretty regularly right up until the end, despite reports to the contrary, but this was the last time Frank and Dad were to see each other. Frank, who had senile dementia by then and couldn't be allowed out on his own for fear he might wander off, was almost deaf and wore a hearing aid. Dad, as mentioned, was deaf on the left.

Tony will never forget that night or the conversation that ensued. It went something like this.

"I saw Bullet Head last week, and he said to say hi," said Frank.

"What?" said Dad, straining to hear.

"I said I saw Don Rickles last week—you know, Bullet Head," Frank said, louder than before.

"What? Tony, tell Frank to speak up, I can't hear him."

Tony passed the message on, and Frank tried again to tell his story, this time almost shouting, without success.

In exasperation, Frank pulled the hearing aid from his ear and stuffed it into Dad's. "Tell him to put this on so he can hear me," he told Tony.

Dad fixed the hearing aid to his ear and Frank tried again.

"I saw Rickles last week, for God's sake," he yelled.

"What are you shouting for, pallie?" Dad asked. "I can hear you just fine."

"What?" said Frank, his hand cupped around his ear. "You'll have to speak up. I can't hear a damn word."

I STOPPED by to see Dad one night with some homemade pasta fagioli, but he told me, "I can't eat it, baby. I don't like the taste anymore." I was shocked. This was his favorite dish.

I noticed that the room wasn't full of its usual tobacco smoke. "Dad, did you stop smoking?" I asked.

"Yes," he replied. "I gave it up. I woke up one day and didn't smoke anymore."

"Great. How did you do that?"

"I don't know."

In all my life, I'd never known Dad without a cigarette in his hand. Although hugely relieved that he'd given it up, something I'd been urging him to do for years, I was taken aback by this sudden transformation.

His house was a shrine to the good times. Jeanne had decorated it with his numerous gold and platinum albums. There were dozens of photographs of him with various people over the years—

presidents, actors, and celebrities. As he used to joke, "I need a grand piano just to put my photos on." He also collected items from his favorite westerns and had a beautiful Remington bronze of a cowboy astride his horse. Jeanne had always been the one who collected art—original works by Ed Moses and Marc Chagall—and Dad would just enjoy looking at them.

"I like this one, Jeanne," he'd tell her. "The colors are real pretty." He'd always liked to be surrounded by pretty things— pretty women, pretty clothes. But when it came to art, he had absolutely no idea whether he was looking at a Monet or a Matisse. Jeanne provided most of the décor for each of his homes, and had some faux masters painted for him because he favored the classic style. He didn't care if they were originals. It didn't matter. He just liked the look of them.

He had a safe built into his bedroom closet wall, in which he kept large amounts of cash, but he didn't attempt to hide it behind a painting or in paneling. On the contrary, it just sat there for everyone to see, and written in marker pen right next to it was the combination. When I first saw it, I was dumbfounded.

"Dad!" I cried. "You can't write the combination next to the safe. That's crazy!"

"Why?" he asked, surprised.

"Because anyone could just come in, open it up, and take the money," I explained.

"Oh, Deana, baby," he said, laughing, "who'd want to steal from me?"

THE TABLOID PRESS, which had previously been reasonably respectful of a man considered a universal icon, smelled blood and ran a series of scare stories about Dad, each one chipping away at my heart. The paparazzi began to hound him whenever he went out. Knowing Dad's health was diminishing, and sensing a good story, they waited outside the restaurants he frequented to flash their cameras in his face as he was leaving for home. If any of us were with him, we'd do what we could to stop them, but Dad would usually intervene.

"No, leave it," he'd say. "Let them get what they want. It's part of the deal."

The resulting photographs in some of the trashy magazine were always awful. Dad would usually be wearing his beige Members Only jacket. Once he didn't have his teeth in, and he was caught so off guard that he looked startled, his eyes vacant. The headlines accompanying the photographs said things like, BELOVED DINO IS WASTING AWAY, or DEAN MARTIN'S TRAGIC LAST DAYS.

I hated to see those pictures, and I never bought the magazines they appeared in, but I couldn't help catching sight of them at the supermarket checkout or on a newsstand. One day, at a grocery checkout, I was emptying my shopping cart when the man in front of me started showing the checkout girl some photographs. He had a camera slung over his shoulder. I looked to see who he'd photographed, when I saw to my horror that it was Dad, looking worse than I'd seen him before. He was wearing his giant glasses, and the poor man looked so frail and unwell. He was emerging from the Hamburger Hamlet, and the photographer had caught it on film.

He had stacks of these glossy prints and was showing them around. Tapping him on the shoulder, I asked, "Can I see one of those?"

"It'll cost you," he said, grinning.

"No, sir," I replied, coldly. "It will cost you, because that man is my father."

Faltering, he peeled a couple of photos off and said, "Here, have some on the house."

My eyes filling with tears, I said, "Please, can't you just destroy these? He's an old man and he's not at all well."

"I'm sorry," he said, backing away. "I can't do that. These are worth good money to me." And with that, he disappeared through the automatic doors.

Twenty-One

I LAST SAW MY FATHER IN DECEMBER 1995, WHEN I popped in as usual to see how he was doing. He was seventy-eight years old and spent most of his days sleeping. Because of a chest infection, he had missed the annual Thanksgiving dinner a few weeks before and was taking a long time to recover.

"Is he awake?" I asked his nurse. She checked before coming back to show me in.

"Hi, Dad," I said cheerily as I walked in to his bedroom. "How you doing?"

"Oh, I'm okay," he said, his face gaunt as he pressed the mute button. The cook told me he'd hardly been eating and was no longer going out to dinner.

"Can I get you something?" I asked, concerned at how small he looked against his big white pillows.

"No, thanks, baby."

"Can I make you something to eat?"

"I'm not hungry." As he spoke, I was amazed at how much he looked like Pop.

"But you've got to eat something, Dad," I said enthusiastically, trying to cheer him up.

"I will, when I'm hungry." His answers were almost inaudible. I only stayed for about ten minutes, sensing that he wanted to sleep. Kissing him on the forehead, I told him I'd drop by again soon, and I would see him at Mom's Christmas party.

"I'll see how I feel," he said.

"But, Dad, you have to come." I reminded him. "You haven't missed one in years. You won't have to chitchat. It'll be fun. I'll see you there, okay? I love you."

"I love you too, baby," he replied, slumping back, staring at the television.

On the afternoon of Christmas Eve, Dad took a call from Frank Sinatra, placed for him by his friend, Tony O. Tony told me later that Frank spoke to Dad, laughed a lot, and then signed off with, "Goodbye, Dag."

"I asked Frank why he was laughing," Tony told me. "Frank smiled and said, 'That cuckoo bastard is still telling jokes. Dean asked me, "What did one casket say to the other casket?" I told him "I dunno." He said, "Is that you coffin?" He's sick and he's still making wisecracks. I love him.'"

I wasn't unduly alarmed when Dad didn't make an appearance that evening at Mother's party. With all the preparations for the holiday season, I did not have a chance to drop in and see him that day. I was kept up to date by Mom and Mort and knew that he was not feeling or looking well at all.

"Well, should I go over and see him?" I asked Mort.

"No, he's fine," he replied. "He has plenty of people there to take care of him. He just wants to have a quiet few days. You know your dad."

True to form, Mother hosted a fabulous party, with a legion of waiters, bartenders, and a hip three-piece band. The backyard was tented and transformed into a magical Christmas wonderland, with three-tiered centerpieces and twinkling lights overhead. The room came alive with a symphony of candlelight dancing on tables filled with crystal, silver, and china. The sounds and smells of Christmas engulfed you. The scene was set for the kingdom of Hollywood and the royals were about to arrive: Angie Dickinson, Shirley MacLaine, Tony Curtis, Rosemary Clooney, Bob Newhart, Janet Leigh, Lew Wasserman, Don Rickles, George Schlatter, Dick Martin, and a cast of other legends whom Dad and Jeanne had known forever.

It was a wonderful evening, filled with love and laughter. Jeanne's Christmas parties are always memorable. The previous year, Oliver Stone, the director, attended. He was a huge fan of Dad's and excited to meet him. Dad regaled him with stories that kept Oliver laughing. I have always been amazed at how people turned into little kids in my father's company. One memorable year, I had the opportunity to sing Christmas carols with Rosemary Clooney. Among others, we sang her song "Have Yourself a Merry Little Christmas." That was definitely a moment to savor.

John and I stayed late with Mom, enjoying a nightcap and reminiscing of Christmas parties past.

"You know, it's not like your father to miss my Christmas Eve party," she told us, her sadness evident.

It was true. Dad's absence was keenly felt. I looked at my watch, and to my surprise, it was nearly 4:00 a.m. We kissed Mom good night and drove home.

♦♦♦

ON CHRISTMAS DAY, I was awakened early by a telephone call. It was our son, Mickey. Answering, I wished him a merry Christmas.

"You haven't heard?" I heard him say. "You haven't had a call?"

"What?" I asked, confused. "Heard what?"

"Pop's dead," he said. "He died at three-fifteen this morning. I'm so sorry, Mom, but I just heard it on television."

I can't remember much about the next few moments, but I do remember sitting up in bed, staring into space, the telephone receiver dropped into my lap, and Mickey's voice somewhere, distantly calling my name.

The next call was from Mort Viner a few minutes later, confirming Mickey's bombshell. Dad passed away at three-fifteen in the morning, Christmas Day. His nurse heard him coughing and checked on him, and then she went back to sleep. The happiest of family occasions now holds bittersweet memories for all of us.

John turned on the television and I sat, cradled in his arms, watching the news bulletins informing the world that Dean Martin was gone. Old footage of Dad was played and replayed—onstage in his tuxedo with Frank and Sammy at The Sands; as a drunken sheriff in *Rio Bravo;* the dapper ex-soldier in *Ocean's Eleven;* impossibly handsome alongside beautiful Jeanne arriving at some glittering premiere or outside 601 Mountain Drive, his seven children at his feet. In almost every frame he stared straight into the camera, a cigarette in one hand, and smiled that sexy, sweet smile, his eyes twinkling.

The phone didn't stop ringing for weeks. Everyone who knew me wanted to call and express their condolences. In the end, I couldn't bear to speak to anyone else. I lay on the bed, my heart breaking, as John took their calls.

The press all rushed to see Jeanne, who was still Mrs. Dean Martin to everyone in Hollywood. She stood on the steps of her house in sunglasses, and she spoke of the man she'd never stopped loving.

I sat and watched, as she told the reporters, "I was with my husband at the end. And I told him, 'Dean, just let go, let go, let God.' I think he understood." Her quote was repeated on every news item and in every newspaper thereafter.

In her mind, I know she wanted to have been there. In her heart, she probably was.

Mort arranged the funeral, which was by invitation only and booked for seven in the evening of December 28 at a small chapel at Pearce Brothers in Westwood. The vaulted room, hung with crystal chandeliers, had first been used for Marilyn Monroe's funeral. It was to be a private service and the press was excluded. Dad would have hated any fuss.

What he would have liked, however, is what the city of Las Vegas did for him. Paying him the ultimate tribute, they turned off the lights on the famous Las Vegas Strip for one minute at seven o'clock p.m. It was a parting toast to the immortal Dean Martin, something the city had done only once before, for Dad's friend Sammy Davis Jr. People lined the streets to watch such an extraordinary sight. Many were crying; others just wanted to pay their respects. The only lights twinkling were the candles lit by his adoring fans. Cars stopped, private planes and commercial jets slowed overhead to show their passengers the sight, and Dad's fans remained silent throughout the sixty seconds it took for the town he so loved to demonstrate its deep affection.

The press, of course, refused to be excluded from such an event as Dean Martin's funeral and erected scaffolding and put up stepladders to peer over a wall and into the chapel with their telephoto lenses. The flashes illuminated the place for several minutes at a time. Inside the chapel, a large photograph of Dad stood at the front, surrounded by two huge floral tributes, one of them depicting the Italian flag in red, green, and white. Mother and Dad's six children sat in the front row with their spouses. Sasha sat behind us. Cathy, her mother, didn't come. I sat staring at the photograph of Dad's smiling face and listened to some of his songs being played distantly in the background.

Rosemary Clooney was to open the service with a song, accompanied by the inimitable Peter Matz. Gail and I spotted Rosemary sitting to one side, waiting for her moment, and we walked over to say hello and to invite her to sit with us.

"I can't," she said, visibly trembling. "I can't face anyone right now. I loved your father very much. I'm just going to sit here until I'm on." When her cue came, she stepped up to the microphone and gave what I believe was the most poignant rendition of "Everybody Loves Somebody Sometime" ever done. It was one of her greatest performances. Dad would have been so proud.

The first person to speak was Shirley MacLaine, who'd just produced the latest of her many books about her strong beliefs in an afterlife. Without flinching, she stood up, took her place on the podium, and said, "Well, the last time I spoke to Dean . . ." she paused, "was about an hour ago and he said everything is fine." Everybody broke into much-needed laughter. She spoke of Dad, whom she had loved and worked with for more than forty years.

Greg Garrison, the producer of *The Dean Martin Show*, spoke lovingly of his years working with Dad. He seemed very nervous.

Jerry Lewis was the next to speak, and as he pulled out his folded speech from his pocket, Jeanne, sitting in the front row, said, "Keep it light, Jerry."

He looked down at her, shook his head sadly, and replied, "I'm sorry, Jeanne, I can't. This is not the time to keep it light." He spoke of the partner he'd known and loved since he was a nineteen-year-old solo comic, and of Dad's "exquisite tranquillity despite a great inner turbulence." He added, "Rest well, Dino, and don't forget to short-sheet my bed when I get there." By the time he'd finished, there wasn't a dry eye in the chapel, including his. It was an incredibly moving tribute from a man who'd loved Dad more than any other.

After delivering his eulogy, Jerry came to each of the family in turn to hug and kiss us. When he hugged John, his knees buckled. Holding him up, John asked, "Are you okay?" and he replied tearfully, "No, no, I'm not. I just lost my partner and my best friend."

Uncle Frank didn't attend the funeral because of ill health and the fact that he was completely overwhelmed. He issued a statement that said, "Dean has been like the air I breathe—always there, always close by. He was my brother, not by blood, but by choice. Our friendship has traveled down many roads over the years, and there will always be a special place in my heart and soul for Dean."

His daughter Nancy and his wife Barbara both came, but sat at separate ends of the chapel. My friend Tina didn't come. "I couldn't face it," she told me. "It's too emotional for me." Other guests included Tony Danza, Bob Newhart, Dom DeLuise, Janet Leigh, Tony Curtis, and Angie Dickinson.

After the service, Dad was interred in a crypt in the wall of the Sanctuary of Love at Westwood Village Memorial Park. Dressed in his best tuxedo, he was placed not far from his parents, Guy and Angela, and a few yards away from his beloved Marilyn Monroe.

Jeanne was asked what should be written on his plaque, and she couldn't decide. Nobody could. Suddenly I spoke up. "I know what it should read. *Everybody loves somebody sometime.*"

"Perfect," Jeanne replied. So his plaque reads, DEAN MARTIN, JUNE 7, 1917–DECEMBER 25, 1995. EVERYBODY LOVES SOMEBODY SOMETIME.

Dedicated fans from around the world regard it as a place of pilgrimage. They come and sit with Dad, place flowers or coins beneath his tomb, and often add a martini glass with a little note rolled up inside.

Dad may be gone, but his spirit remains. He's always with me. I walk into a store and I hear him singing, or I turn on the television and he'll be there in one of his movies. At first it would upset me, but now I see it as a good omen, a way of his reaching out to me to tell me he still loves his little Deana.

A COUPLE of weeks after Dad's funeral, I had a mass celebrated for him at the Church of the Good Shepherd. It was a chance for all those friends and family who hadn't been able to attend the funeral to pay their respects and say a few words. Afterward we adjourned to the sacristy and ate cookies, drank coffee, and cried together. It was intensely moving, and a chance for me to say good-bye to Dad surrounded by the people we loved most.

As a family, we were sent letters and mass cards from fans around the world when Dad died. Mort and the staff in his office divided them among us, so that we each had a few of our own to look through. There were people who'd never known Dad personally who spoke of their abiding affection. Several who had met him told us how meeting him had affected them. One man who'd once worked for him wrote, "Humor was a quality of his that he used to convey something more fundamental: communicating to those around him a sense of their worth. There were no 'little people' as far as Dean Martin was concerned."

Another fan told a story of how he and his children were in a pizzeria out by Malibu one night when his daughter asked for some coins to play video games. "I said I was sorry but I hadn't brought along any cash," he wrote. "Then I suddenly heard someone behind me saying, 'I've got some.' Sitting at a table nearby was Dean Martin, who had undoubtedly seen the disappointment on my daughter's face. Tanned, casually but elegantly dressed, he reached into his pocket and produced a fistful of change. 'Take it all,' he offered with a shrug, as if to say, hey, it's no big deal.

"Later, on the drive home, my daughter asked, 'Who was the nice man?'

" 'That was Dean Martin,' I said. 'He's a terrific entertainer.'

" 'Do you know him?' she asked.

" 'Everybody knows Dino,' I replied."

ONE NIGHT, about a month after Dad's death, I hit a real low. I couldn't believe he was gone, I couldn't imagine life without the man who had dominated my life and my heart for so long.

"I know what will make you feel better," John said, reaching for the pile of mass cards. "Pick a card, any card." He fanned them out in his hand like a deck of playing cards and, sighing, I reached for one and read it.

The card was from a couple in the Bronx, New York, who said they'd been lifelong fans of Dad's and that although they'd never met him, they just wanted to send their condolences. Their names were Carmine and Alice Materasso. John called their church and got their address, and then he called information and found their number. Before I could stop him, he was dialing it.

"Is this Alice Materasso?" he asked, when the phone was picked up. "My name is John Griffeth and I'm calling on behalf of Dean Martin's daughter Deana. She'd like to speak with you."

There was a short silence. "Who put you up to this?" the New York–accented voice asked suspiciously. "What kind of trick is this?"

"It's no trick, Alice," John said. Carmine picked up the extension and yelled, "What do you want?"

"I don't want anything," John explained. "You sent a mass card when Dean Martin passed away, and his daughter simply wants to say 'thank you.' Wait a moment, let me read the card you sent." John proceeded to read the words Carmine and his wife had written. When he'd finished, he said, "We don't wish to bother you, but would you like to speak to Deana Martin?"

"Yes," came the sheepish reply. Then he handed the telephone over to me.

Drying my eyes, I smiled and spoke into the receiver. "Hello, this is Deana Martin," I said.

The reception I got on the other end of the phone couldn't have been warmer or more surprised. Alice shrieked at me down the line that she couldn't believe she was actually talking to Dean Martin's daughter. She told me she had a shrine to Dad in her living room, with his photograph and a candle burning next to it.

"Now, I thought you looked lovely in the photograph of your sister's wedding," she told me, "but I didn't like it when you cut your hair so short." She seemed to know everything about my family, and she regularly clipped articles about us from the newspapers. We talked for almost thirty minutes, and I promised to visit them next time we were in New York.

I put down the phone feeling completely rejuvenated. Dad might have gone, but his memory and the overwhelming love for him lived on. As his daughter, I suddenly realized, I could be instrumental in keeping his memory alive.

Twenty-Two

DAD WAS GREAT AT MAKING MONEY, AND PROVIDING for his family. He'd worked hard his entire life and made enough money to keep all of his children and wives looked after for the rest of their lives.

He was never terribly interested in the business side of things, and left that to other people. His policy was "Tell me where to stand, what to do, and I'll do it." That was him through and through, and what he did, he did very well. He never wanted to do anything else.

He had conquered the entertainment industry, but he knew his limitations and left financial matters to the professionals.

He joked, "I'm so bad at business that Michael Douglas brought me the script for *One Flew Over the Cuckoo's Nest* to invest in, and I turned him down four times." The truth was that he made some very clever investments in real estate and stocks that would stand the test of time. He had more than enough for his own lifetime, and he'd left us plenty.

"I only do this for you kids" was his most commonly repeated expression. "As long as the kids are taken care of, nothing else matters."

At various times toward the end of his life, his personal wealth was estimated at well in excess of $150 million. His estate included vast tracts of land in the San Fernando Valley, and property from Ventura County to Beverly Hills. He owned the Solvang Ranch in Santa Barbara, bought from his friend Jimmy Stewart, rental property in San Francisco, and was the largest shareholder of RCA stock. He also owned a share of a lemon growers' cooperative, and several hundred acres of land in places as far afield as Camarillo and Tarzana.

Toward the end he told me, "I've provided well for you all, Deana. The rights to *The Dean Martin Show* are for you kids. There's $33 million there alone, and that gets split equally among you when I'm gone."

He'd repeatedly led each of us to believe that, after Jeanne and Cathy had been taken care of, his estate would be split seven ways, among his seven children (including Sasha) or, if they were deceased, their offspring. Ellie, his accountant and a longtime friend, confided that to me a few years before Dad passed away. The trouble with Dad was that he was far too trusting.

Ricci tells a story that in the late seventies, when Dad was approaching sixty, he announced that he was going to buy himself a new car. "He called his business office to check out some detail, and one of the accountants in the office told him, 'But Dean, you've only got $250 in the bank.' Dad was stunned. While he had a lot of money on paper—real estate, stocks, bonds, and notes—his liquid funds had disappeared. Dad was always very trusting of his business people, and this time that trust had been taken advantage of, because there had been serious mishandling of his funds."

By the time the final details of Dad's estate had been worked out and inheritance taxes paid, Dad left in excess of $23 million. Where the rest of it went, we may never know. The house he "owned" on Loma Vista, the one we'd all gone back to after Dean Paul's funeral, wasn't his. Mort told us, "Oh, no, I owned that. I just let your Dad live in it. If people thought Dean Martin wanted to buy their house, they'd charge double, so I'd buy it instead. It was done like that for tax reasons. Your Dad knew all about it."

Dad once asked me, "Oh Deana, baby, who'd want to steal from me?"

Well, Dad, the answer is everyone.

◆◆◆

DAD'S FINAL will was written and signed eleven days before he died. The original will it replaced disappeared and has never been found. Mort Viner, Dad's executor, arrived at his house with the new will just before Christmas, and asked one of Dad's security guards to witness it. The guard, an ex-cop, refused. He later told Jeanne that he thought Dad, who was in bed and dying, had diminished mental capacity at the time. Mort had to get someone else to sign, a complete stranger who scribbled his name along with Dad's housekeeper and an on-call nurse. A specific clause written into the will said that if any of the beneficiaries ever challenged it, they'd be cut out of the estate without recourse.

The first I knew of how much had been left and exactly to whom was when Gail called me when we were on holiday in Aspen, where John had taken me skiing to cheer me up.

"I've just received the papers from the lawyers," Gail said, "and you're not going to like this."

"What?" I asked, my heart racing.

"The percentages are quite different from what Dad said he wanted."

"They are?"

Gail went on to explain that, somehow, all the percentages were suddenly changed. They were no longer evenly split among the children; some received a great deal more than others.

"But how could this have happened?" I asked her. "Why the sudden change?"

My eyes filling with tears, I quelled the feelings of hurt. I was unable to speak.

A big part of me knows that to inherit anything from a parent is a gift. To come into as much as we did from Dad's estate was truly wonderful and meant that none of us ever had to work again. His wish to look after us all once he was gone was certainly fulfilled. Every day I count my blessings and thank Dad for the great gift he gave me, the gift of choice, of freedom, and of the ability to live my life the way I want.

However, a part of me wishes that the division of his estate would have been equal, the way Dad had said it would be. I can't imagine him wanting to make such radical changes a few days before he died. I don't believe for one minute that he truly understood what was going on. The sad part is, I'll never know for sure.

◆◆◆

FAR BETTER than any money or income we received from Dad's estate were the personal belongings that meant so much to each of us. I was delighted to be given some of his silk pocket squares and trademark cashmere sweaters, which he wore playing golf and which still smell like him. I keep them in my closet, and sometimes I slip one on and spend a day in it, just to feel close to him again.

Best of all, John bought me the red button tufted leather chair Dad always sat in at the Hamburger Hamlet on Sundays. The owners agreed that it wouldn't be right for anyone else to have it, and it sits in a special place in my living room. It was one of the most thoughtful gifts anyone ever bought me, and it always makes me smile.

Dad's precious golf bag and clubs came up for sale on the eBay Internet auction site one day, and I was staggered. Sasha was selling them. Mort told me she'd gone to the Riviera Country Club after Dad died, and she emptied his locker. The bag and clubs brought in over $10,000. Gail was so cross she sent Sasha a scathing letter. I was too upset even to communicate my anger. Those sorts of belongings should have remained in the family and been preserved for all time. There has long been talk of setting up a Dean Martin Museum, and they would have been perfect for that.

The gold signet ring with a large emerald-cut diamond that Frank gave Dad, and that he wore on the pinkie finger of his right hand, was left to Ricci. Some years later I heard through the grapevine that it was being put up for auction at Sotheby's. Ricci took out full-page ads in the auction brochure, with a photo of Dad wearing it at The Sands. I would have loved the ring to go to our son Mickey, but Ricci said it was sad, but he was unfortunately in a position where he needed the money and it could sell for up to a hundred thousand dollars.

John and I went to the auction with a view to buying it, but in the end I couldn't bid. I sat there with the paddle in my hand, my heart breaking, as an integral part of my father's life was sold to a private buyer for $17,000.

When Mort Viner died, we finally discovered who that private bidder was. It was him. Before he passed away, he told a friend, "You'll know when the time is right to give this back to Ricci." I'm happy to say, thanks to Mort, the ring is back in our family and proudly worn by Ricci.

◆◆◆

IT WAS Thanksgiving at Gail's. Her home was decorated like something out of *House and Garden*, with pumpkins spilling over with flowers, a huge turkey, and all the trimmings. We ate and drank, laughed and chatted, and celebrated.

Sitting around the table were about twenty people, including friends of Gail's daughters, Cappy and Liza. One was a beautiful blonde from Chile named Paola who was talking with John. Eyeing them across the table, I wondered what my husband was up to. Walking over to where they were sitting, I heard him ask her, "Do you have a boyfriend? Are you dating anyone?"

"No," she replied.

"And you'd be asking her this why?" I inquired.

John beamed up at me and winked. "She'd be perfect for Mickey," he said. So we invited her to join us for Christmas dinner at our house.

He was right. Paola and Mickey fell in love, and within a year she and our son were making plans to get married. Mickey was attending UCLA as a history major, and he promised us that he would not get married until after he graduated. He graduated June 16, 1996, at 12:00 noon. At 5:00 p.m. on that same day, Mickey and Paola were married. It was the happiest family celebration since Dad had died.

The ceremony took place in the garden of his uncle's Beverly Hills home. Terry walked Paola down the aisle, and John was Mickey's best man. The whole family was gathered around—Craig, Claudia, Gail, Jeanne, Ricci, and Gina were all there for Mickey, to celebrate Mickey and Paola's happiness. Not only was he getting married to a wonderful lady, but he was the second Martin to graduate from college. It was a beautiful day, and we were immensely proud.

My baby boy, my little Mickey, born twenty-six years earlier, was standing in front of a justice of the peace, exchanging vows. I would always be his mother, but now there was another woman in his life.

♦♦♦

UNCLE FRANK had been ill for some time. There were numerous false alarms. Television entertainment shows would call to ask me what I knew of his condition. "Nothing," I said. "You'll have to contact the family for any information." Frightened to know the answer myself, I'd call Tina and see if something was wrong.

"No, he's still with us," she'd tell me. "Don't worry. He just had a bad day. I'll call you when the time comes, I promise. You'll be one of the first to know."

Poor Tina was having to deal with not only the physical and mental deterioration of her father, but difficult events within her own family. Amid painful infighting, Frank's wife, Barbara, was selling many of his personal possessions, family heirlooms. I know Tina and Nancy were terribly hurt and upset. Sometimes Frank knew what was going on and would try to save some things for his kids. Tony O was Frank's Mack Gray and had been with him for years. Tony told me Frank would give him something on the quiet, like a lighter or a set of gold cuff links, and say, "Make sure Tina gets this, will you?"

"Consider it done," Tony O would reply.

On November 26, 1996, The Sands Hotel, which had hosted the golden age of the Rat Pack was finally demolished to make way for the Venetian Hotel and Casino. Jack Entratter, The Sands's manager who'd given Dad and Jerry one of their first breaks in New York's Copacabana, had died of a brain hemorrhage at the age of fifty-seven. As the very fabric of the historic Sands returned to dust, it was truly the end of an era. Fans scrabbled for a piece of the legendary hotel, once it was leveled. In its archives were stacks of some of the best black-and-white glossy photos of the Rat Pack in their finest years. They were donated to the University of Nevada. Uncle Frank, the only surviving member of the triad, was too ill to attend the presentation ceremony. I'm certain he would have loved every minute of it.

In May 1998, Uncle Frank passed away, at eighty-two. Tina phoned that day to tell me the news and asked me to pass on the information. His death was devastating for many, just like Dad's was. Frank, "The Voice," was the consummate entertainer, and an Oscar-winning actor. There was no one quite like him in the world. I will always treasure my relationship with him and the times we spent together.

"If you ever need anything, Deana," he told me, "you just call me and I'll make it happen." I knew he would.

Tina telephoned to tell me about the funeral arrangements.

"I'm sorry, but because of security and the number of people going, I won't be able to messenger over your tickets. You will have to pick them up at Ticketmaster on Sunset."

"Excuse me?"

"Deana, it's become so overwhelming. So many people want to come and pay their respects, we've had to issue tickets for the funeral," she explained. "Take some ID," she added.

Security insisted that everybody had to go to Ticketmaster to pick up their tickets in person, even Nancy Reagan. There was a line. When I reached the window I was handed two envelopes with two tickets in each, one blue and one lavender, one for the Vigil Mass on Tuesday evening, and one for the Funeral Mass on Wednesday. Unless you had your ticket, you would not get in.

In the church I saw many familiar faces, such as Kirk Douglas, who was an honorary pallbearer. The official pallbearers were Steve Lawrence, Don Rickles, Sonny Golden, Eliot Weisman, Tony Oppedisano, Frank Sinatra Jr., Bobby Marx, and Tom Dreesen. Tom Dreesen was also the host of the evening. The tone was light-hearted, which was comforting. As we were leaving, I saw Liza Minnelli on the steps, someone I hadn't seen in years. I went up to her and peered into her tear-streaked face.

"Liza, it's Deana," I said.

"Oh, Deana, Deana!" she said, hugging me to her, crying and stroking my hair. "My lovely Deana, my lifelong friend!" I pulled myself together and smiled. Liza turned to a man at her side, someone I didn't recognize, and introduced us. "This is Dena," she told her friend. "Dena Kaye."

"Martin," I corrected her. "Deana Martin. Dena Kaye is Danny's daughter. I'm Dean's daughter."

"Deana, oh, Deana!" Liza started again, embracing me once more. "Your father! Oh my God, I loved your father! My dearest friend. This is Deana, Deana Martin." She turned to her companion

Twenty-Three

IN NOVEMBER 1999, I WAS INVITED TO NEW YORK TO accept the Broadcasting & Cable Hall of Fame Award that was to be given to my father. I'd told Mort Viner that I wanted to become an ambassador for Dean Martin and would gladly attend any ceremony or service in his name. I was honored to accept this award and proud to be instrumental in keeping my father's heritage alive.

John and I flew into JFK airport in New York and took a car into town. We had a day and a night to prepare for the gala at the Marriott Marquis Hotel and the Hall of Fame induction awards. On the way into town, John suddenly turned to me and said, "I just saw a sign to the Bronx. Why don't we call Carmine and Alice

Materasso and see if they are in town. I'm certain they would be delighted."

Smiling, I agreed.

John was right. The Materassos couldn't have been more pleased. They lived in an apartment building near the Long Island Expressway. As the limo pulled up outside, Carmine was waiting to greet us. He escorted us inside and when Alice opened the door, I was transported straight back to my childhood—with the aromas of pasta and fresh prosciutto and Italian cheese. Alice came toward me with tears streaming down her face and embraced me.

"I can't believe it," she cried. "I can't believe you're here. Come, come and sit down. Eat something." She showed me inside, led me to her sweet shrine to Dad, with its candle permanently lit, and offered us a glass of wine. She insisted that we have something to eat, and it was delicious. Mostly the two of them just kept staring at me, telling me how much I looked like Dad.

Carmine told me, "You don't know how hard it was for me to persuade Alice not to have a hundred people here to meet you. We have to take some pictures or none of our friends will believe us." So we posed for photos with them and spent some time in their company, telling them why we were in New York, and soaked up the love they felt for Dad. It made me realize, once again, how much his legacy lived on.

Just as we were about to leave for our hotel, John had an idea. "Hey, Carmine, do you have a tuxedo?" he asked. To Alice, he said, "Do you have an evening gown?"

Both of them shook their heads, but assured us they could get the garments. Without hesitating, John invited them to the black-tie awards ceremony the following evening as our guests. We had also invited Rose and Rich Angelica from Steubenville, where Rose is the director of the annual Dean Martin Festival.

It was an incredible night. Rose and Rich, whom we'd never met before, were just as warm and devoted to Dad as Carmine and Alice. The Hall of Fame compiled a wonderful video montage of Dad's career and showed it to an appreciative audience. Afterward, as I took the stage to make my speech and accept the award, I felt surrounded by love and affection. A little shaken by the fact that the announcer said just about everything I was going to say about Dad, I thanked them and told them how much Dad would have enjoyed the evening.

Finally, I concluded, "I would like to end my acceptance of this award as I feel Dad would have. I then sang the line "Everybody Loves Somebody Sometime." As the audience rose to its feet for a standing ovation, with Carmine and Alice and Rose and Rich making the most noise, I leaned into the microphone, just the way Dad used to, and said, "Keep those cards and letters coming in, folks!"

◆◆◆

MY SISTER Claudia was a remarkable woman. Dad had always adored her. She bought him that Saint Christopher medal as a young child, and he never took it off to the day he died.

Claudia was gorgeous. She'd worn the most makeup and the tightest slacks, and had dated the most boys. She was the first to break into films, and with her Sophia Loren looks, she'd broken quite a few hearts. She filled her life with love and laughter.

Claudia loved her husband Tom Brown and was brokenhearted when he passed away. A few years later, fate smiled on her and she met a wonderful man named Jim Roberts, who simply adored her. Claudia and Jim married in 1996 and ran a printing company in Reno. They were together for just a few years before she became ill.

We were at our grandson Hunter's first birthday party in January 1998, when Gail told us the news: "Claudia's found a lump and she's having a biopsy today." She and Claudia were very close and spoke to each other almost every day.

Shocked, I rang Claudia that night to offer my support. The doctors quickly discovered that she had left it unchecked for too long, and the cancer was already in her bones. Her back had been hurting her for some time, but she'd never made the connection. There was little they could do. The high-dosage chemotherapy they gave her almost killed her.

John and I went to see her in the hospital and she was happy to see us. We sat with her, doing crossword puzzles, while her lovely husband, Jim, investigated every possible alternative and holistic treatment under the sun. Between chemo treatments, she came to L.A. to stay with Gail. She had one of her legendary luau parties, just like Mother's, with tiki torches and cocktails. I really loved my big sister and her wry sense of humor. She never missed an opportunity to rib me. Seeing how the dampness had made my hair go all funny and curly, she said: "Deana, your hair looks like Harpo Marx's," and adjusting her wig, she said, "Mine, on the other hand, looks fabulous."

It was a bittersweet day.

One day early in 2000, Jim called and said, "I think you should come to Reno."

Jeanne, the woman who Claudia called Mother since the age of eleven, said she just couldn't go: "I couldn't possibly see her like that." As if any of us wanted to. It was a very painful and stressful time. I was furious with Jeanne at the time, at what appeared to be her selfishness. I have since come to understand that each of us responds differently to sickness and death, and every response is equally valid.

♦♦♦

CLAUDIA LIVED just long enough to see her granddaughter Sophia born. Jesse, her daughter by Kiel, gave birth that January. Claudia died on February 16, 2001. She was fifty-six years old. The funeral was held at Our Mother of Sorrow Cemetery Chapel in Reno. It was raining and cold. The cloud cover was so low that our flight was nearly canceled. It obstructed the mountains and covered the tops of the streetlights. In all directions, the sky was overcast, with sleet and driving rain.

Inside the chapel it was very beautiful and calm, with stained-glass windows and a carved wooden altar. Claudia was in a white casket adorned with lilies and roses, her favorite flowers.

The priest gave a touching eulogy and then asked if anyone would like to speak. Nearly everyone was weeping so hard that they couldn't say anything. I sat there and listened to the silence, and was suddenly compelled to stand up and say something. With tears streaming down my face, I stepped to the altar and said, "I'd like everyone to know what a wonderful sister and woman Claudia was, and how much we love her. I'm sure Claudia is looking down on us today, and I want her to know how much I truly love her and that we're all here for her today."

It was early afternoon, but the skies outside the chapel were black. As I spoke those words, a tiny opening filtered through the clouds, and a thin beam of sunlight shone through the window and onto the white coffin, completely illuminating the room. People gasped audibly.

"Did you see that? Oh my God," I heard someone say.

The minute I stopped speaking and returned to my seat, the light vanished. Everything seemed suddenly very dark. Music filled the church right on cue, and the voice of Dad soared soothingly out of the speakers. It was as if he were there, singing "Return to Me," one of Claudia's favorite songs.

I knew, there and then, that he and Claudia had been reunited and were together for eternity.

IN THE summer of 2002, when I was looking through some of Dad's old photographs and newspaper clippings, I came across a file relating to his ten years with Martin & Lewis. There was Dad, eyebrow arched, the epitome of suave sophistication, and alongside him, looking devotedly into his eyes, was the zany Jerry. They were the number-one comedy team of all time, outshining Abbott and Costello and Laurel and Hardy in box-office receipts and television ratings.

Before things changed, Dad and Jerry had enjoyed the finest moments in comic history together, laughing spontaneously until their sides ached, allowing everyone watching them to laugh along. In many ways, Dad's time with Jerry was his happiest. He knew he'd made it by then. He had a wife and four kids, and was well on his way to becoming the big Hollywood star he'd always dreamed about.

I decided to get in touch with Jerry. He had spoken so movingly at Dad's funeral that I felt I wanted to keep in touch with him.

"He's seventy-six now," I told John, "and he's not going to be around forever. I don't want to hear that he's gone and not have had a chance to sit down and talk with him about Dad."

So I called Jerry and asked if I he would like to get together and chat. He was delighted and invited John and me to his yacht, which was docked in San Diego harbor. We were overwhelmed by the warm reception given us by Jerry and his wife, Samantha. Within a few minutes of our arrival, tears were streaming down Jerry's cheeks as he hugged me and said, "Gee, you sure look like your Dad. I look at you and I see my partner. It's so wonderful."

Jerry has had to endure some horrific medical and physical problems, but is a natural survivor. He has an indomitable spirit and an infectious love of life. He suffers from agonizing back pain that is eased by a hi-tech device that administers an electrical charge. He referred to Dad as his "partner" and spoke openly of his deep love for him. He showed us the book he was writing on the Martin & Lewis years, some three thousand manuscript pages already, and he was only in the early part of their career.

Jerry looked very different from the man whose photographs I had been studying so closely just a few days before. Gone was the child's voice he put on for the act, gone were the crazy physical antics that had him jumping wildly around the stage. Instead, that agility and dexterity could be seen only in the mind of this brilliant man I am proud to call my friend.

Devoted to his wife, he played us a CD he'd recorded for her, in which he sang "Time After Time." "I love this woman," he told us.

"She saved my life and gave me my daughter Dani. I try to do something special for her every week. The CD was this week's gift."

The CD began with Jerry singing a capella, then a piano came in softly in the background. "Oh, I love this song," I told him. Before I knew it, I was singing along, too, harmonizing with his recording.

"That's beautiful, Deana, do you sing professionally?" Jerry asked.

"I used to, years ago," I laughed. "We should record this as a duet, and then it would be Martin & Lewis together again."

"Deana!" Jerry cried, as his face lit up. "What an idea! We could sing this together on my next telethon. It would be a show-stopper! Will you do it?"

Seeing the enthusiasm in his eyes, I knew I had no choice.

"Sure," I said, trying not to panic at the thought of singing live with Jerry Lewis in front of millions of television viewers.

He gave me the CD so that I could practice at home, and we agreed to sing it just the way it was on the disc, with me doing the harmony. It was a little high for me, but with help from my voice coach, Bob Garrett, I got there.

Jerry couldn't have been more excited. He immediately picked up the phone and called everyone from the show to tell them the news. "Deana Martin and Jerry Lewis are going to be singing a duet!" he announced. "It'll be Martin & Lewis together again!" No pressure, I thought.

I arrived for the telethon rehearsal with trepidation. It had been years since I'd last performed live. Jerry was a complete professional. He put me at ease. We laughed together, we cried together, and we sang together. We had a sensational few hours. When it came time to work, we took our positions and he started to sing. I'd studied the CD and was singing along just as we agreed.

Suddenly, Jerry stopped and waved his hand at the pianist. "No, no, no," he said. "Let's change this. I'm going to take it down a key. Deana, sweetheart, I don't want you doing the harmony here. I want you to sing the melody. I'm thinking we'll have a camera there, another one over there, coming over my shoulder for your face, and it would be better if I sang a line and then you sang a line, and then we did one line together in harmony, with the full camera coming in this way, and then we could fade in at the end with a picture of your Dad. That's it."

The producer, who was clearly used to this way of working, scribbled down some notes. For a moment I knew what it was like to be Dad, being directed and redirected by this creative genius and told exactly where to stand and what to sing and how to sing it.

Smiling, I said, "Okay, so what exactly am I supposed to do?"

Jerry began again. "Okay, let's run through that," he said in the same methodical way. Then he changed the key again. I could feel a headache coming on.

I worked very hard over the next two days to get that song right. I asked Colin Freeman, Lorna Luft's husband and musical director, to transpose the key for me. Tony O came by and with his help, I rehearsed and rehearsed until I hoped I had it right.

The telethon was to be broadcast on Labor Day, September 1, 2002. I had just emerged from Hair and Makeup that evening when I ran into Jerry.

"Are you ready, Deana?" he asked, smiling broadly.

"Absolutely," I replied.

"Great, see you on stage in a few minutes." Turning to go, he added, "Oh, and by the way, I think the key we started with is better. I told the pianist, and that's what we'll be singing it in now."

Raising my eyes to the heavens, I couldn't help smiling. "Okay, Dad," I thought. "I hope you're enjoying this."

I walked on stage, sat on a stool next to Jerry, and smiled.

"This is my partner's daughter, Deana Martin," he announced to the nation and the world, "and tonight, for the first time, Martin & Lewis will be together again."

As he was introducing us, my mind was racing. I thought back to all those wonderful years that Dad and Jerry had spent together. From their earliest shows in Atlantic City to Slapsy Maxie's in L.A., where Dad was onstage the night I was born, playing as much to each other as to the audience.

Their natural humor and exuberance, their love for each other and for making each other laugh, was unique. Now, for one special night, I was being allowed to share in that magic. Side by side with Jerry in front of millions of viewers, I sang along with my father's old friend and partner, and relished every moment.

I never wanted the magic to end.

Epilogue

THE DEAN MARTIN FESTIVAL BEGAN IN STEUBENVILLE, Ohio, the year after Dad died. The town's mayor, Domenick Mucci, was bombarded with calls from around the world, from people spontaneously expressing their grief and wanting to mark the event in a meaningful way. He decided to do something official. He phoned Rose Angelica, a high school music teacher known to the town for her ability to successfully produce shows and events. She was the best person to handle this difficult task. Between them, they came up with the idea for a "Dean Martin Festival" on the nearest weekend to Dad's birthday, June 7.

That first year, 1996, was mostly a gathering of local people who loved Dad and wanted to remember him. A special mass was held at St. Anthony's, the church where my grandparents Guy and Angela were married, and where Dad and his brother Bill were baptized.

Candles were lit, and Father Tim led the mass in a moving and intensely personal service.

They wanted to do something special to remember Dean Martin, Steubenville's favorite son. The regular guy who became a superstar, but never forgot the state, the town, or the people where he was born. Rose had an idea: to paint a giant mural on the front of a building at the local mall. But that would be very expensive and the town couldn't afford it, so it would have to be accomplished with donations. "What could be better?" she queried. So the following year the festival grew into a full-blown extravaganza.

There were impersonators of Dad, Uncle Frank, and Sammy, memorabilia for sale, an auction, Dean Martin dinners, discos, and nightclub events. The city collected the funds raised, and after just a few years it had enough to commission a massive mural of Dad on the wall of a local mall, not far from the highway that bore his name.

Thousands of people now come from all over the world to participate. Thanks to Rose, the Dean Martin Committee, and George Borden of the Ridgefield Group, the festival has its own website.

I established the Deana Martin Foundation to carry on the charitable works my father started. Each year, all the monies raised at the festival go toward a college scholarship for one local girl and boy. I present a check to the winners every year at the festival. We also continue to support the charitable causes Dad contributed to throughout his life.

Dad was very proud to be from Ohio, and a town called Steubenville. He never missed an opportunity to brag about his hometown, and when the town fathers dedicated the highway to him in 1968, he flew the mayor of Steubenville to L.A. to present him with the certificate. Over the years, he also hosted two other Steubenville mayors onto his television show.

There is still much for fans to see in Dad's hometown. The funny little two-story house that he was born in was knocked down long ago, but the house where his parents lived on Sixth Street is still standing, opposite the hospital.

The Naples Spaghetti House where he used to eat is still there. Dad finally received his high school diploma when Steubenville High School recently bestowed upon him the honor. In the local museum is a wedding dress made by my Grandmother Angela. Rich Delatore, a Jefferson county commissioner, and his wife, Ladonna, a councilwoman, have the very roulette wheel on which Dad learned how to be a stickman at the Half Moon Casino. The plaque dedicating the cobalt wing to my grandmother Angela's memory is still on the wall at the local hospital. The Steubenville Bakery is still open and run by Louis Tripodi, the grandson of the original owner, who would sometimes let Dad sleep on the sacks of flour if he got home too late. He makes the finest bread I have ever eaten.

Every time we go to Steubenville, we are overwhelmed by the warmth and generosity of its townspeople, who open their homes and their hearts to us.

THE FIRST time I went to Steubenville for the festival, I was so nervous, I didn't know what to expect. Rose Angelica collected John and me from the airport in a scarlet and gray van with the words GO BUCKS painted on the side—a testimony to her love of the Ohio State football team. She took us to the local hotel, a Holiday Inn, where she filled our room with drink, snacks, and gifts to make us feel welcome. Every minute of every day that we were to be in Steubenville was spoken for. My first official engagement was just a short time after we arrived, when I made a surprise guest appearance at the Dean Martin film festival held at the Jefferson Community College. The auditorium was packed, and Rose Angelica brought me quietly into the back to listen as Neil Daniels, head of the Dean Martin Fan Center, addressed the audience.

During a question-and-answer session, someone put up his hand and asked, "Why doesn't anyone from Dean's family ever come to this festival to show their support?"

Neil looked up to where I was standing, leaned into the microphone, and said, "Well, why don't you ask them?" As everyone turned in their seats, he announced, "Ladies and gentlemen, we are delighted to welcome Dean's daughter, Deana Martin."

The reaction was electric. People jumped to their feet, whistling and cheering as I stepped to the front of the auditorium. I was grabbed and patted, and people reached for my hand and thanked me for coming. By the time I reached the podium, I was close to tears, completely bowled over by the welcome and amazed at the open display of affection.

"Good evening," I said, choking back my emotion. "On behalf of my father, welcome. And may I say that no one from the family came until now because no one ever asked us before. Rose Angelica did this year, and so here I am."

After saying a few well-chosen words about Dad, I invited questions from the audience and was bombarded. What were my favorite films and favorite songs of his? What had been his favorites? What really caused the breakup with Jerry Lewis? What was my father really like? Some older fans, like Mario Camerlengo, got to their feet to tell me some stories of the man they remembered fondly as a childhood companion. I promised to speak with each one later, and I did. We videotaped interviews with Joe Perone, the retired police captain who knew Dad as a young boy, Anna Yannon, in whose wedding Dad was a groomsman, and Mindy Costanza, Mario and Mitzi Camerlengo, Violet Nelson, and other childhood friends. It was a pleasure and a privilege to meet these remarkable people.

When I simply couldn't answer any more questions that night, I officially opened the film festival, which began with a movie tribute to Dad, showing the broad expanse of acting roles he undertook in his sixty movies, everything from Matt Helm and his comic duets with Jerry Lewis to serious wartime pictures and westerns. He played cowboys and drunks and pilots, secret agents, and a disillusioned soldier, clowns, and suave hoteliers, with equal ease. When called upon to sing, his easy voice just burst out of that golden throat we were always warned never to accidentally harm, and his eyes sparkled like diamonds.

Standing there, watching him up on the silver screen, my heart filled with such pride and happiness that I felt it might burst.

OUR NEXT port of call was to the smoky, split-level Spot Bar. There I met the owner Joey (JoJo) DiAlbert and a whole host of Dean Martin impersonators. JoJo could not have been nicer, but the impersonators—now, that was weird. I'd seen several on television before, but had never met any live. It was the strangest feeling, sitting there watching someone who looked like Dad, singing and talking like him, cracking his jokes and playing the audience just as he did. Some of the impersonators were sweet; it was hilarious watching them trying to convince the audience that they were Dean Martin. Dad would have gotten a real kick out of those guys.

Everyone wanted to meet me, have his photograph taken, buy me a drink, or dance with me. I almost wore out a pair of shoes. One woman grabbed hold of me, and with a grip like a vise, her face inches from mine, told me, "I loved your father. I *really* loved him." John had to rescue me from her clutches, and I bore the bruises on my arms for several days.

The next day there was standing room only at a mass at St. Anthony's. Father Tim introduced me, and I stood up in front of the entire congregation and spoke, while a huge photograph of Dad stood on a podium to the left of the altar. His presence filled the church as sunlight poured in through the stained glass windows.

Afterward, the festival moved into the open, to a parking lot outside the Jagging Around restaurant, with stalls and stands, music and impersonators. There was a special birthday cake for Dad, and fans could buy everything from key chains to T-shirts, homemade cookies to Christmas tree decorations with Dad's image on them. Every dime went to charity. Everyone was very excited and having a terrific time. I spent the day smiling, talking, and raising money for the Dean Martin charity.

At first I was a little taken aback by the fans who poured into town. People lined up to shake my hand or have their photographs taken with me. Some showed me their Dean Martin tattoos or cherished memorabilia. Everyone seemed to have a hat or a pad, a shirt or a CD they wanted me to sign. Many people cried when they saw me.

"Oh, Deana," they said, smiling through their tears. "Your father. We loved him so." Sometimes they just came toward me, their hands outstretched, saying, "I just want to touch you." It was overwhelming.

Among them were some truly wonderful people, like Jim Monaco and his wife, Debbie, from New Jersey, who must have one of the largest collections of Dean Martin memorabilia in the world, and who run the Dean Martin Collectors Club website. Jim, a fan for over forty years, brought along his most cherished posters of Dad's films and club dates. He also had Dean Martin puppets, Dean Martin jackets, and an extraordinary Martin & Lewis table lamp. He invited John and me to see his collection. His was a lifelong passion, that began with his mother's own devotion to Dad.

"When I was a kid," Jim said, "all the other kids were out in the backyard playing ball, and I was inside, cutting clippings about Dean Martin and his family from celebrity magazines. How sad am I?"

"Not sad at all," I told him. "It's very impressive and thank you for sharing."

I continued chatting with people, and discovered how devoted they were to Dad. Most of them were exclusively Dino fans who only followed the Rat Pack because of Dad's involvement. Some loved Frank Sinatra equally, and wanted to know all I could tell them about him and his friendship with my family. At one point yet another group, this time from Australia, descended on me, autograph books open and cameras at the ready, and I found myself with a new and interesting set of fans. They were absolutely terrific.

I couldn't believe how exhausted I was by all the attention. I was so beat I virtually fell asleep standing up that night. I felt a little stifled by it all, and John had to whisk me off somewhere and get me a glass of water or a respite from the endless offers of prosciutto and wine. I was thankful for my police bodyguards, Joel Walker and Roger Badger, who kindly protected me from those who wanted to get just a little too familiar.

One year we took our son Mickey, his wife Paola, and our grandson Hunter along. Everyone was over the moon to meet Dean Martin's grandson and great-grandson. It was a good thing for Mickey to come along, so that he could begin to understand for himself what Dad meant to people. Mickey's next child, Jagger, was conceived that year in Steubenville. We say he's a true Ohioan.

A film crew from the popular television show *Entertainment Tonight* followed us around and aired a segment about the festival.

Renzo Gallerati, the mayor of Montesilvano and a distant cousin of mine, came all the way from Italy, along with a group of representatives from the town where "Pop" Crocetti was born. Unable to speak a word of English, they brought along a copy of Pop's birth certificate, and gifts from the town that is proud to call itself Dean Martin's ancestral home. They even showed off photos of their Dean Martin Piazza. They were taken to the Mountaineer racetrack, where a Dean Martin Memorial Race raised money for the foundation. The Ohioans welcomed the Italian dignitaries warmly, and several celebrations took place to mark the twinning of the two cities almost a hundred years ago. We were invited by the mayor to travel to Italy and see for ourselves where my wonderful grandfather was born.

Once I grew accustomed to the adulation people expressed of my father, and the fact that the town had embraced him as their favorite son, I came to realize just what a legacy Dad had left to his millions of fans. That knowledge helped me to work through my own grief and often overpowering sense of loss.

Drinking martinis in Mario's at a private dinner on the last night of the festival, I found myself eating delicious linguine and shrimp, dancing and laughing and listening to Dad singing "Volare" or "That's Amore." I couldn't help marveling again at the man and his music, and the sheer joy he brought to so many over the years. I relish my contact with all of Dad's fans and the people of Steubenville, and the tremendous sense of satisfaction they have given me. Through them, I am allowed the greatest honor of all, to be able to represent my father.

◆◆◆

JOHN AND I fought for two years to change the laws in Ohio to allow Dean Martin Day to be celebrated as an official state holiday each year on Dad's birthday. John was tireless in his campaigning, and I went to address the state senate in 2001 on what was a very emotional day for me.

"When people speak of my father, they call him a legend, an icon, and the King of Cool," I told the packed senate house. "My father was proud of his vast body of work, but I believe he should also be remembered for his other accomplishments: for standing up against racial prejudice . . . for co-founding the Muscular Dystrophy Association Telethon, and for his humanitarian contributions, made with the request of anonymity, too numerous to mention."

I concluded, "He was someone who instilled in all of his children the greatest thing a man can give, love, morals, and ethics, which in turn we will pass on to our children and grandchildren. It was here that my father learned these principles, here in the heartland of our country, the place my father so proudly called home—Ohio, and a town called Steubenville."

◆◆◆

SEVERAL SENATORS stood and spoke in favor of the bill, and Senator Greg DiDonato was the sponsor. One Senator, C. J.

Prentiss, spoke of Dad's quiet but effective campaign to stop racial segregation in Las Vegas. She recounted the story of Dad's refusal to perform at The Sands unless his friend Sammy Davis Jr. was allowed to eat and sleep in that same hotel. Another representative claimed that Dad had done more to promote the state of Ohio than anyone in history. The senate passed the motion unanimously. Our next hurdle was the house of representatives.

The bill was sponsored by Representative Eileen Krupinski, and when it was brought to the floor, three of the representatives, known as "The Three Tenors," printed up copies of Dad's hit song "That's Amore" and handed them out. The bill was passed on an unprecedented vote, and when it was carried, the entire house of representatives stood up and sang the song. I couldn't be there in person that day, but the vote was broadcast live on the Internet, and John called me in my car on my cell phone.

"Stop the car and listen to this," he said from his computer at home. "The entire Ohio House of Representatives is singing one of your Dad's songs."

Sitting in the parking lot of a shopping center, I pressed the telephone to my ear and heard the words "When the moon hits your eye like a big pizza pie, that's amore" being belted out two thousand miles away by a roomful of politicians. It was a remarkable moment, and one I will never forget.

The bill was passed in 2002, and we flew back to Columbus, Ohio, to be with Governor Bob Taft when it was signed into law and stamped with the great seal of the state of Ohio. The new law designates June 7 as Dean Martin Day "in honor of the Steubenville, Ohio, native Dino Paul Crocetti, born on that day in 1917, for his achievements as a national and international singer, actor and radio and television personality." The event was marked with the post office issue of a special stamp, and the holiday is now an annual fixture of the Ohio state calendar. Dad has the distinction of being the only entertainer honored with his own national day in the entire United States.

Our next goal was to create the Dean Martin Music Scholarship, which we launched in 2002 at the National Italian American

Foundation (NIAF). Two students from around the world, one of Italian descent and one of any other nationality, can apply and receive funding through college, majoring in music. Dad would have been very proud.

He was honored by NIAF at a gala event at the Hilton Hotel in Washington, D.C., attended by such celebrities as Tommy Mottola, Sophia Loren, and Robert De Niro—all honored for lifetime achievement awards as outstanding Italians. Representing Dad, I stood in front of three thousand people and launched the scholarship on his behalf. Jerry Lewis had agreed to come with me, but he was taken ill at the last minute and recorded a video tribute instead.

In it he said, "I'm not looking my best, I know, but I'm doing this for my partner, my darling Dean." His tear-jerking tribute, coupled with my simple speech, received a heartfelt standing ovation.

♦♦♦

I HAVE just one precious bottle of Dad's Fabergé Woodhue left, a product that has long since been discontinued. It was in his bathroom cabinet when he died, and I was fortunate enough to inherit it. I keep it wrapped in cellophane to preserve the precious few ounces that remain. Now and then, when I'm feeling especially nostalgic, I peel back the cellophane, unscrew the heavily grained wooden top, and inhale deeply.

Within seconds I am transported back to Dad's happier times when my father was at the very top of his profession, living on Mountain Drive with his beloved family all around him. He was making movies, singing songs, and keeping us all in luxurious style. Closing my eyes, I can see him sitting on the couch eating his sandwich, or remember rubbing his shoulders and neck after a long day at the studio. Best of all, I can recall the times he wrapped his arms around me on the driving range, teaching me how to swing, as I inhaled his cologne and cherished every moment.

To know Dad was to love him. To love him was to forgive him. He was the sun and the moon to those fortunate enough to have been in his orbit. Underneath that polished Hollywood veneer beat the heart of a man who came from an industrial engine of steel mills and sweat—from hardworking, wholesome people, decent Italian folks to whom family meant everything. In his own inimitable way, Dad adored his wives and doted on his many children, who gladly reciprocated that affection, despite everything.

He provided the soundtrack for countless generations with his thousand plus heartwarming songs, which endure in popularity to this day. His melodic baritone voice was seamless, his charm legendary, his talents multifaceted. Men wanted to be like him, and women wanted to be with him. He became an international icon, idolized by millions.

For a time he was literally the most successful performer in the world, conquering more media than any of his rivals. It is a record that has never been beaten. More than that, he achieved immortality—of the best possible kind.

The man with the smiling eyes brought a tremendous amount of happiness into this world, and even though he's gone, that happiness lingers, like the unmistakable scent of his favorite cologne.

The great thing about Dad was that he enjoyed every minute of the blessings that life bestowed upon him. Although it took him years of hard work to get there, he never lost his sense of childlike wonder that all this good fortune had come his way. His favorite cartoon was pinned to the wall of whichever dressing room he was in. It showed two disgruntled office workers bemoaning their lot. One says to the other, "When I die, I want to come back as Dean Martin."

Dad couldn't have agreed more. "I wouldn't change places with anyone in the world," he once said. "It's unbelievable that all this could happen to me. I was destined to be a gambler. Nobody ever figured me for this. Nobody."

With such self-effacing honesty, I defy anyone to think of the name Dean Martin and not smile.

Now, *that's* amore.

ONE NEVER knows what tomorrow will bring. Life moves us in many directions. The passion I once had for flying has returned. On October 11, 2003, I'm proud to say I became a licensed pilot.

GRANDMA ANGELA'S PASTA FAGIOLI

2 tablespoons extra virgin olive oil
1 onion, finely chopped
2 (15-ounce) cans cannellini beans
6 cups water
Salt and pepper to taste
1/4 teaspoon ground cinnamon
(HER SECRET INGREDIENT)
8 ounces tubetini pasta
1/4 cup grated Parmesan or Romano cheese

Heat the oil in a large pan and sauté the onion for a minute. Add the two cans of beans with the six cups of water. Season with salt and pepper to taste. Add the cinnamon, cover, and bring to a boil. Boil for 15 minutes, then reduce heat and simmer for one and a half hours. Simmer very slowly. Check occasionally and add boiling water as necessary. Add the pasta and continue simmering until the pasta is *al dente*. Remove from heat and serve with grated cheese sprinkled on top.

– SERVES FOUR –

Index